CONTENTS

DOGS COLORING BOOK

By Roberto Barondi

DEDICATION

To our fellow dog lover,

Thank you for bringing our canine companions to life through the colors of your imagination. In these pages, you'll find a world of wagging tails, boundless energy, and unwavering loyalty.

May the colors you choose reflect the joy and love that dogs bring into our lives every day. As you embark on this coloring adventure, remember that each stroke of your brush or pencil is a celebration of the bond we share with our four-legged friends.

Happy coloring, and may your days be as vibrant and joyful as the dogs you color!

With heartfelt appreciation,

Roberto Barondi

AKITA INU

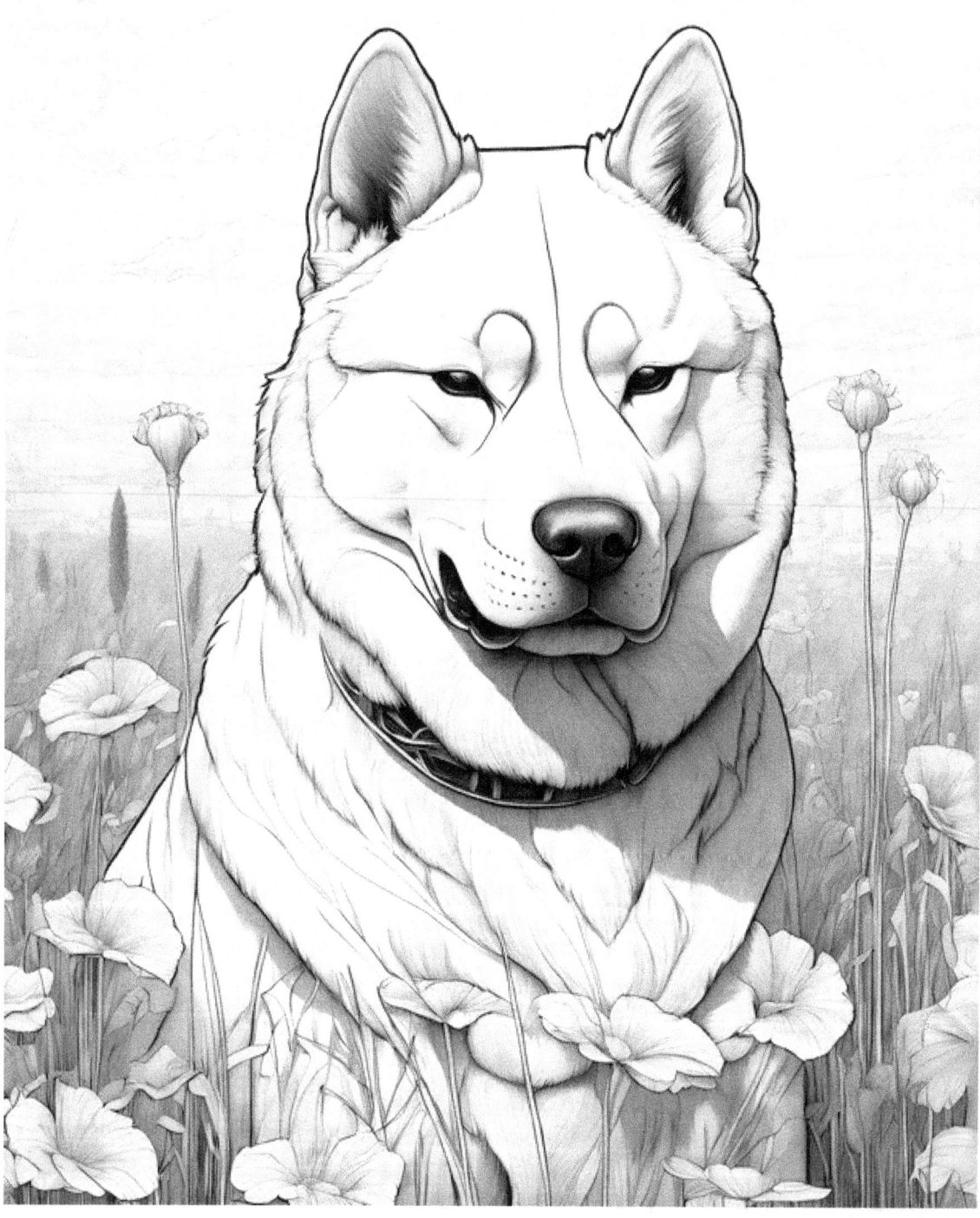

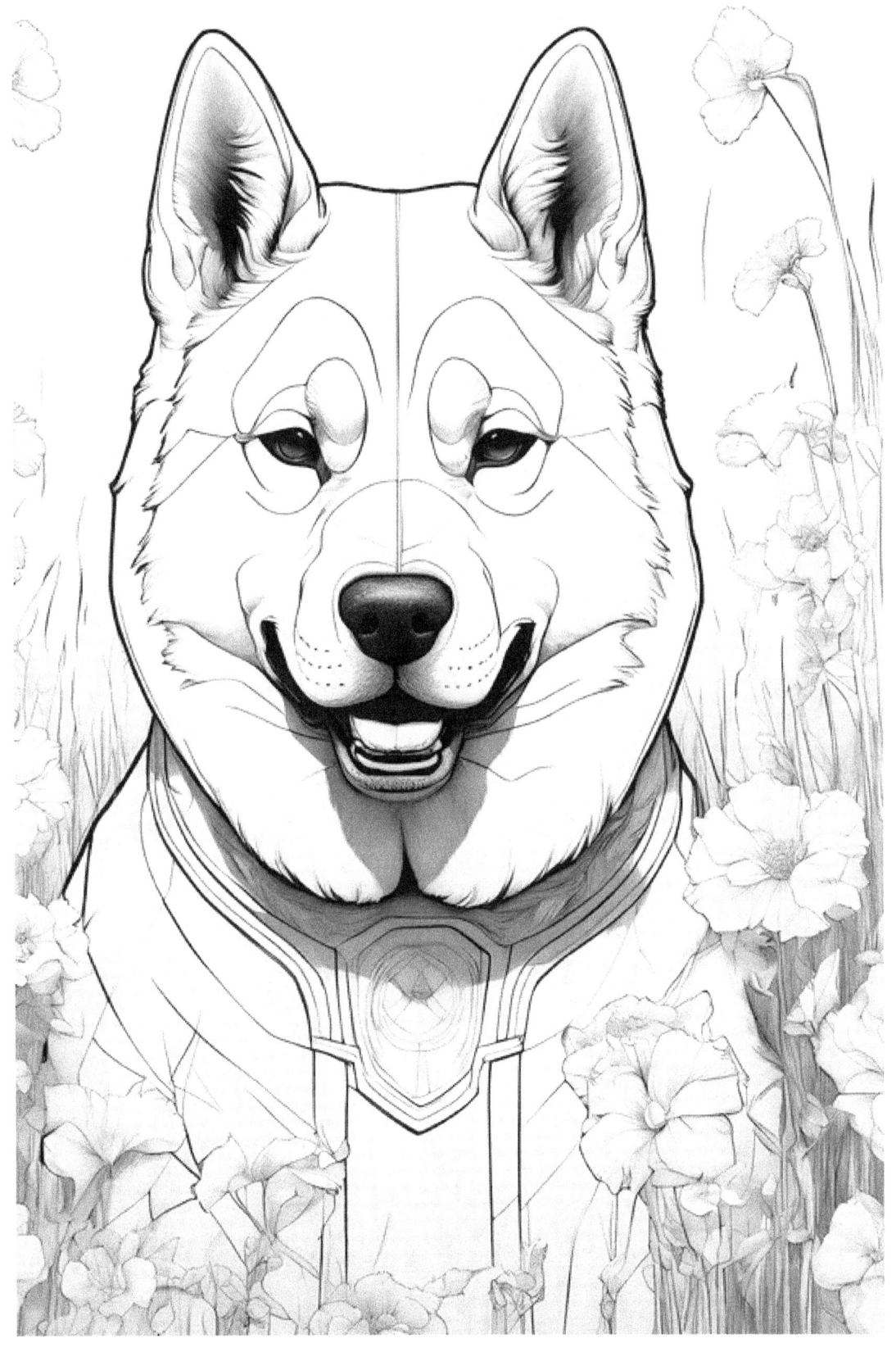

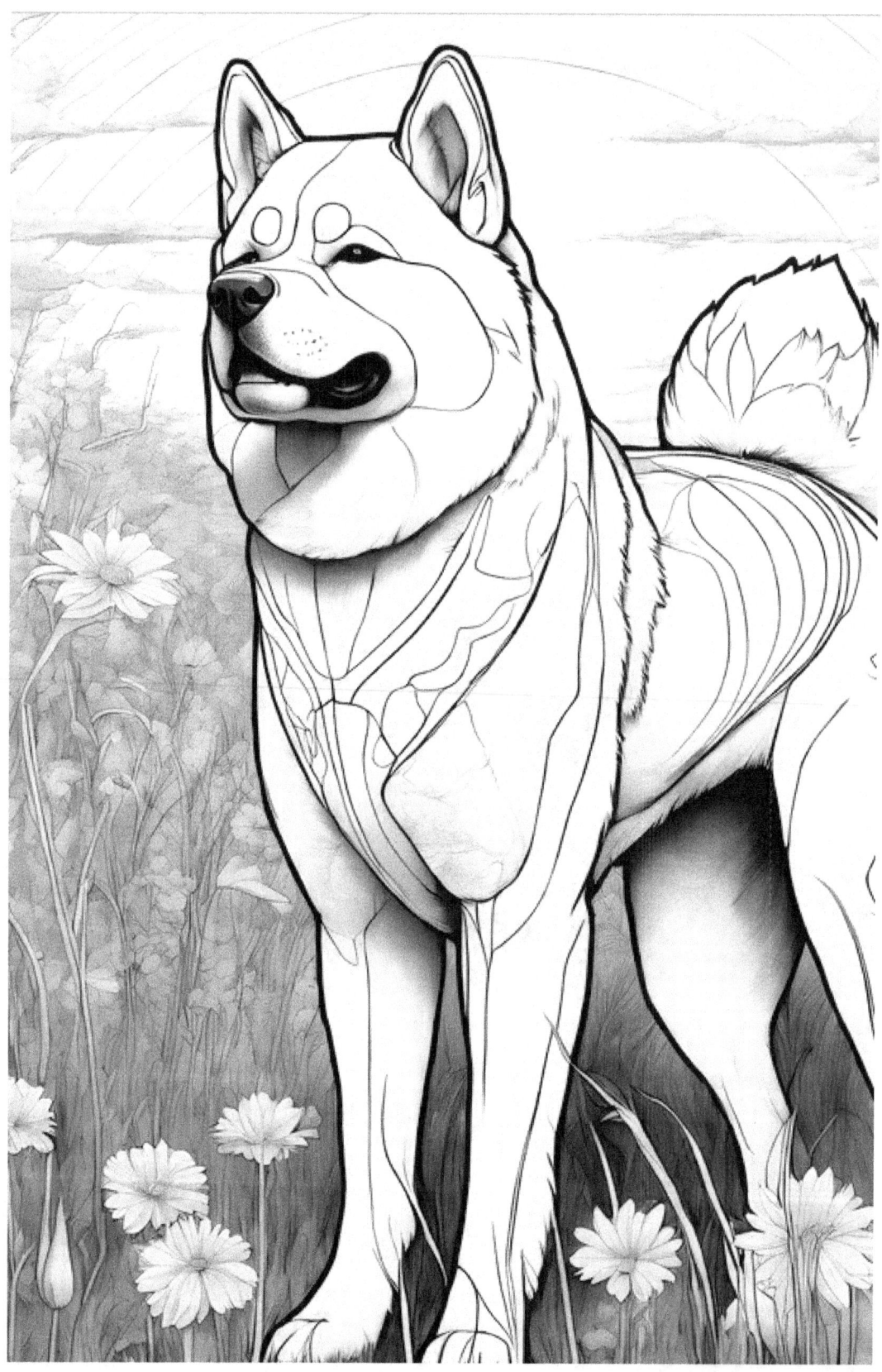

BASENJI

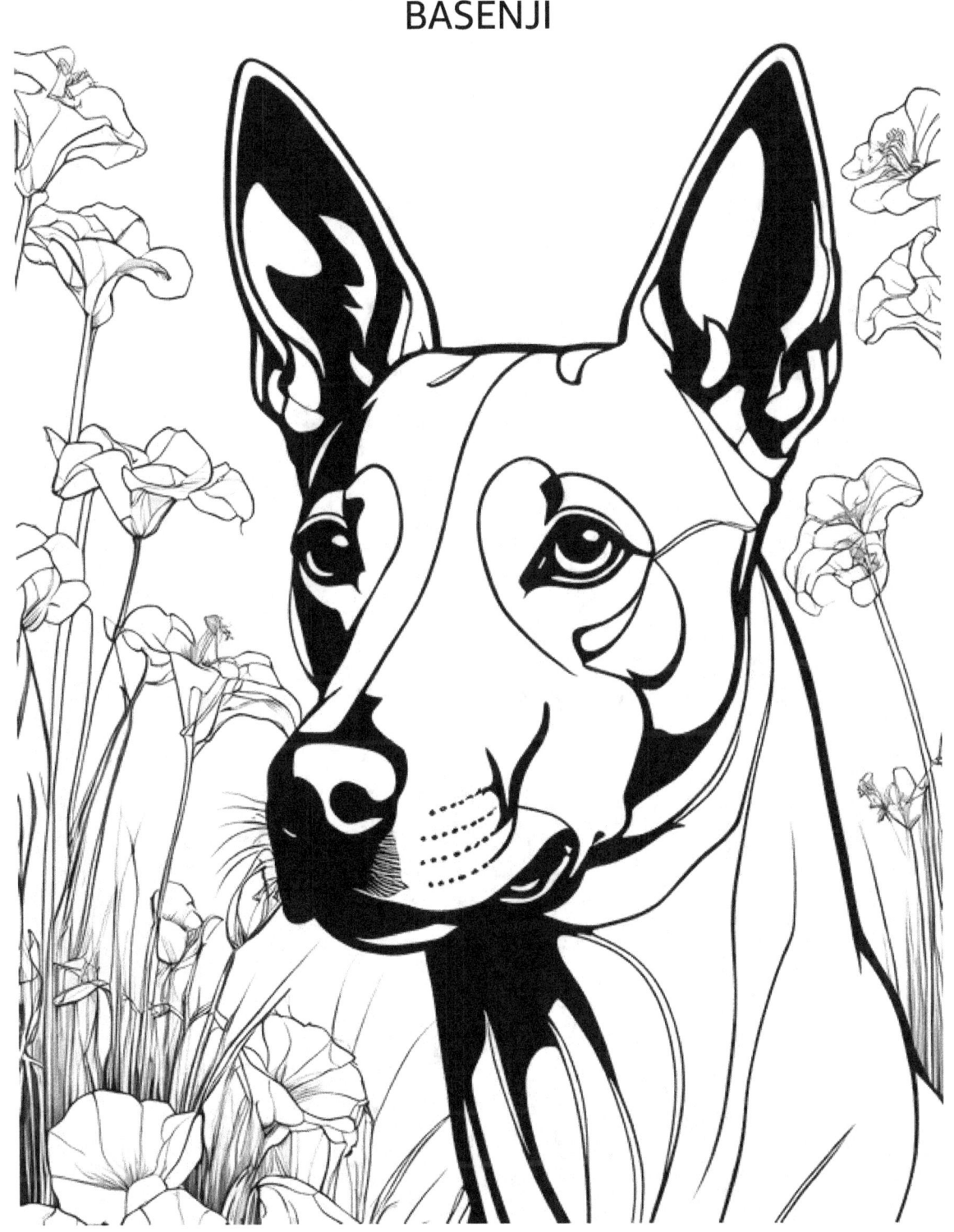

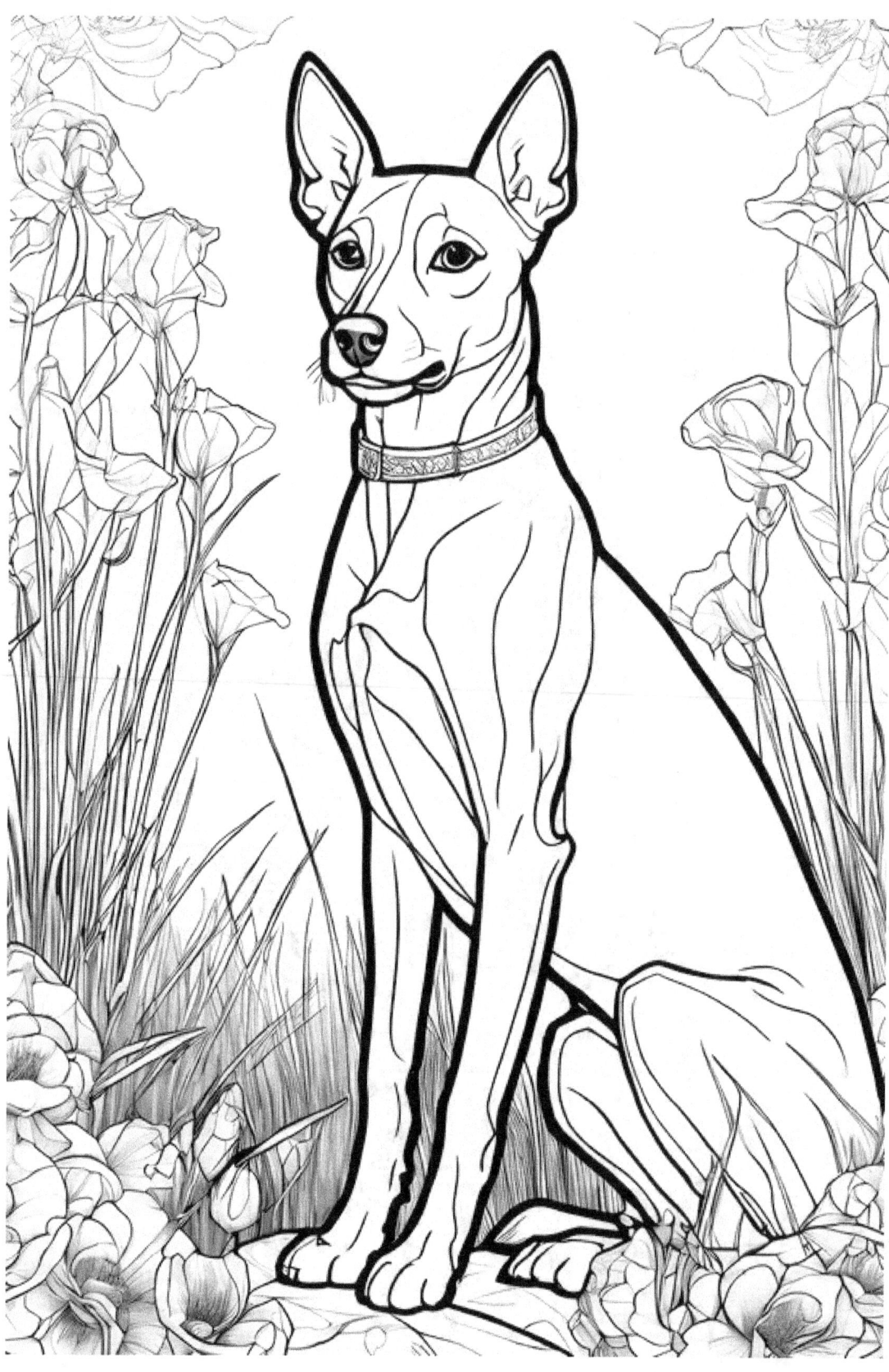

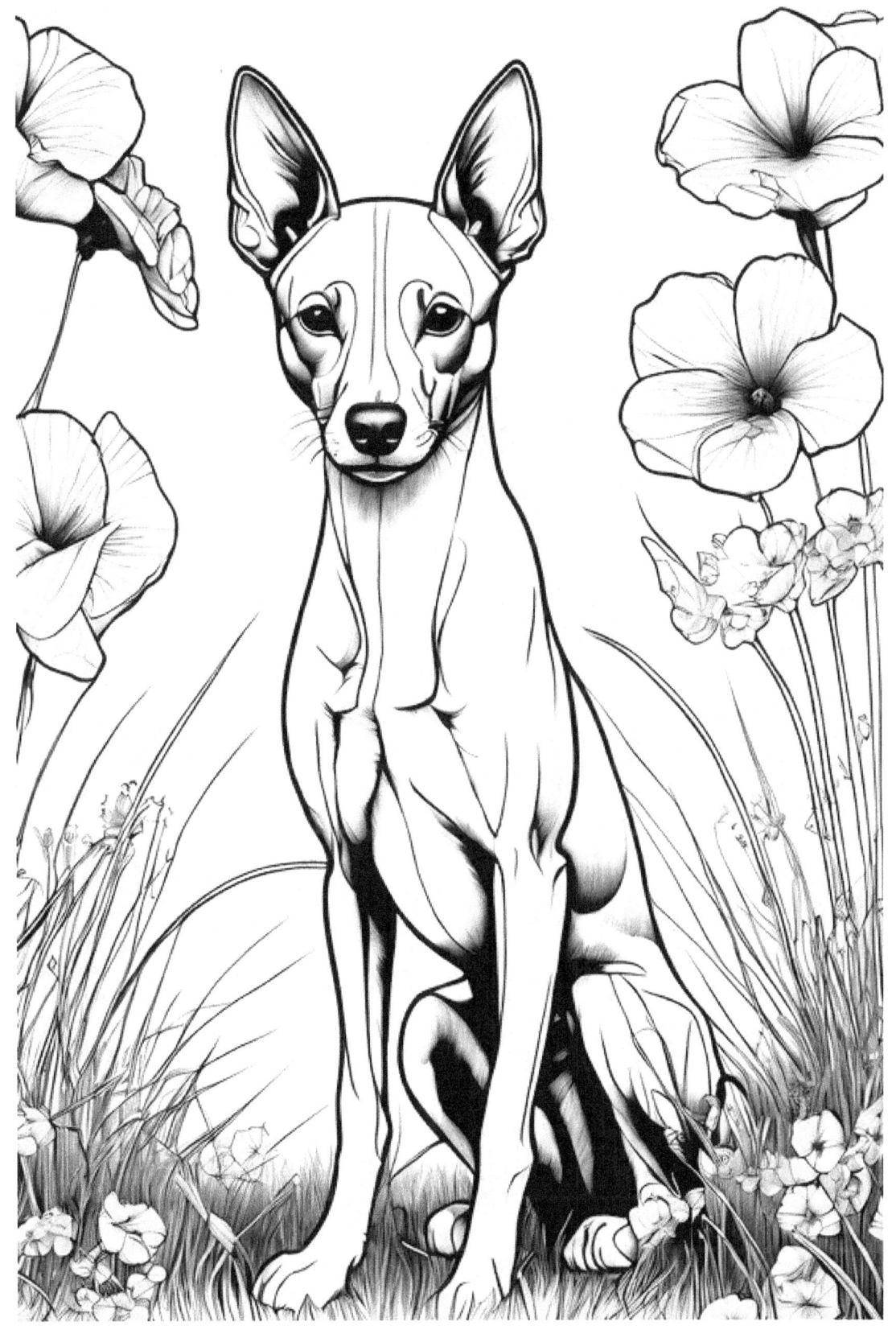

BEAGLE

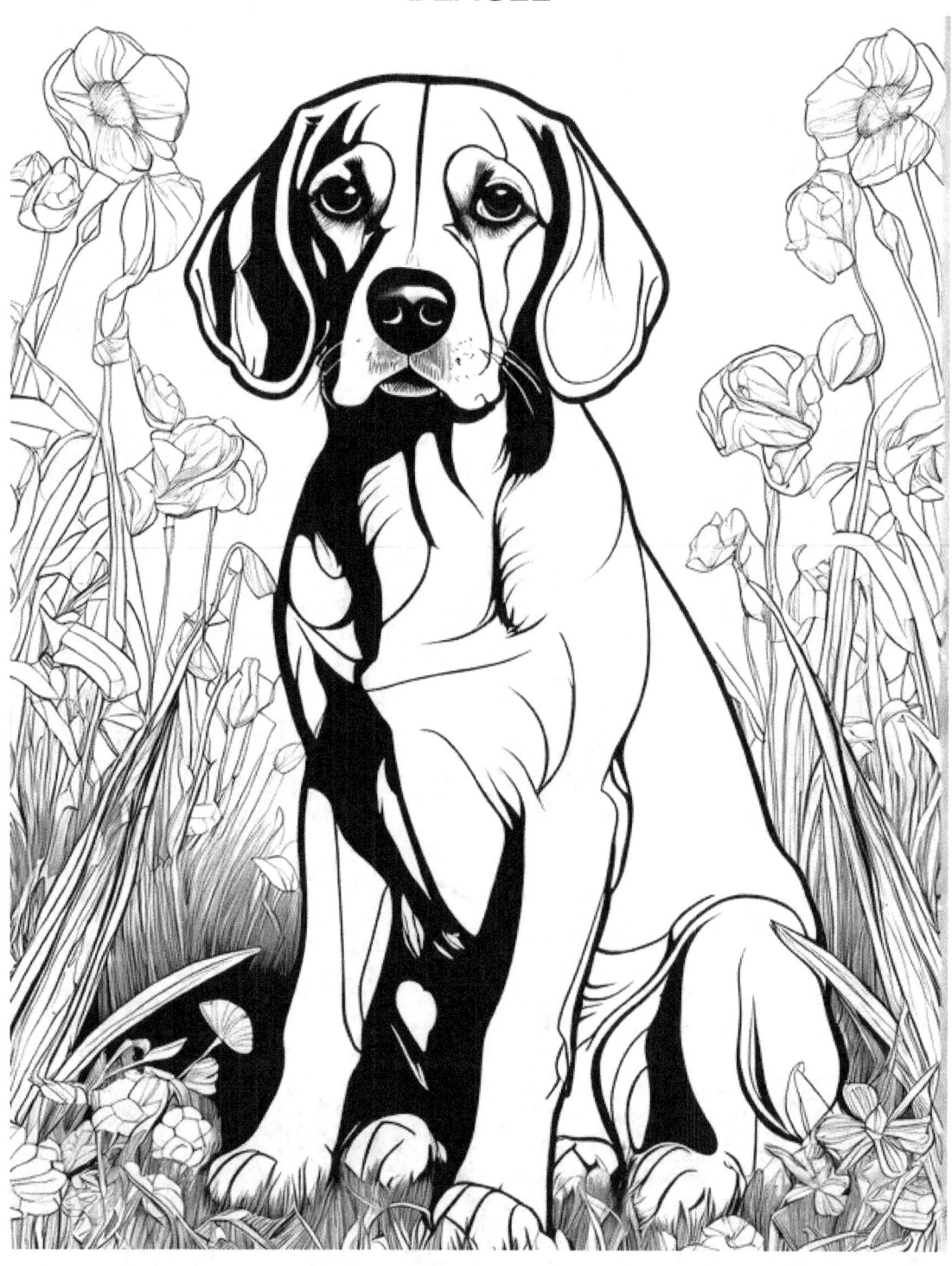

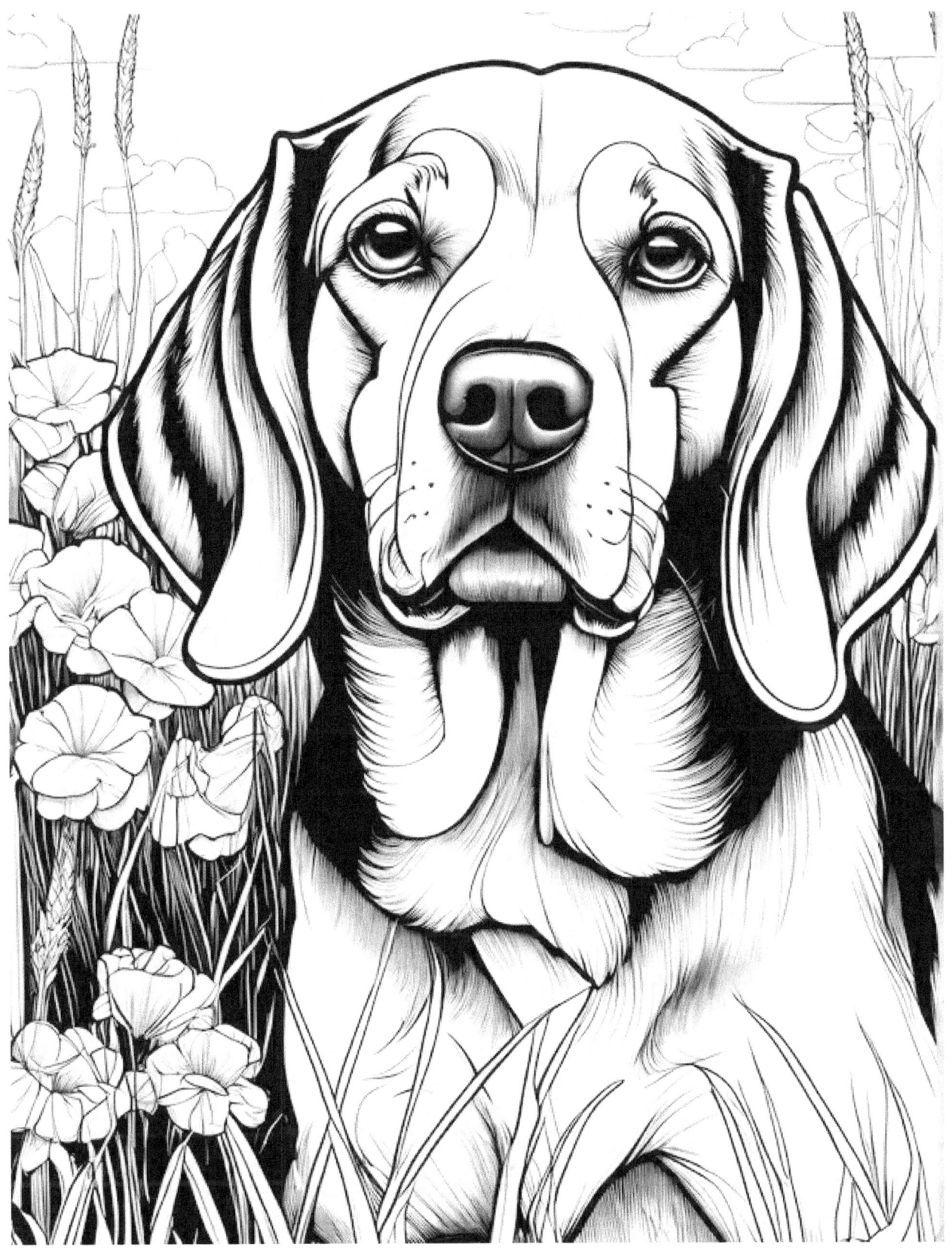

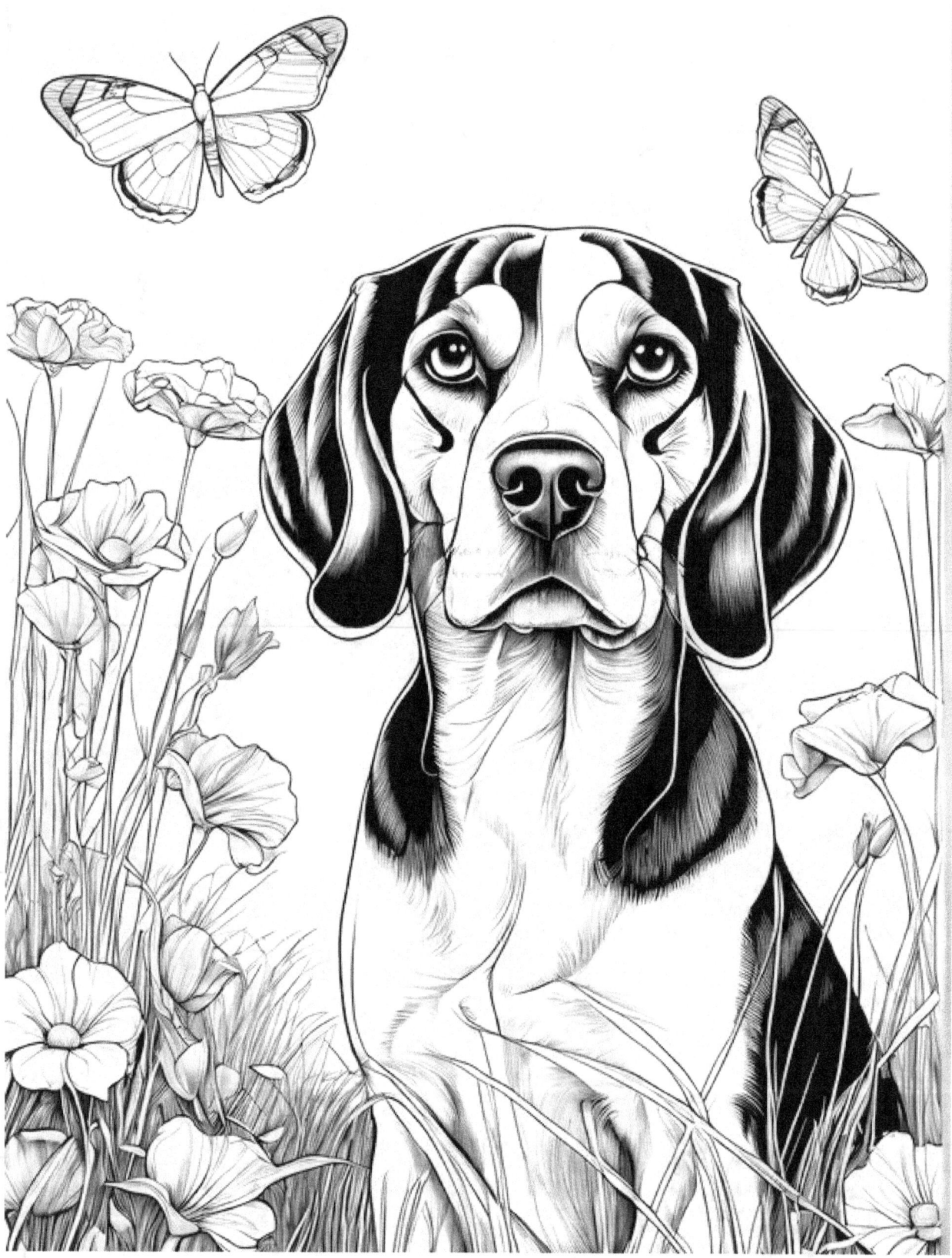

BEDLINGTON TERRIER

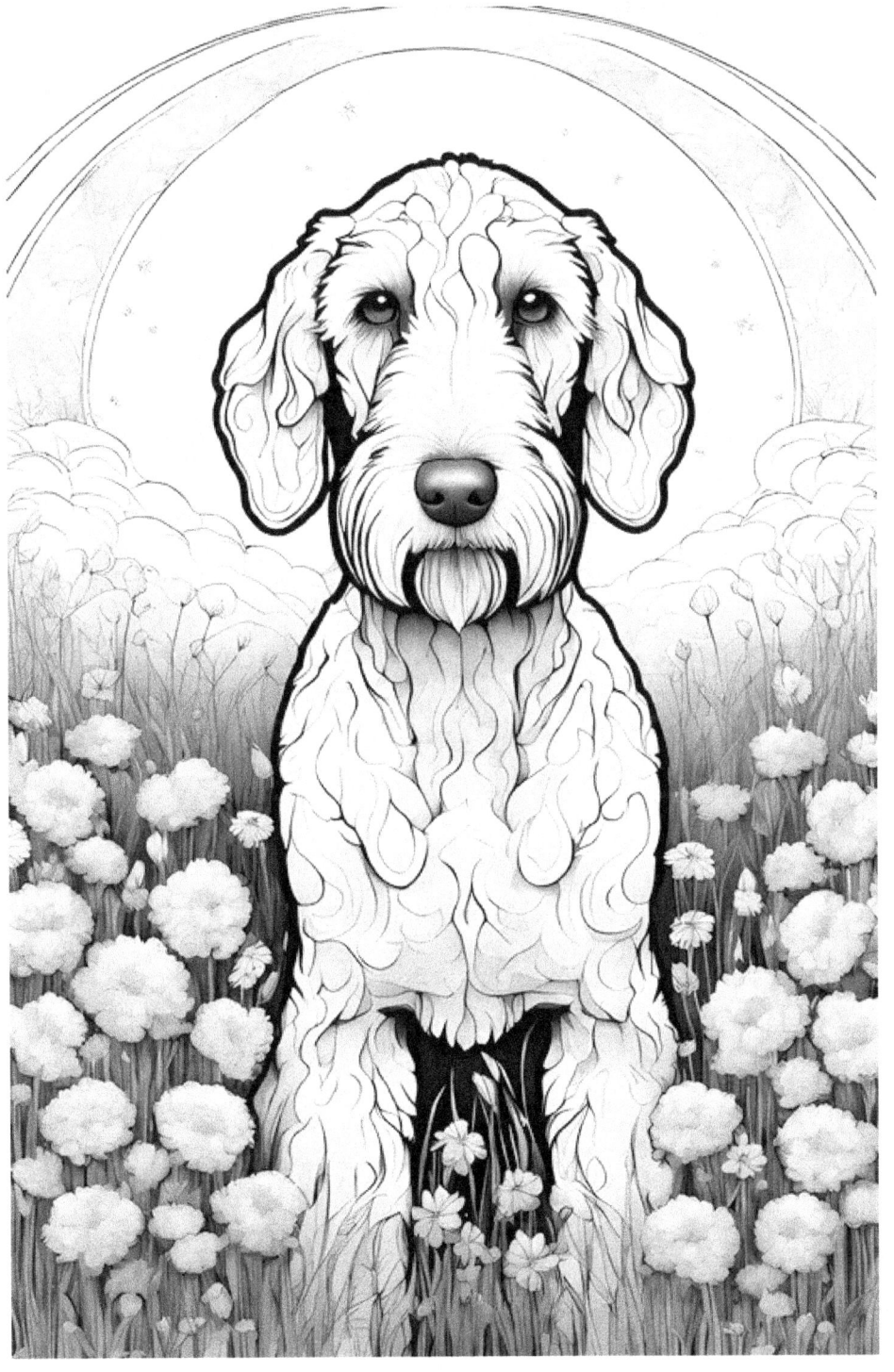

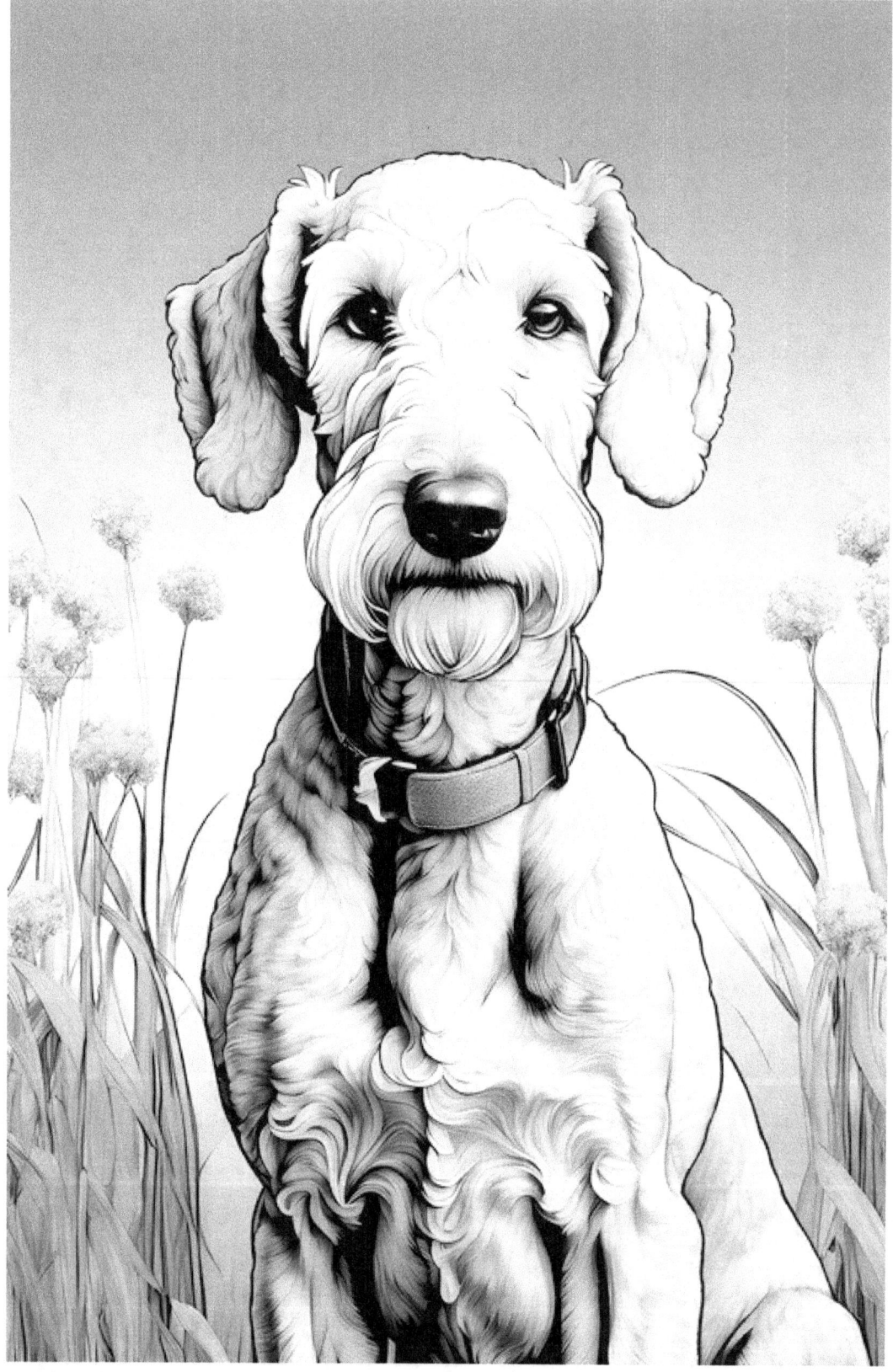

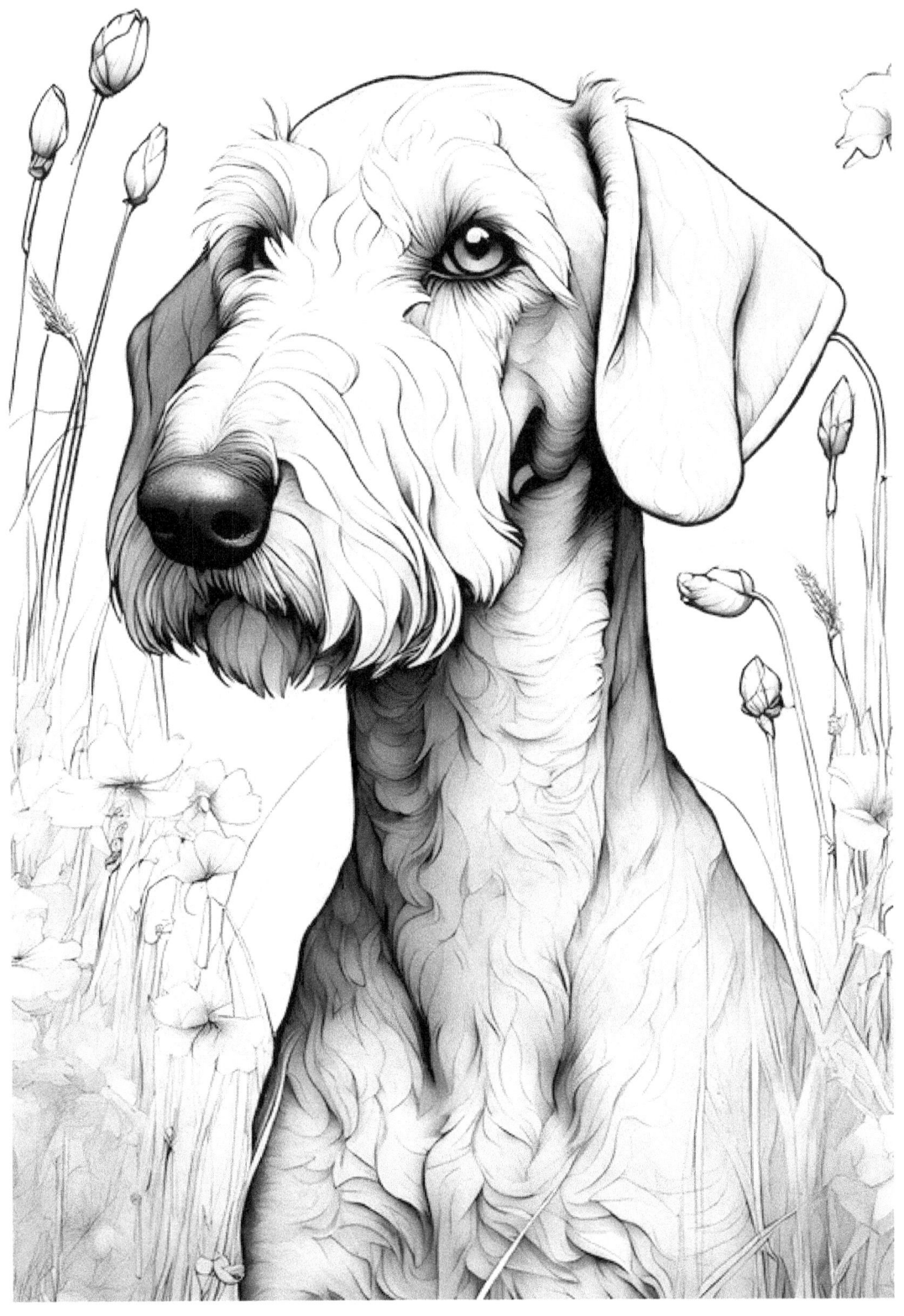

BELGIAN SHEPHERD

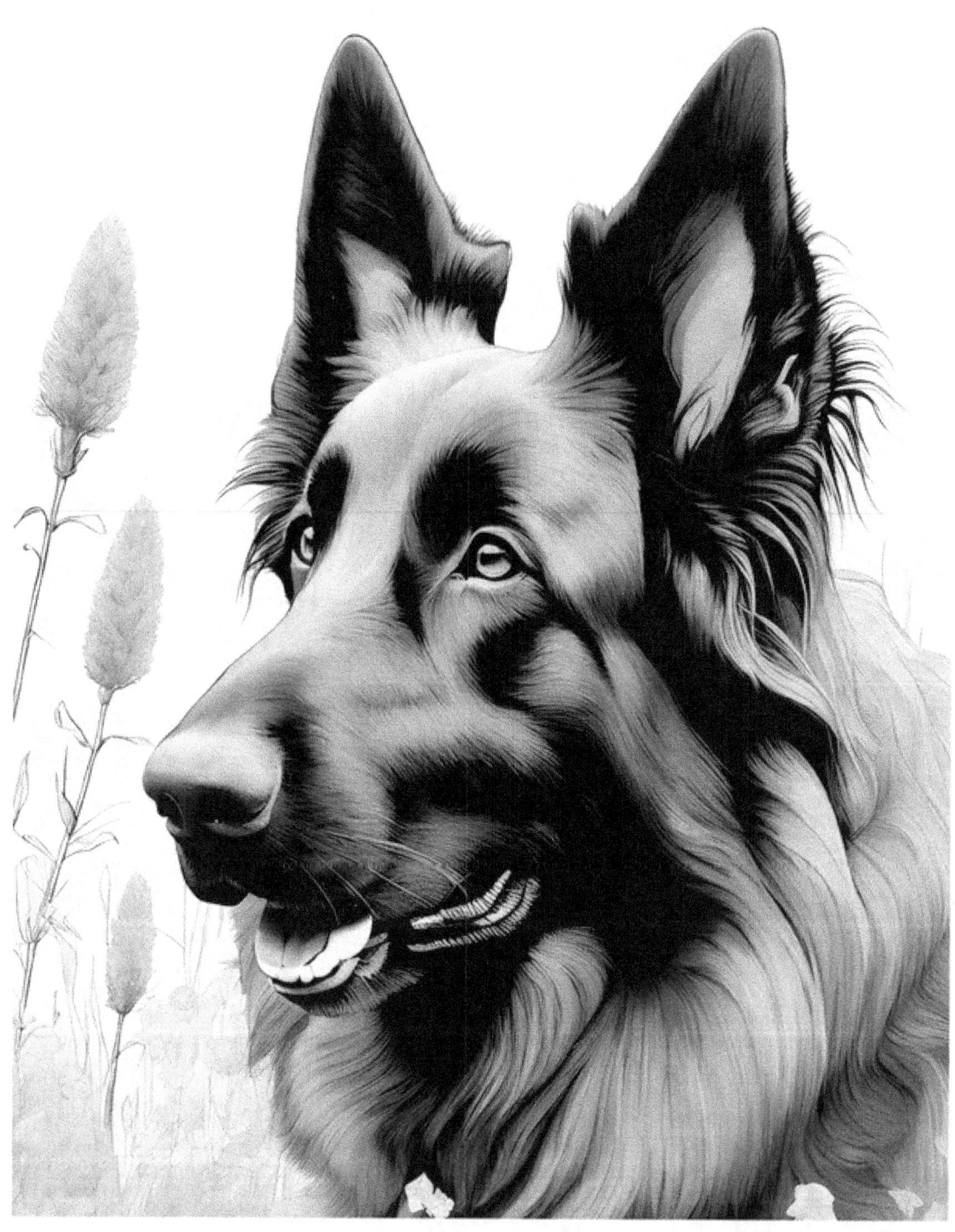

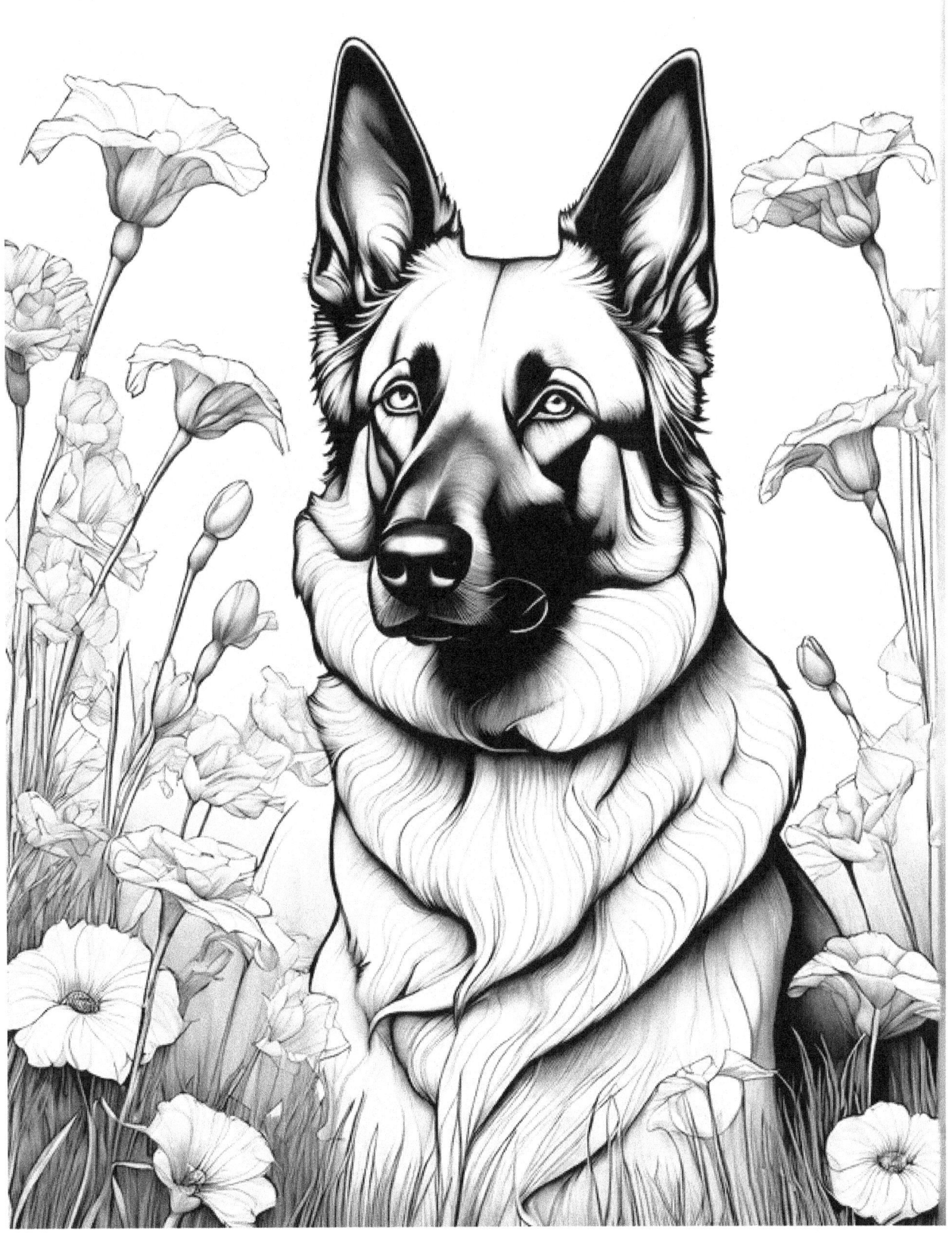

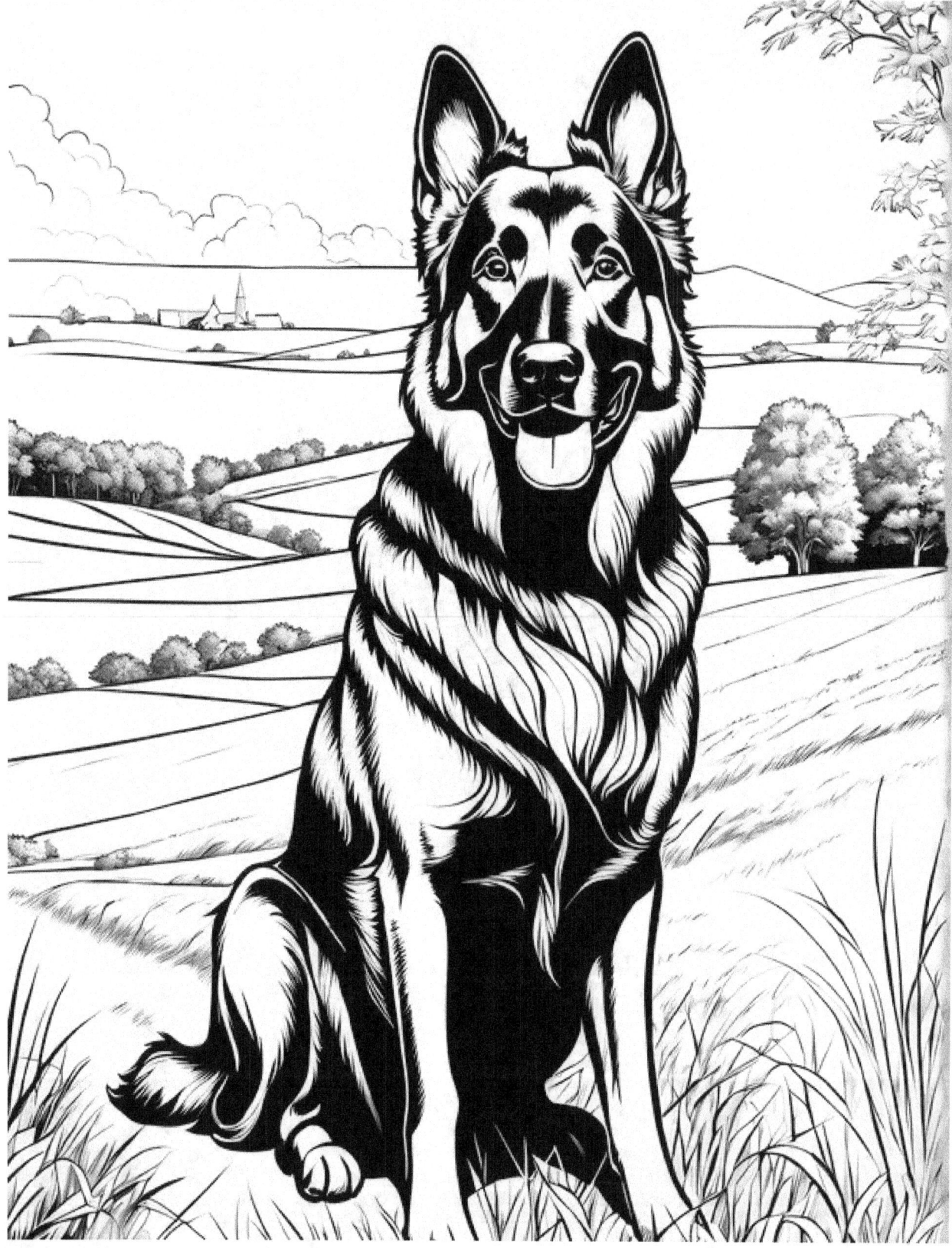

BERGAMASCO

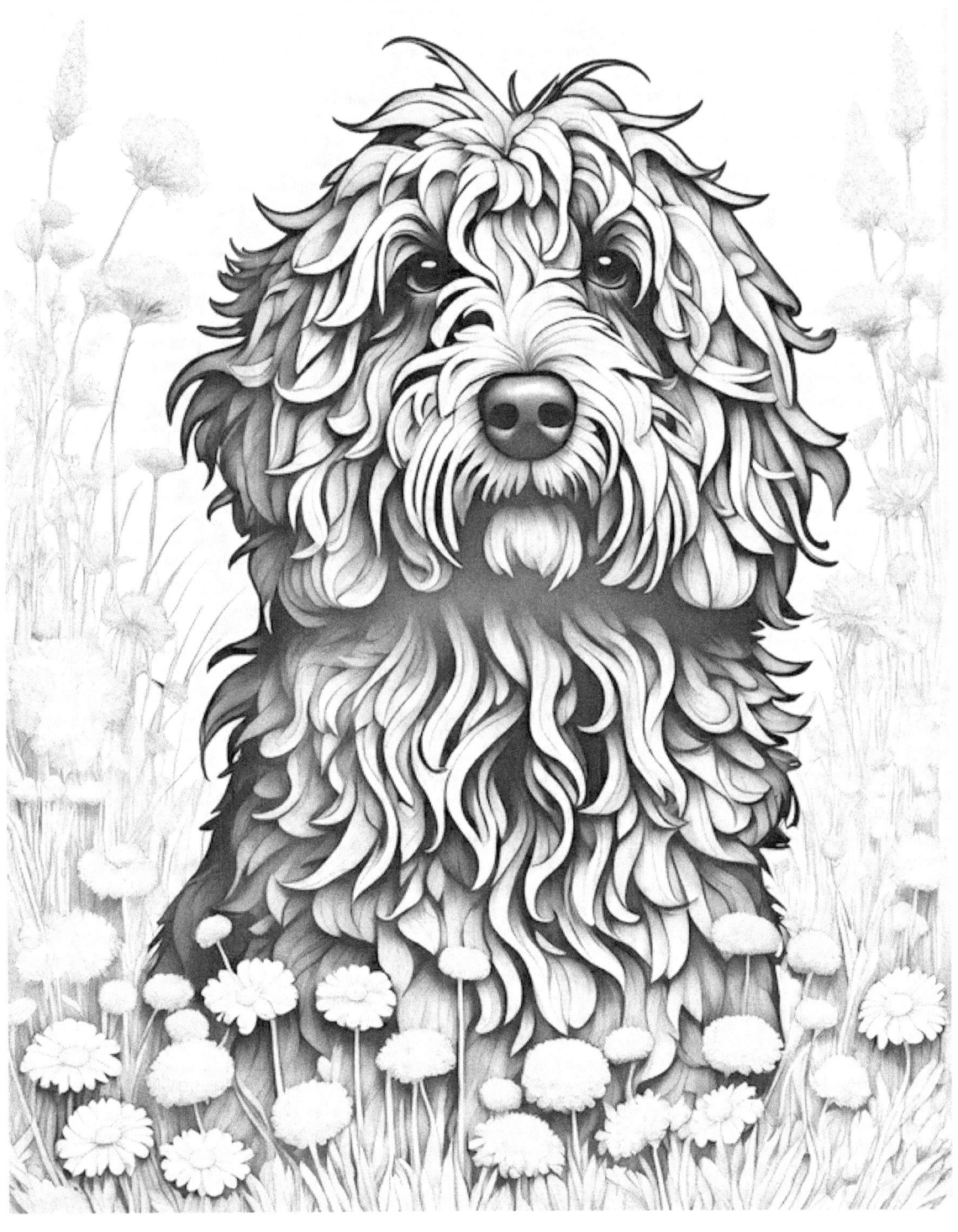

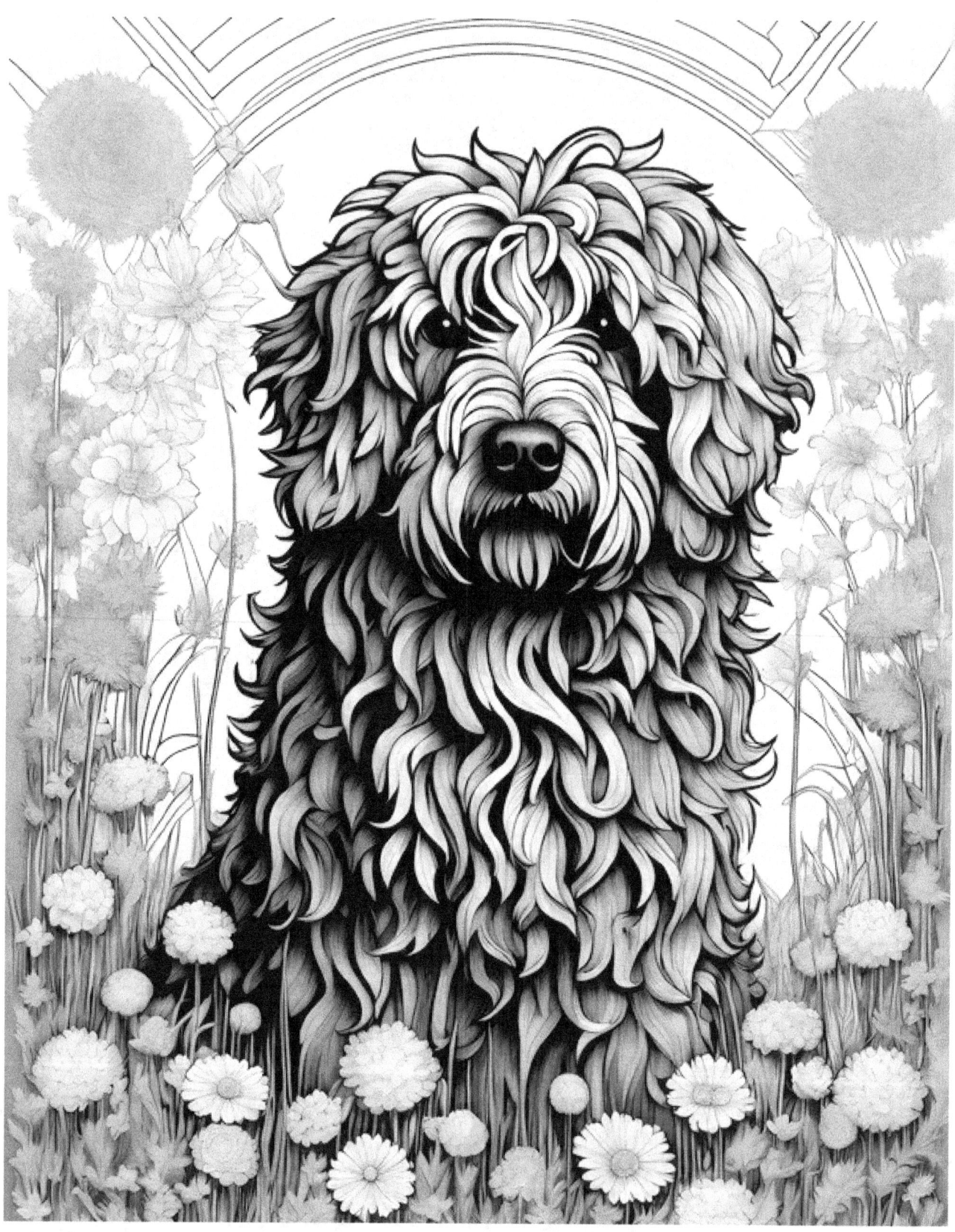

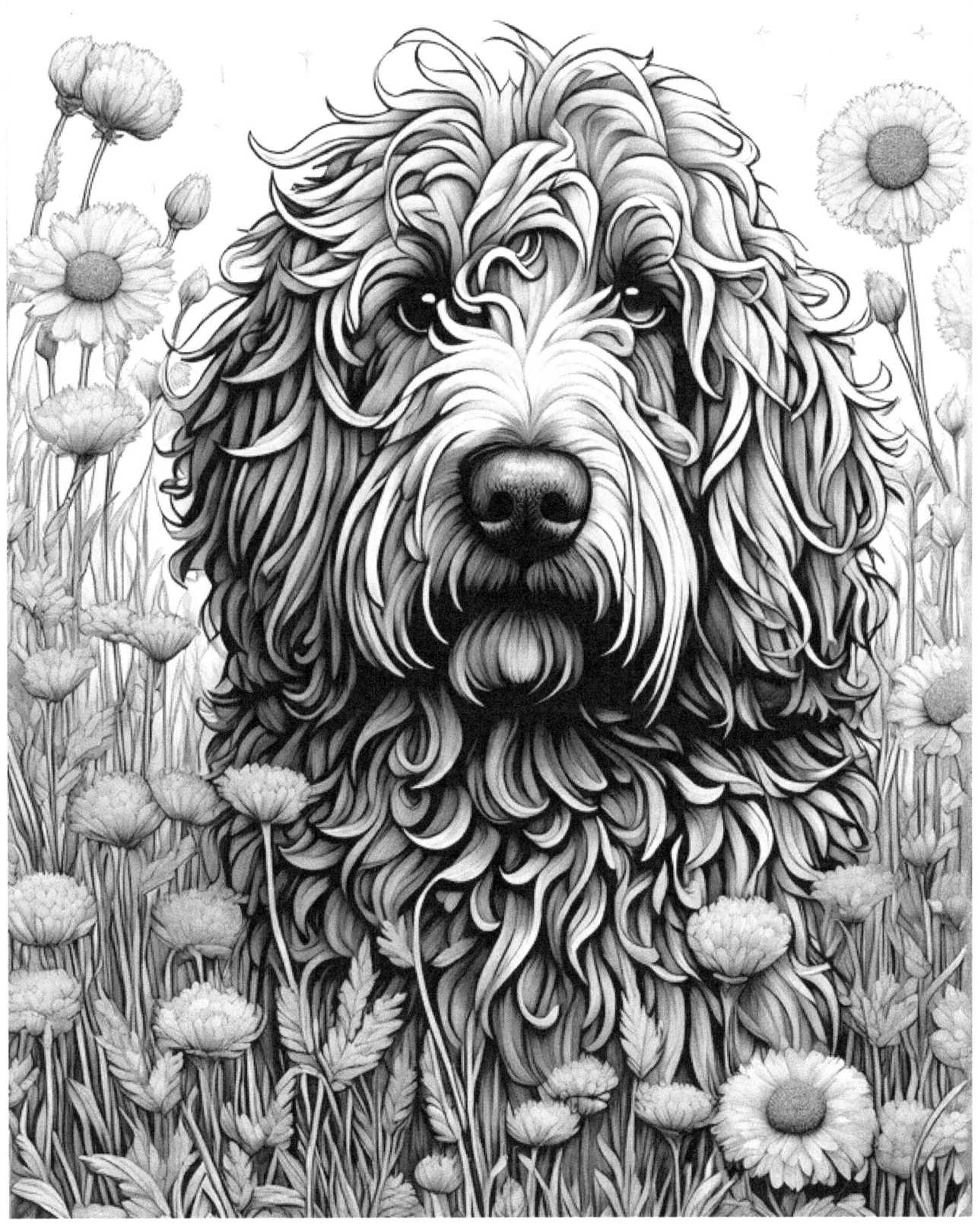

BICHON FRIS

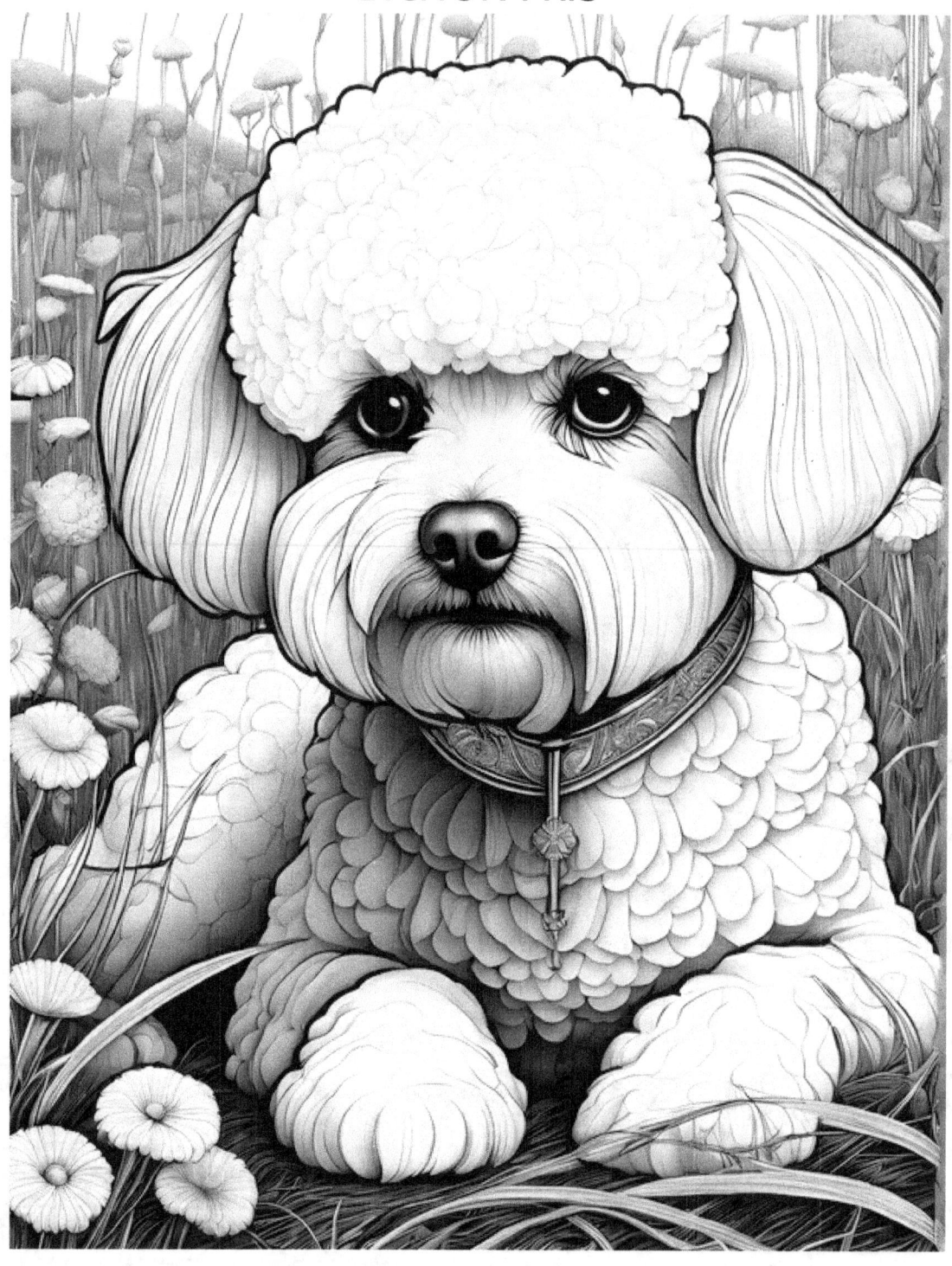

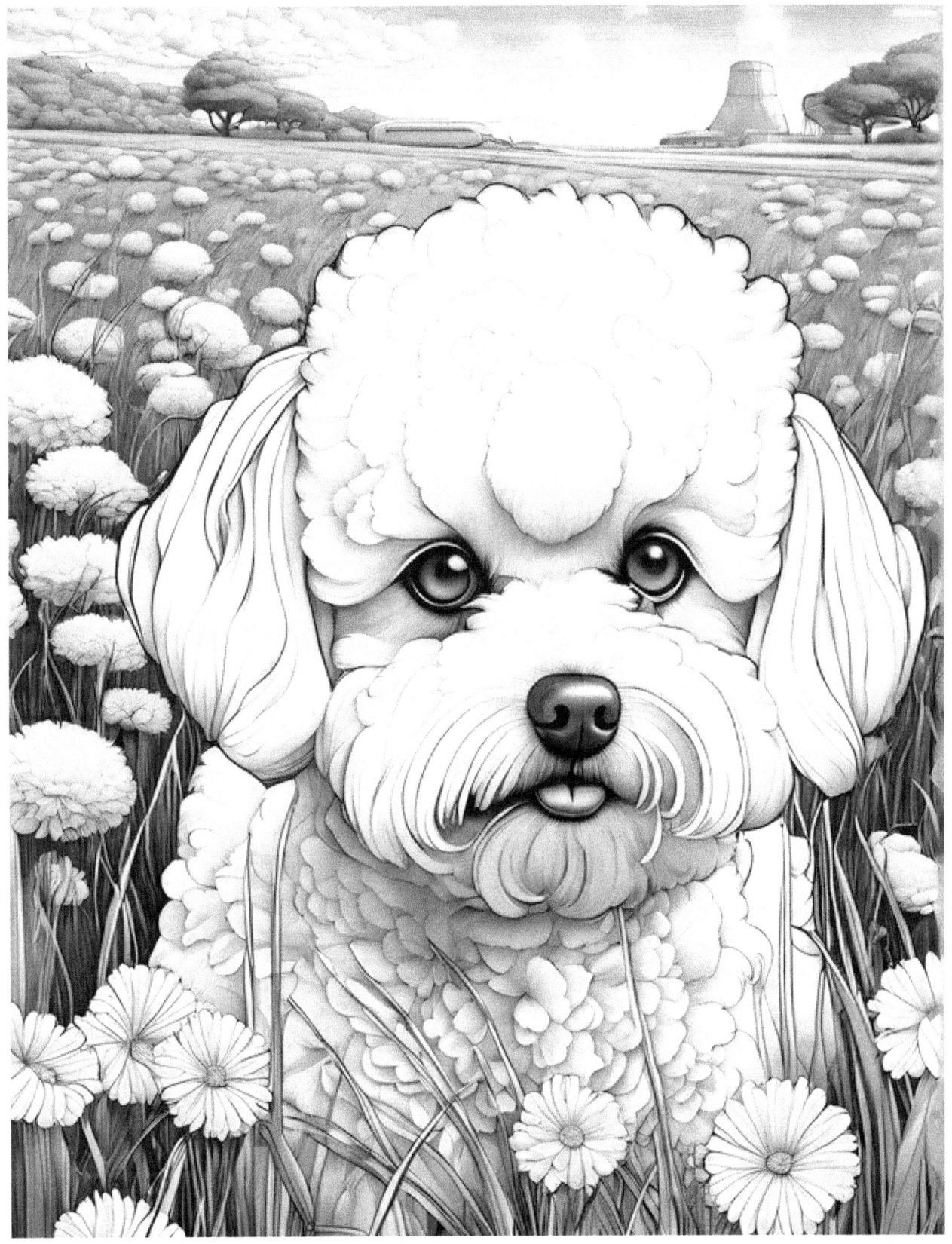

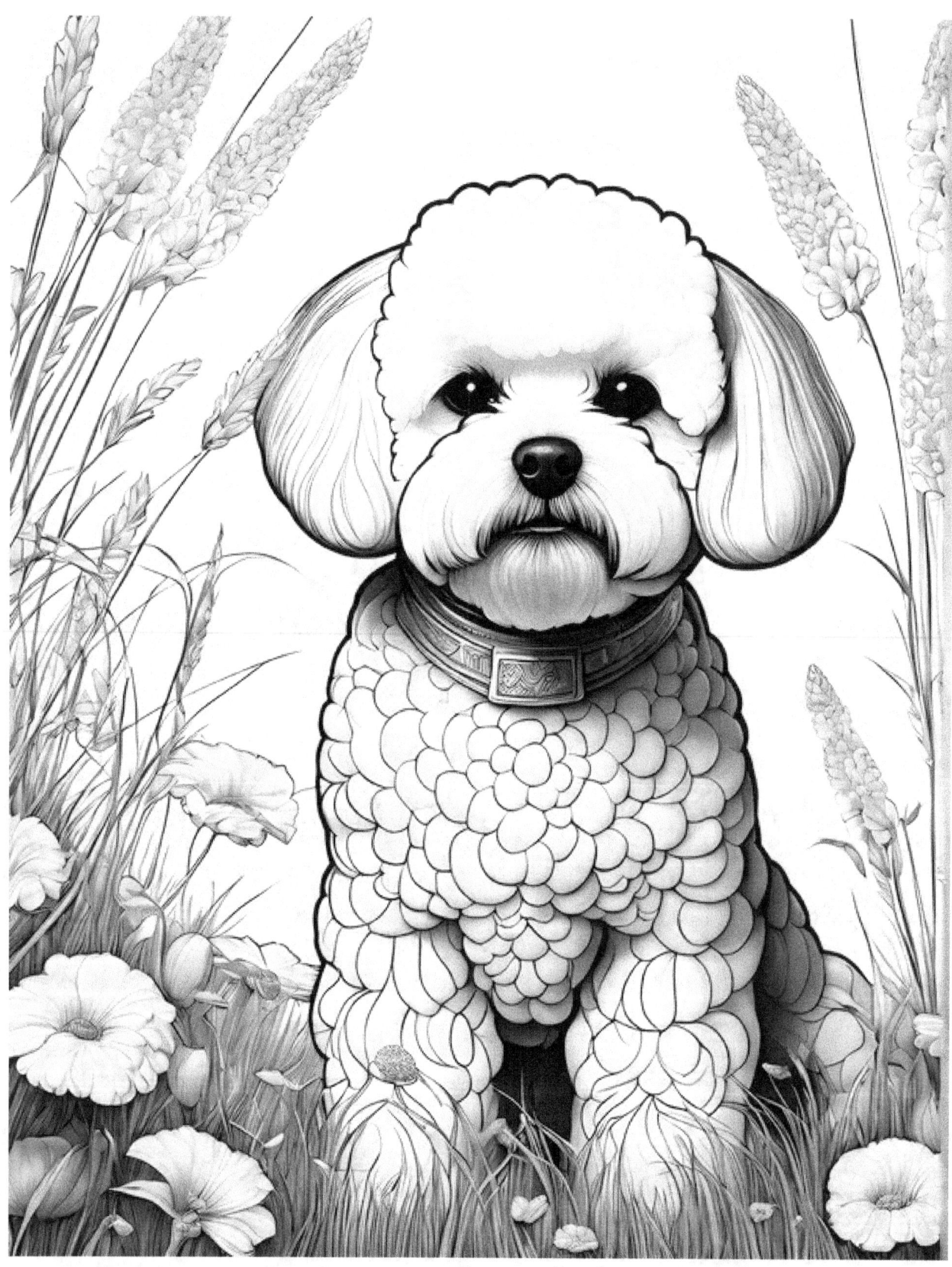

BORDER COLLIE

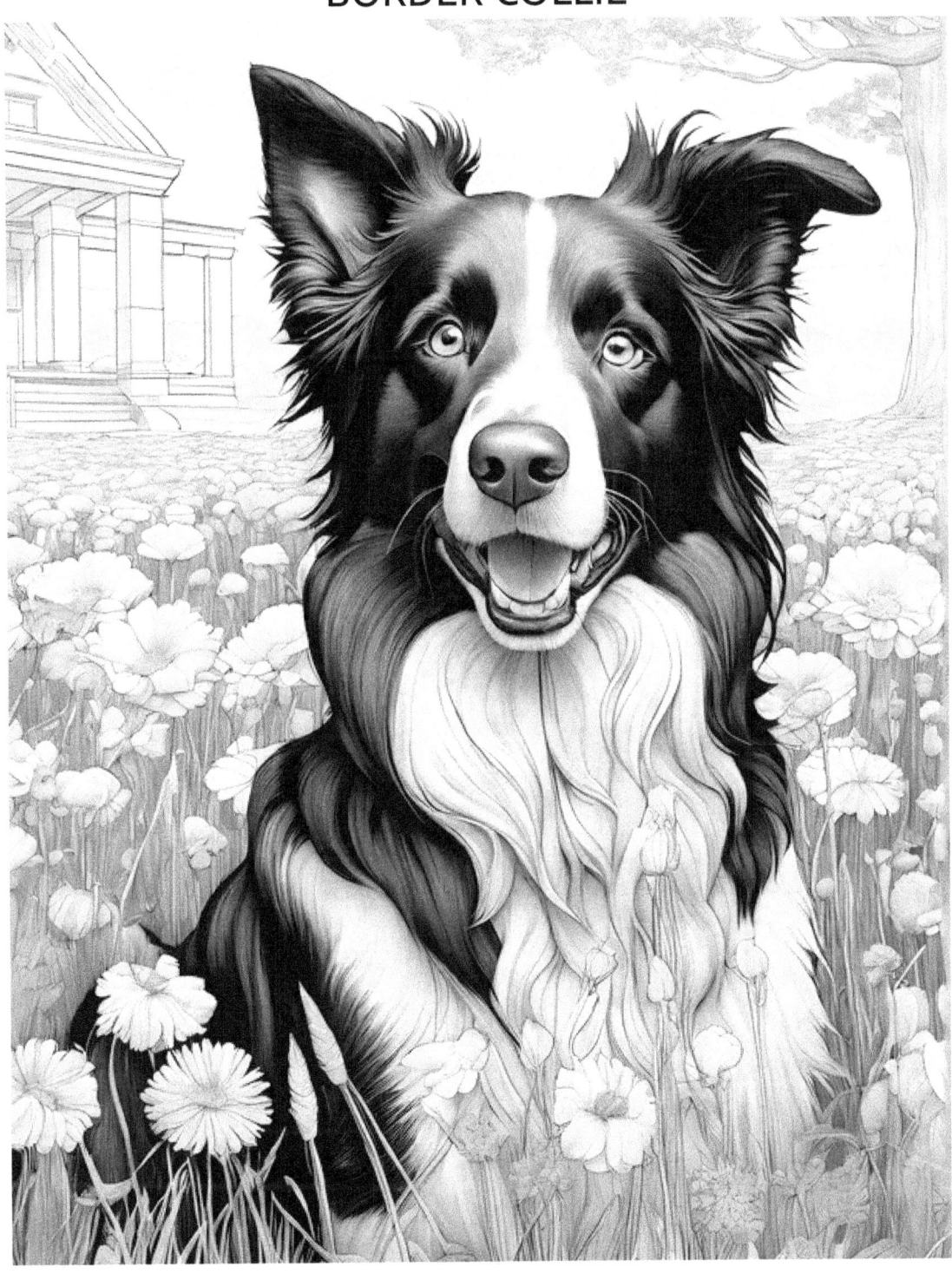

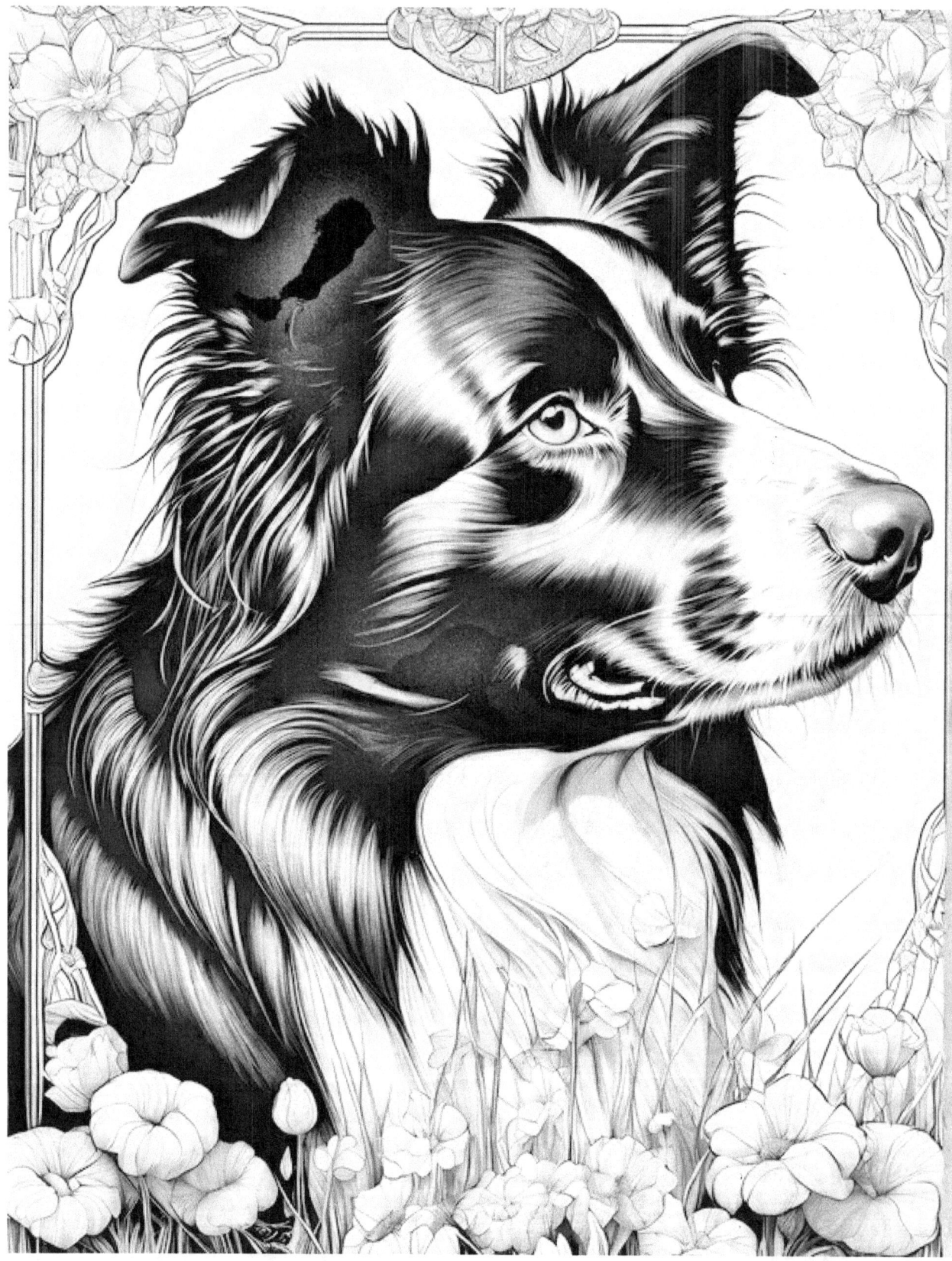

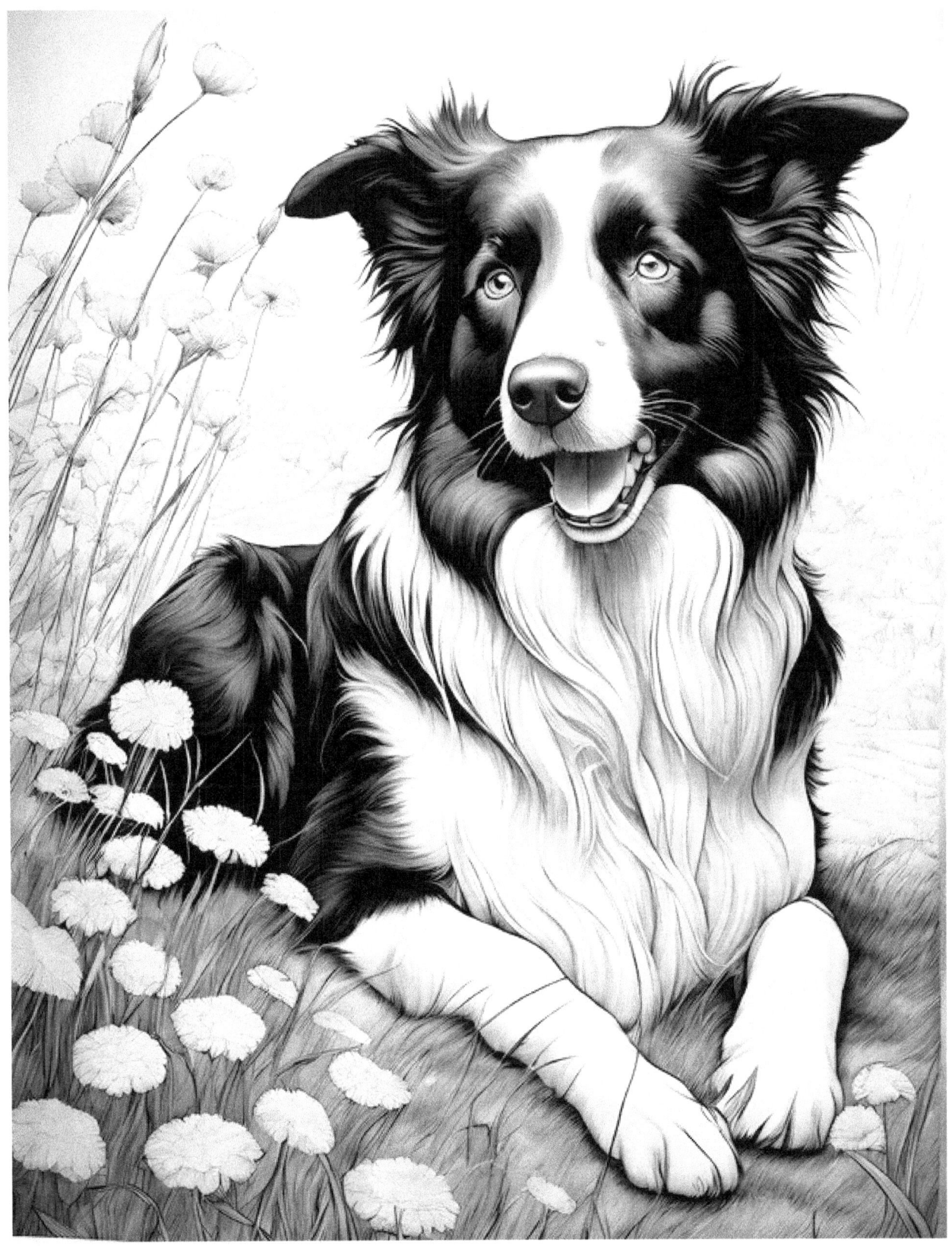

BORZOI

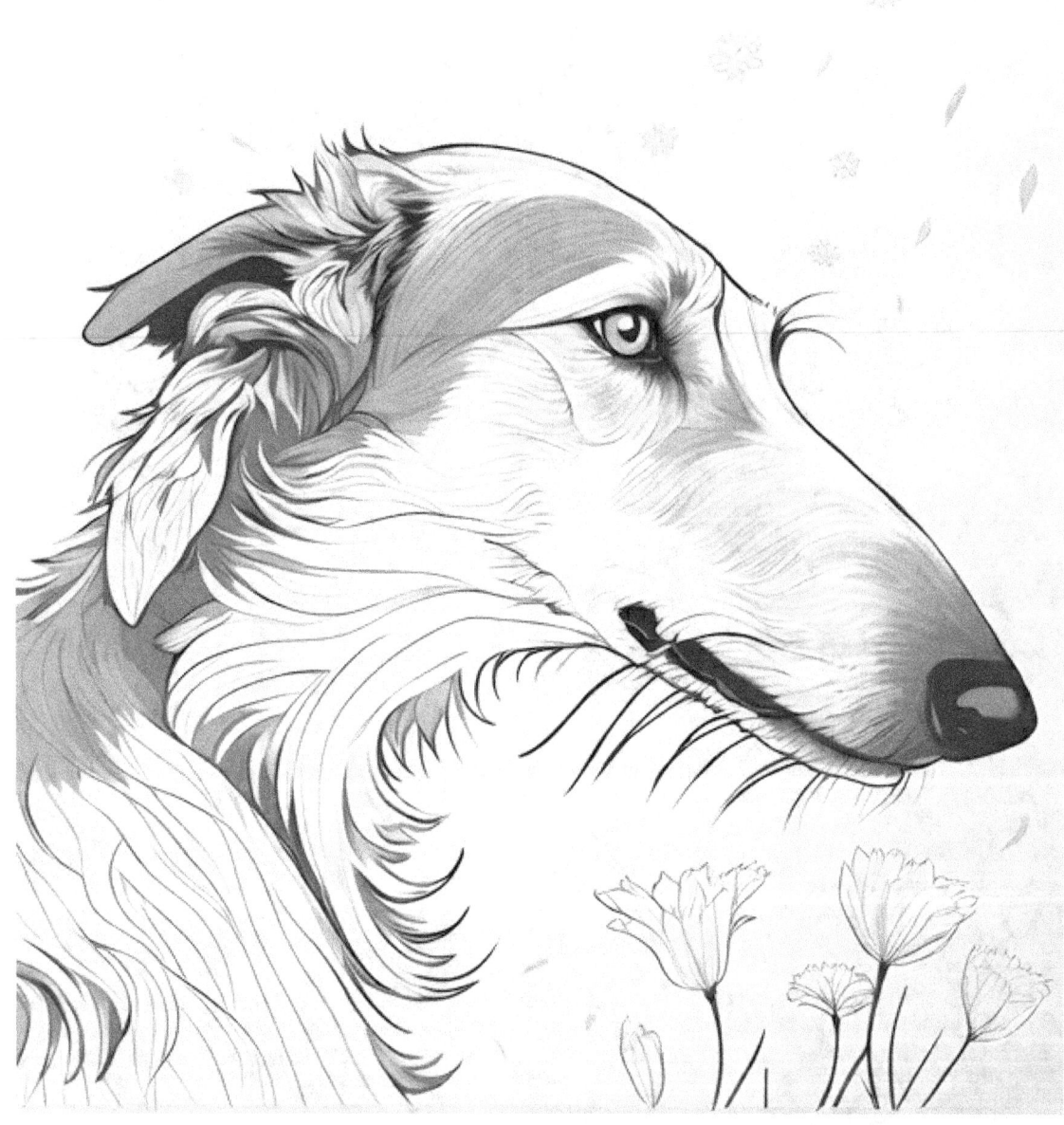

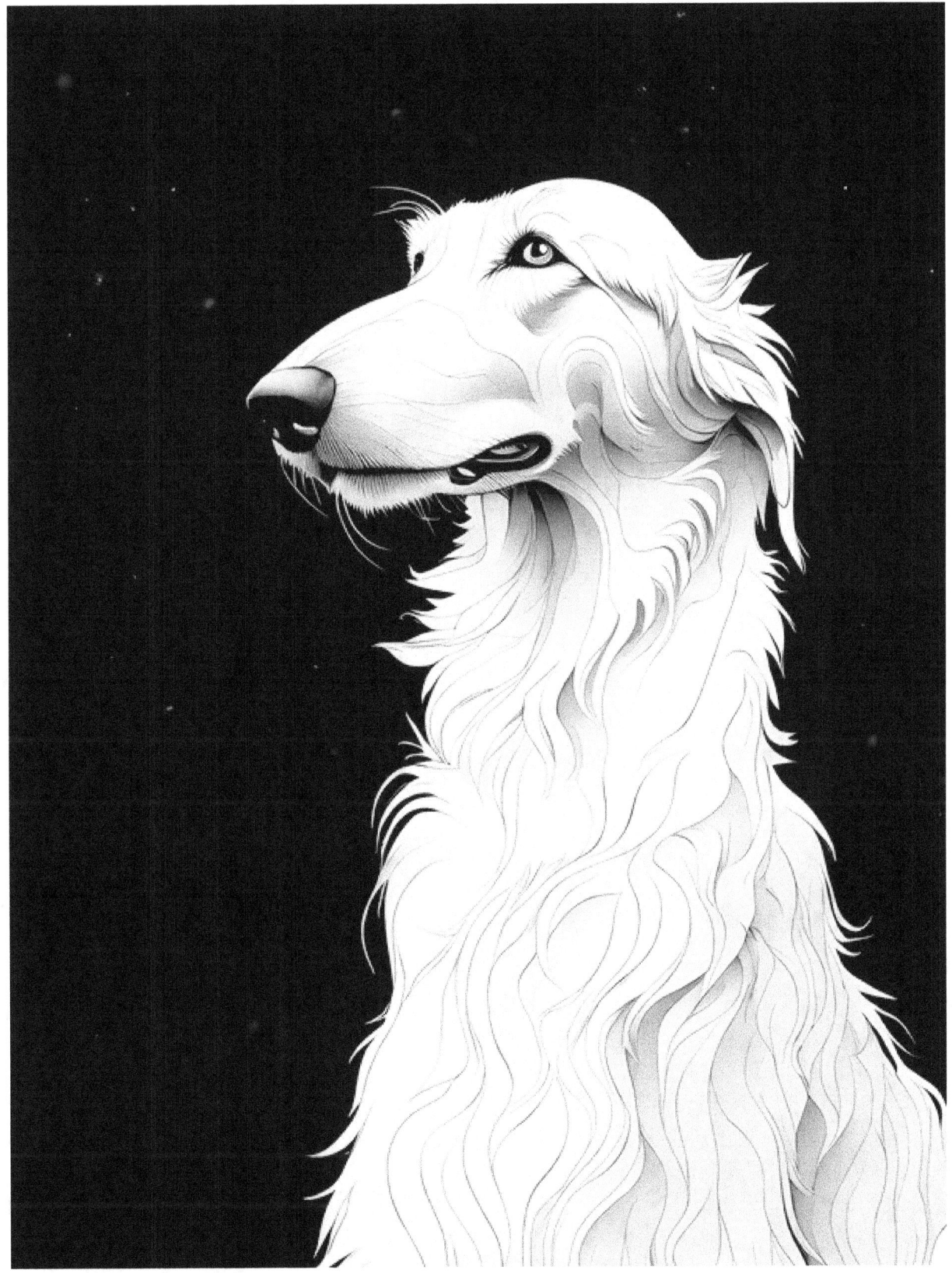

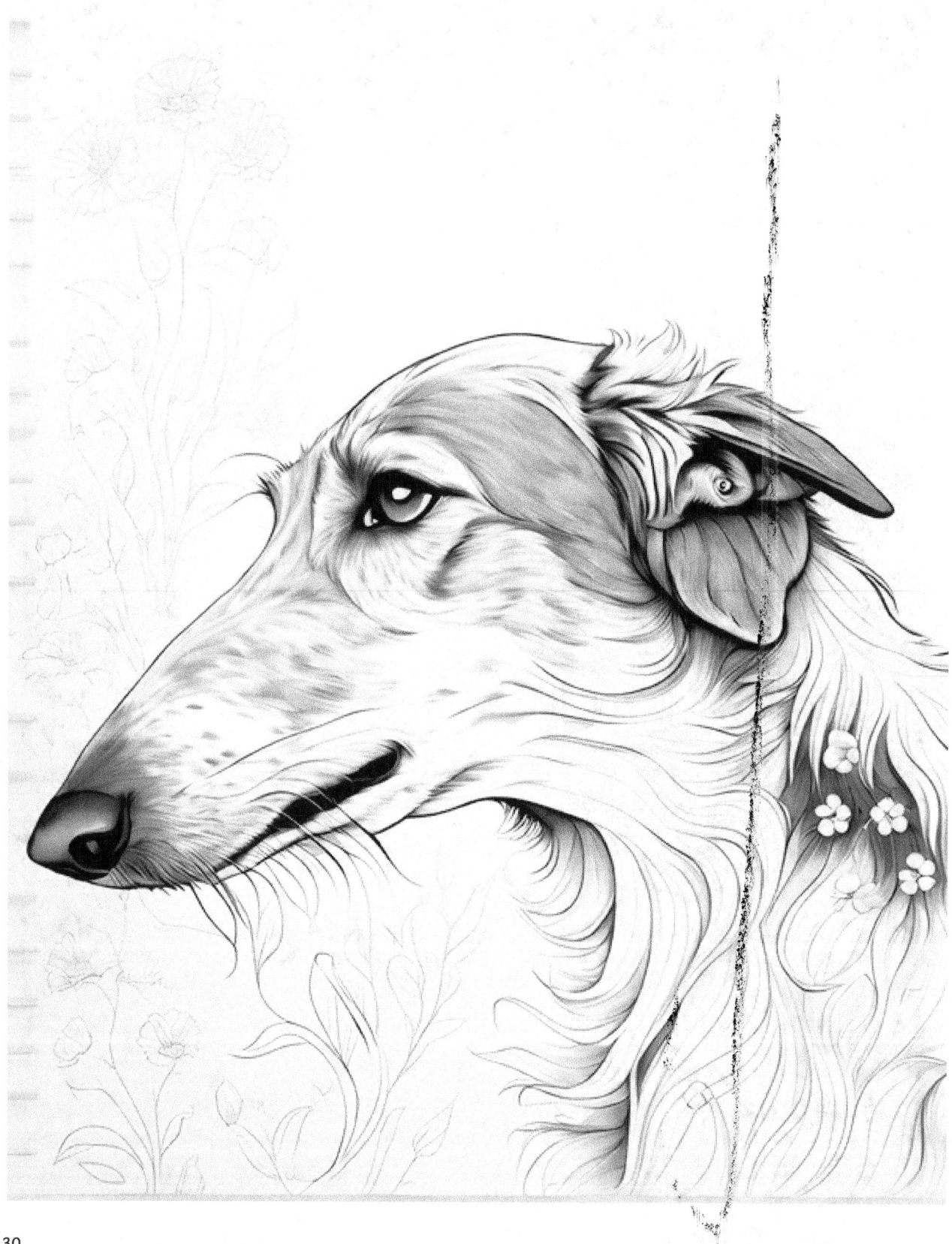

BOXER

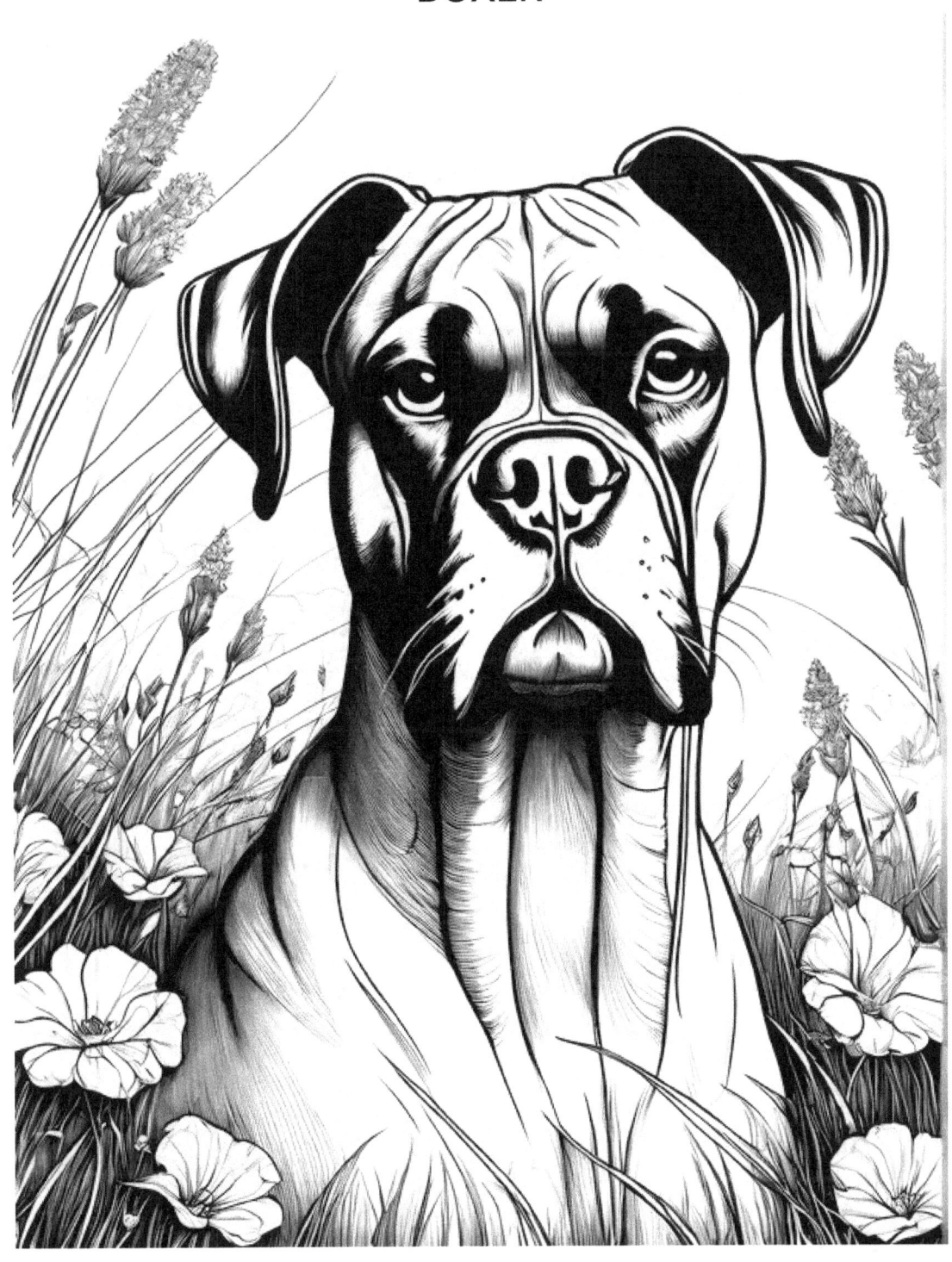

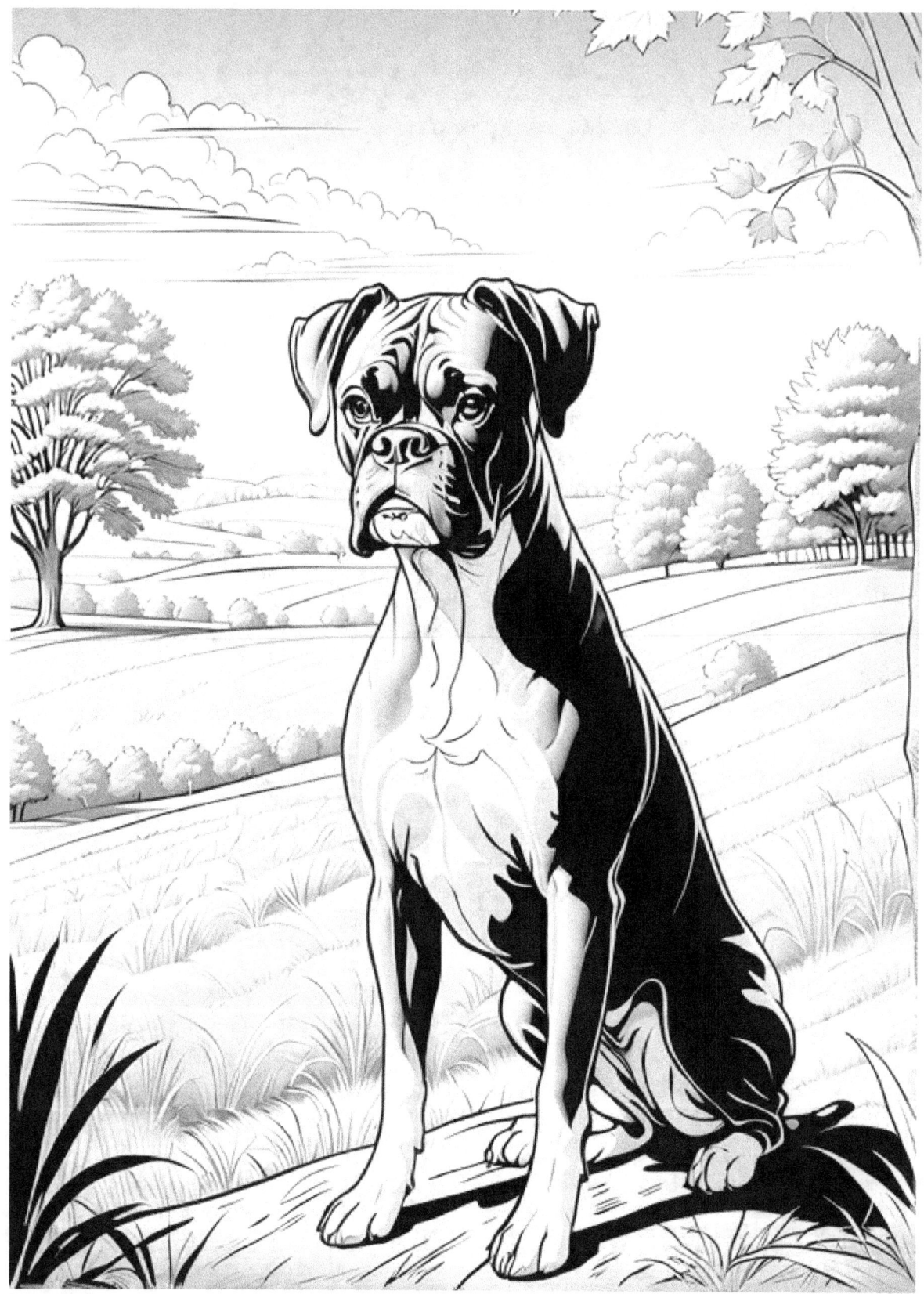

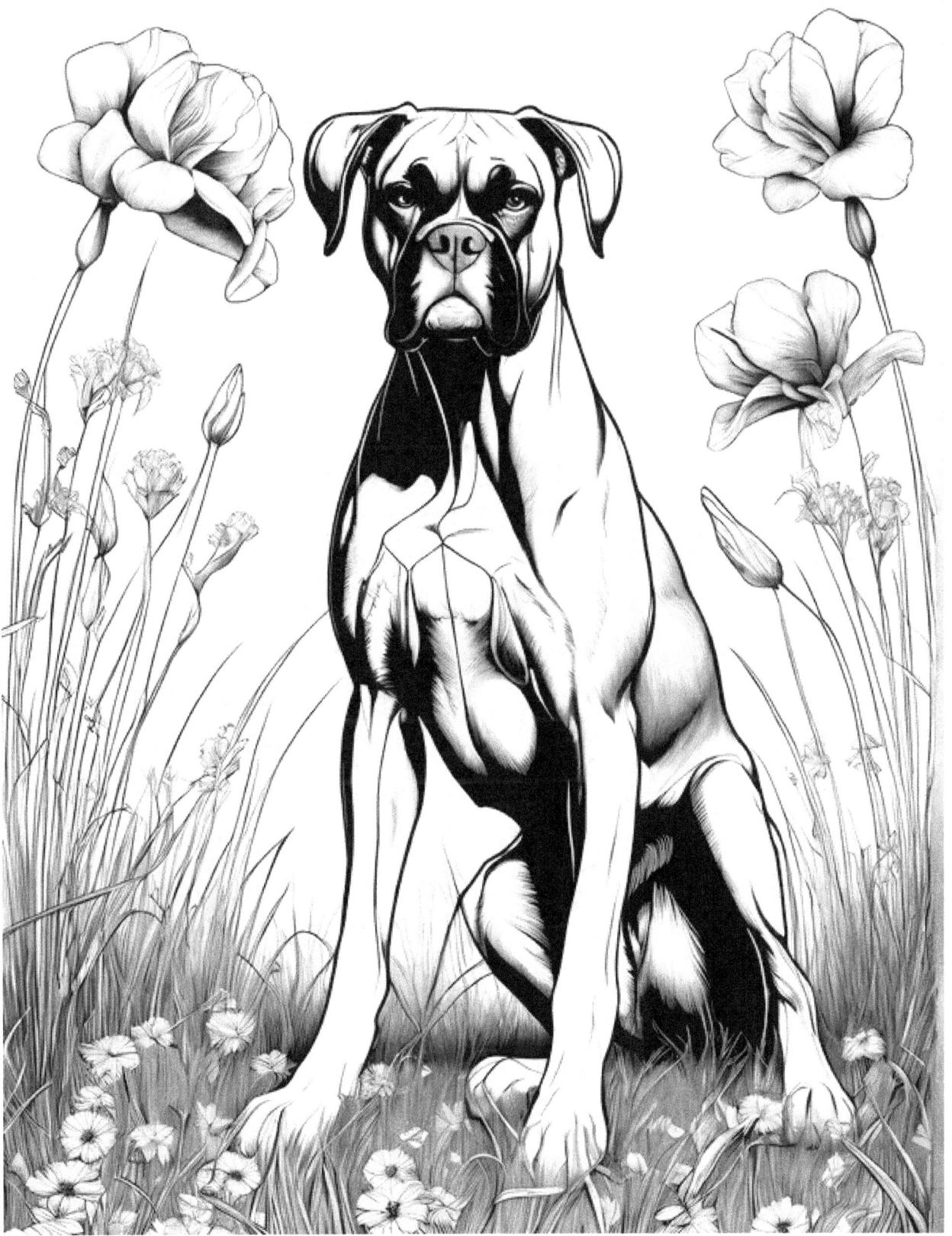

BRUSSELS GRIFFON

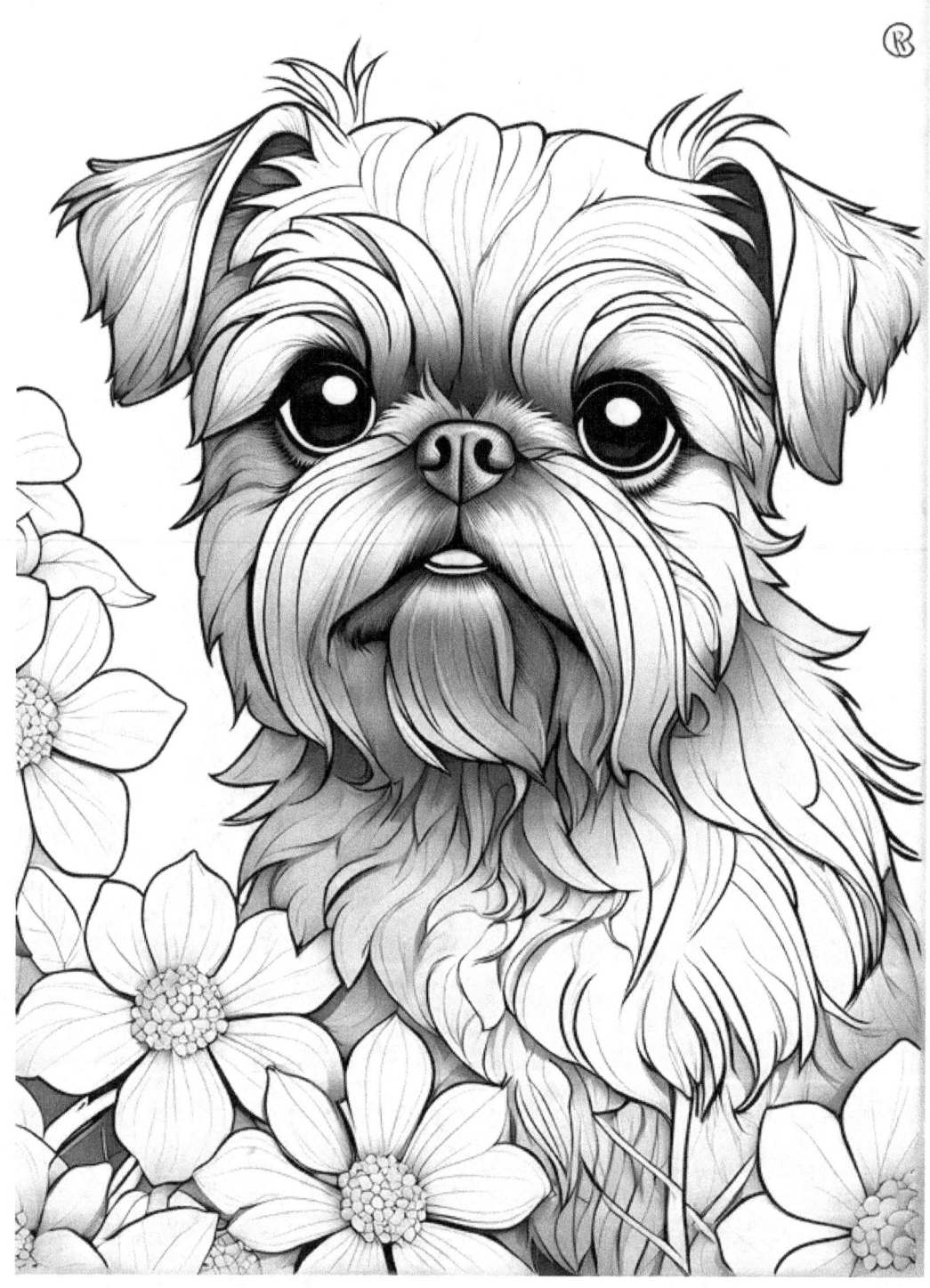

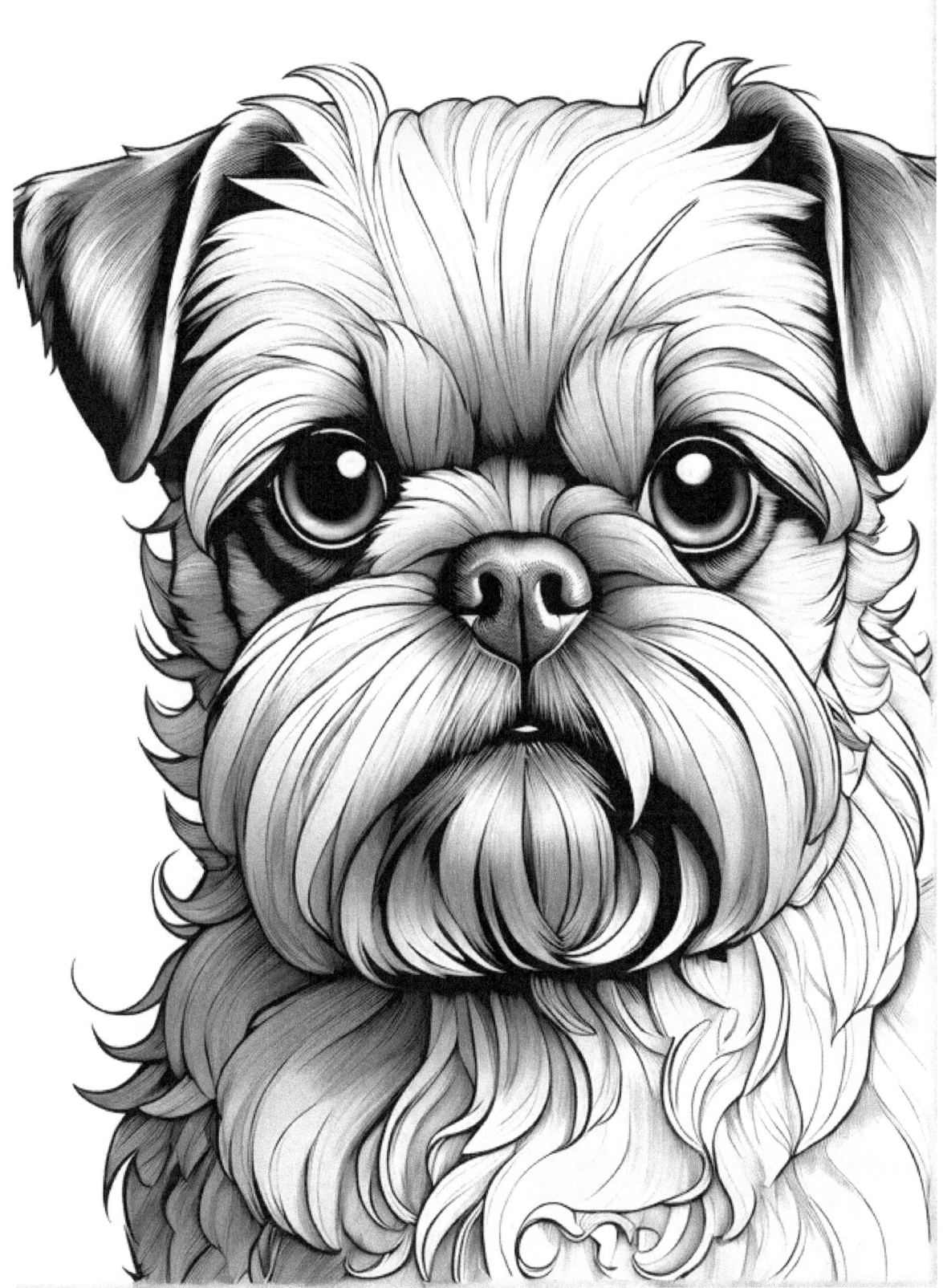

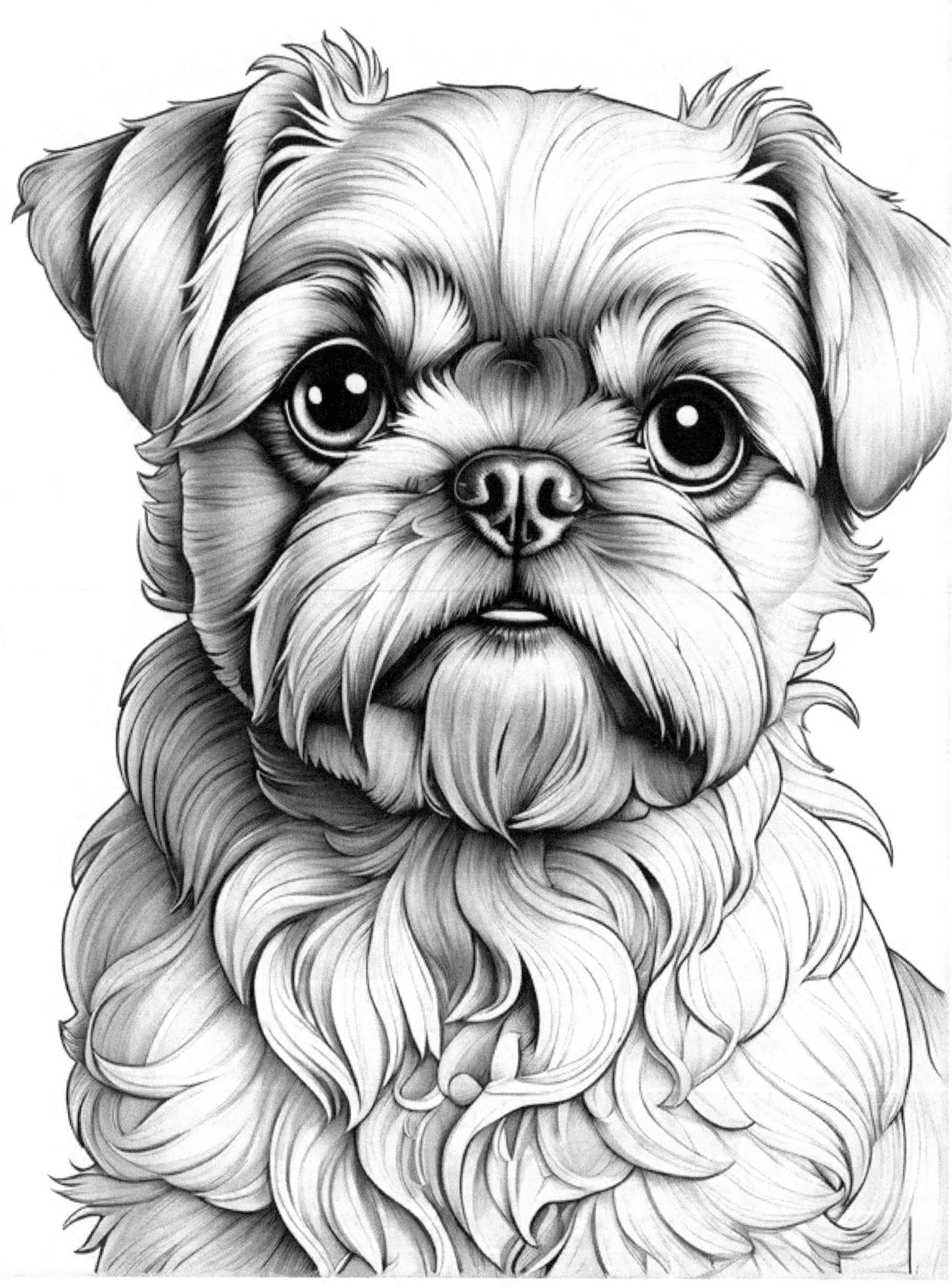

BULLDOG

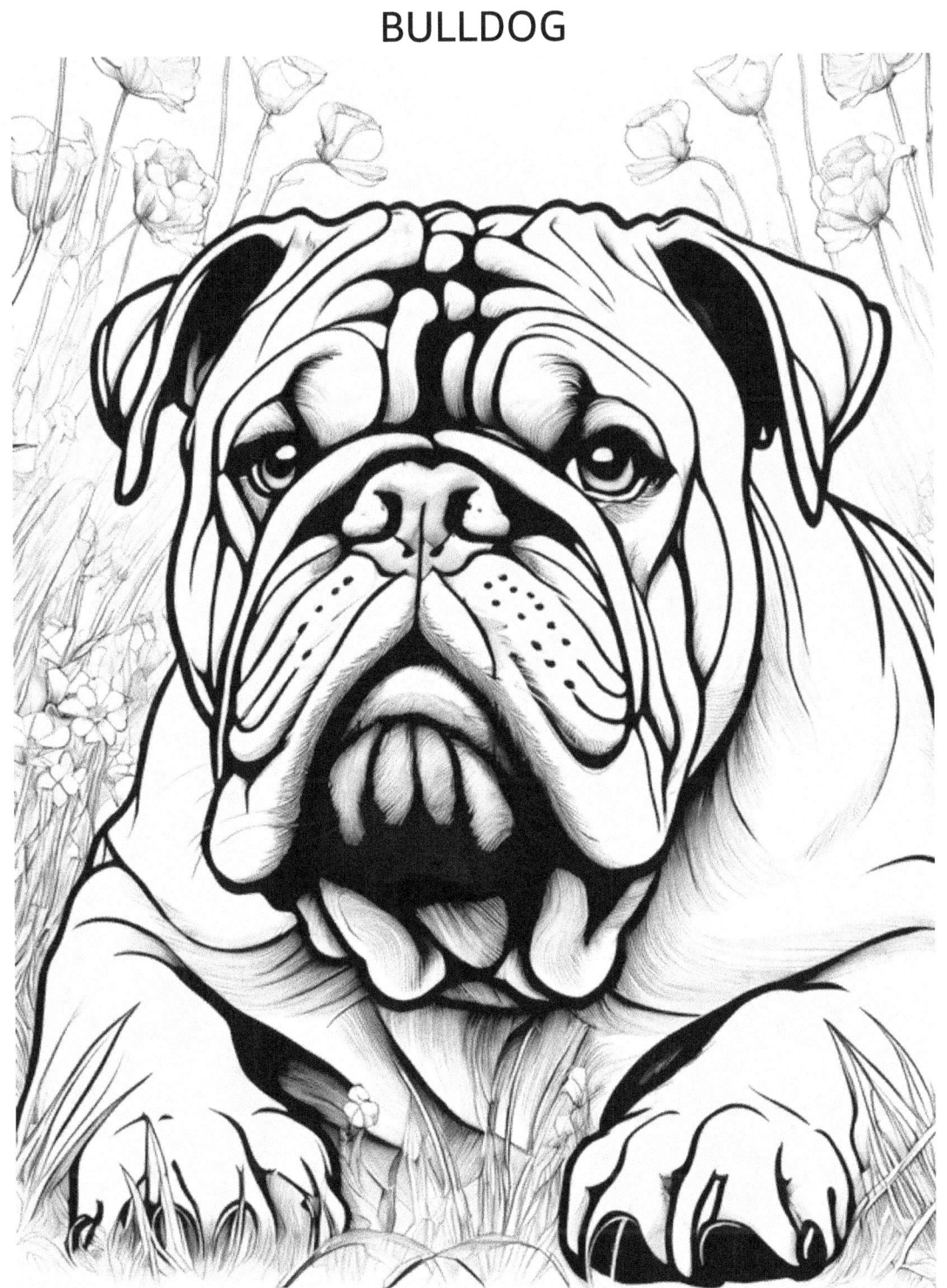

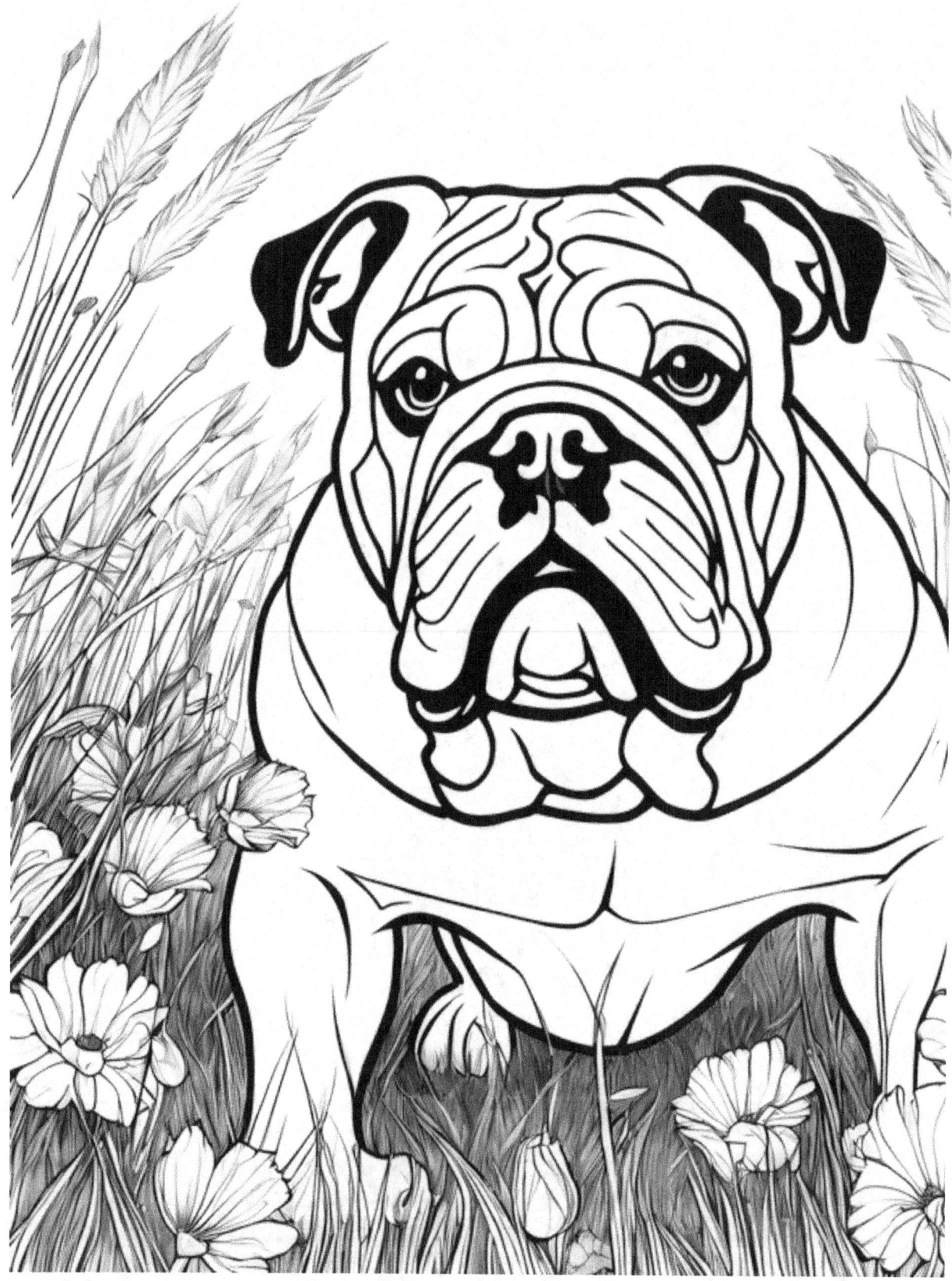

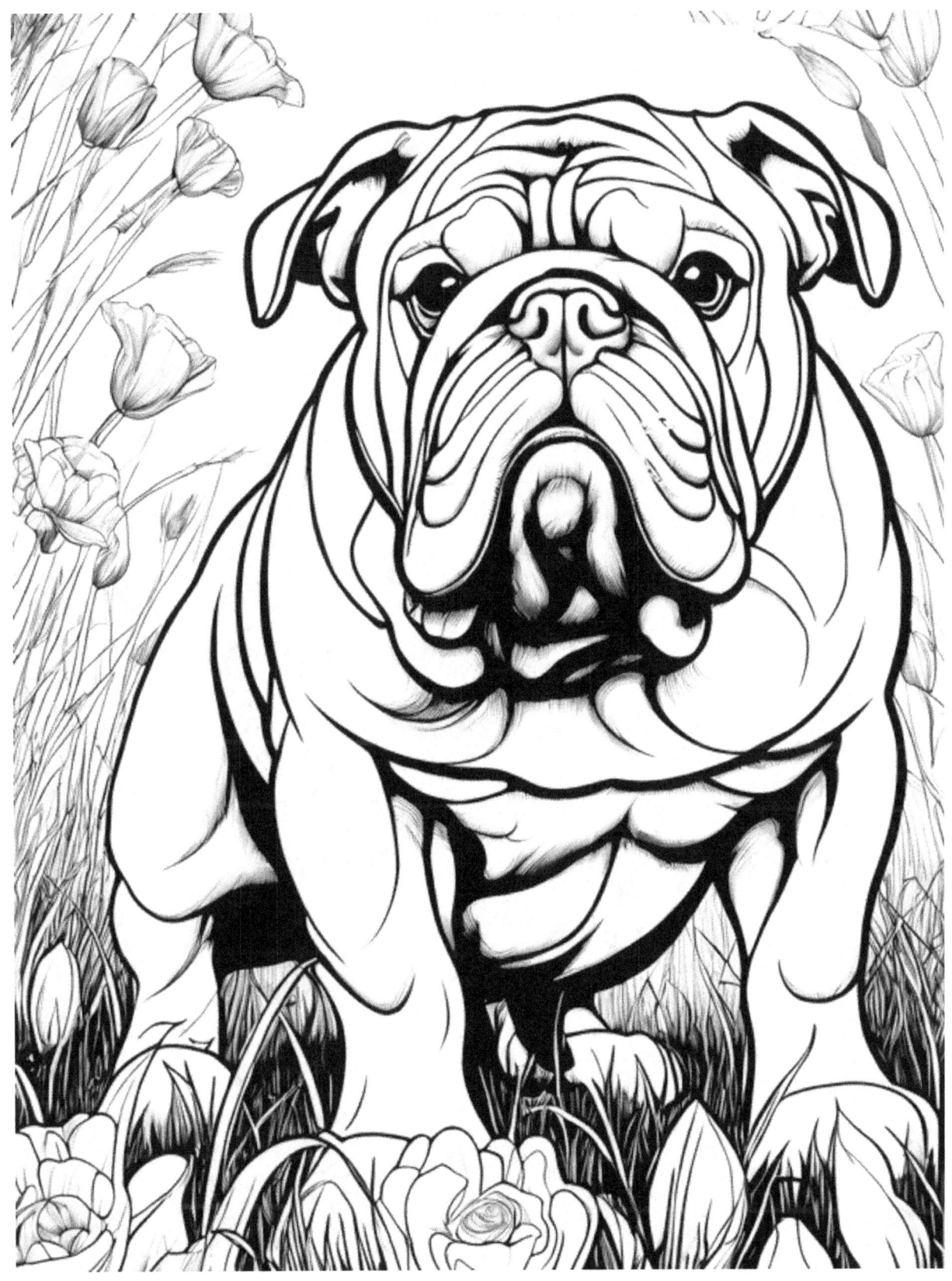

CHIHUAHUA

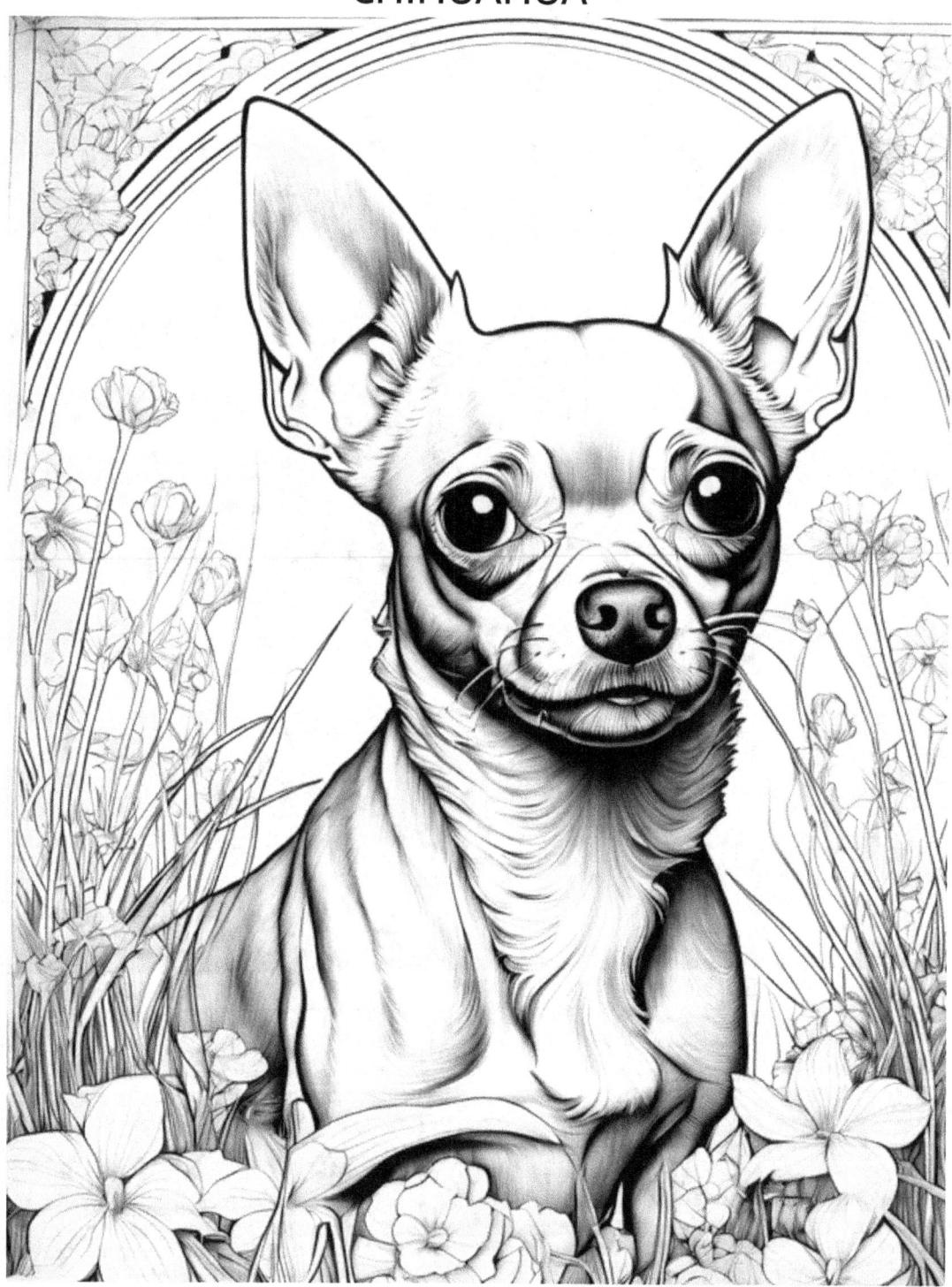

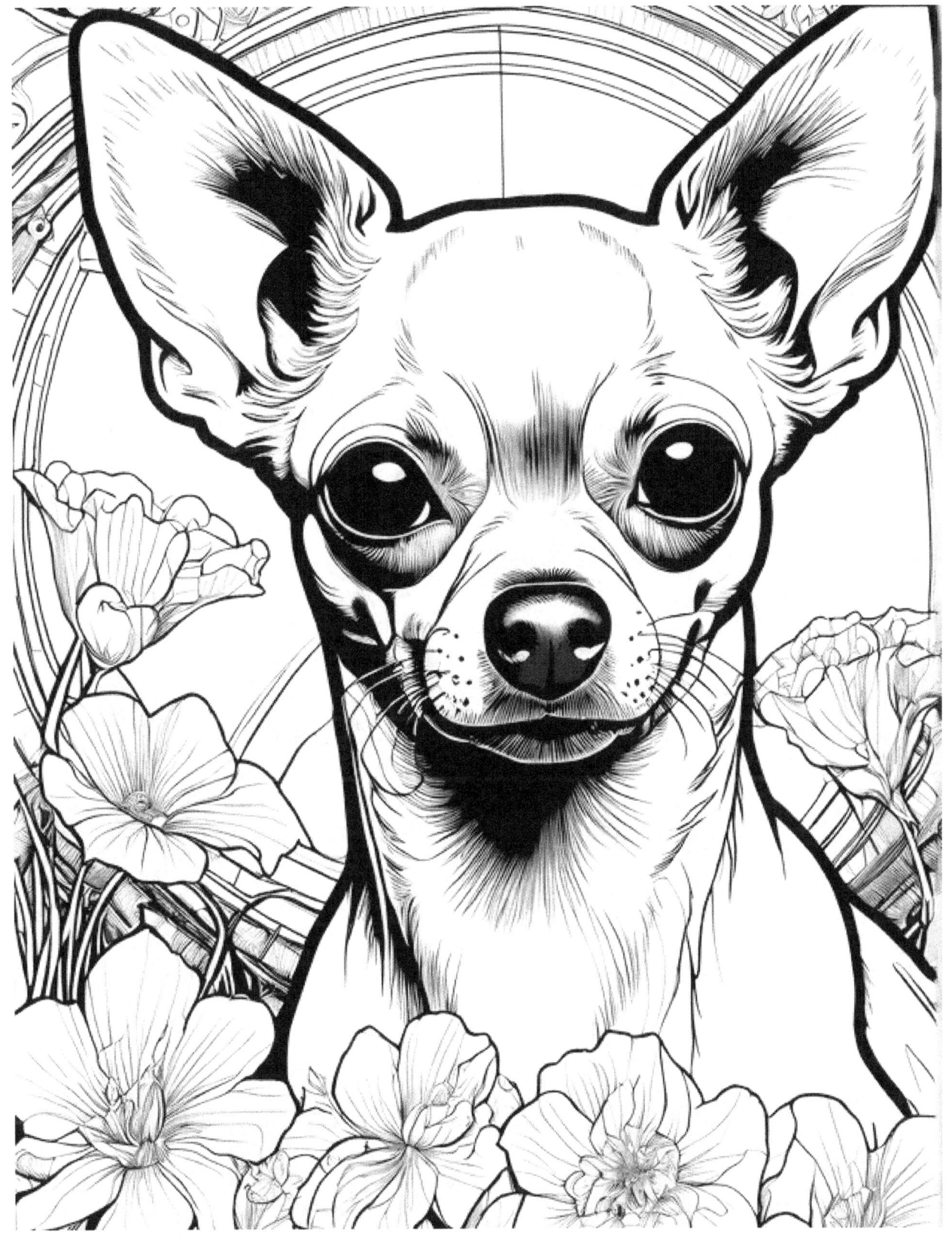

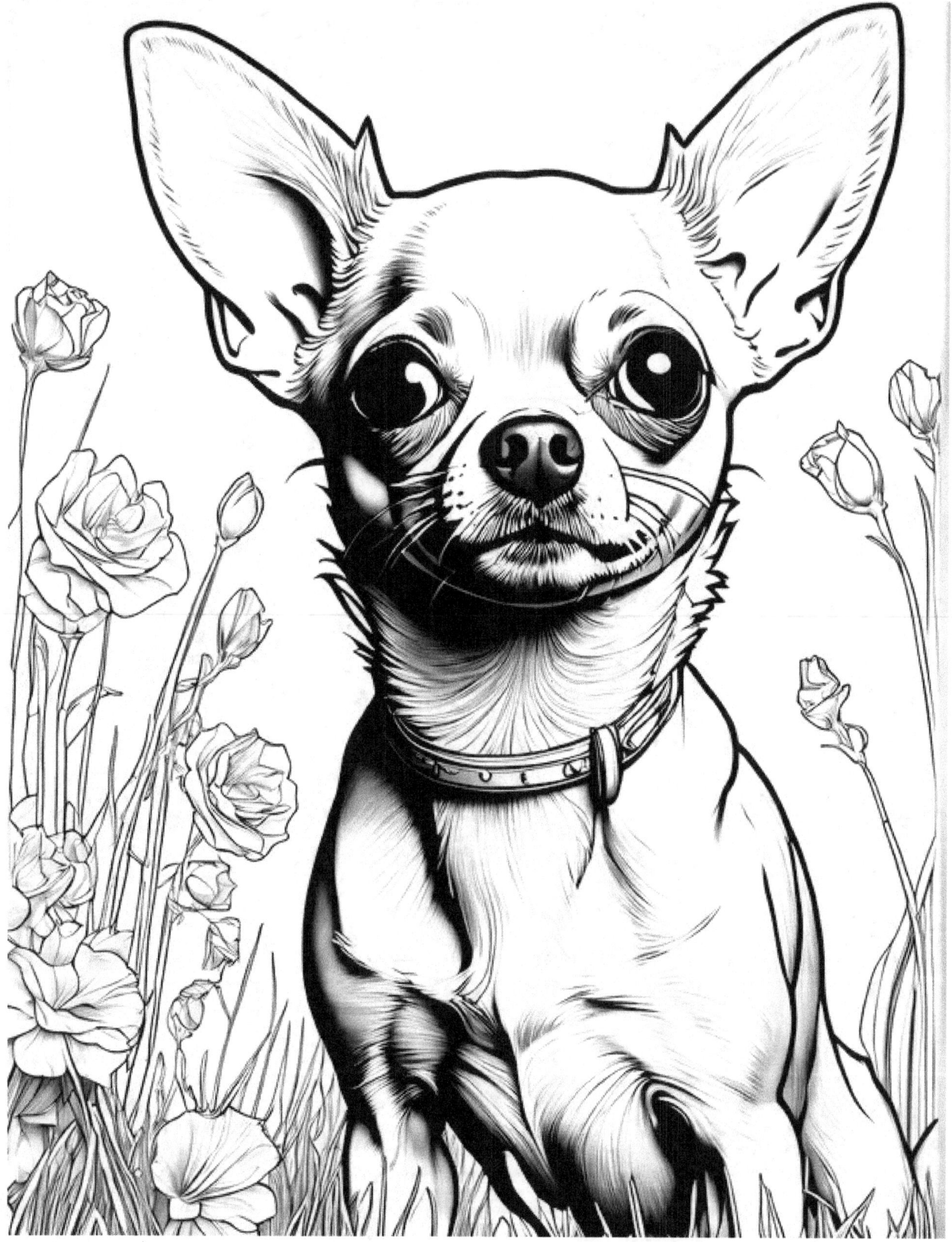

CHINESE CRESTED

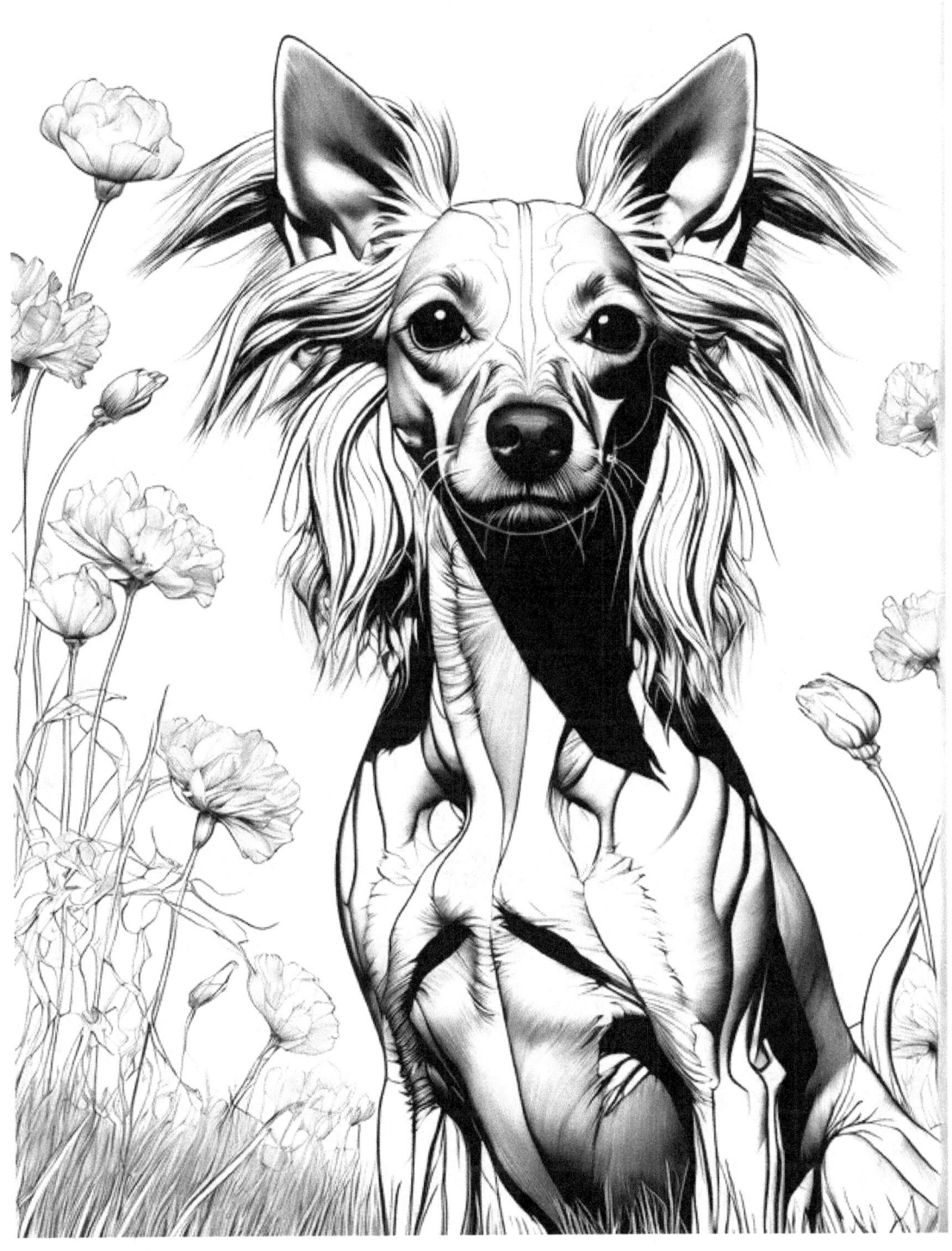

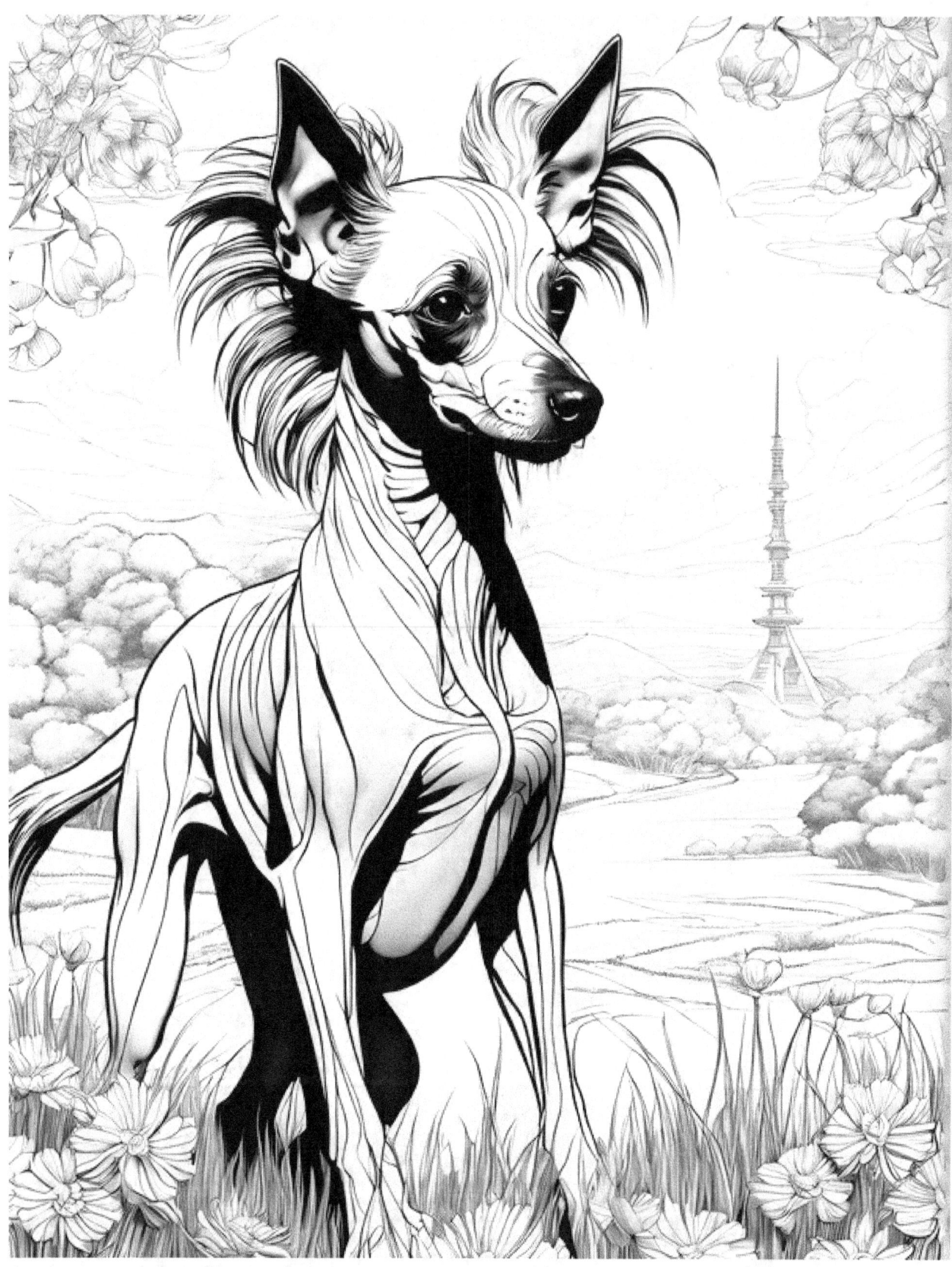

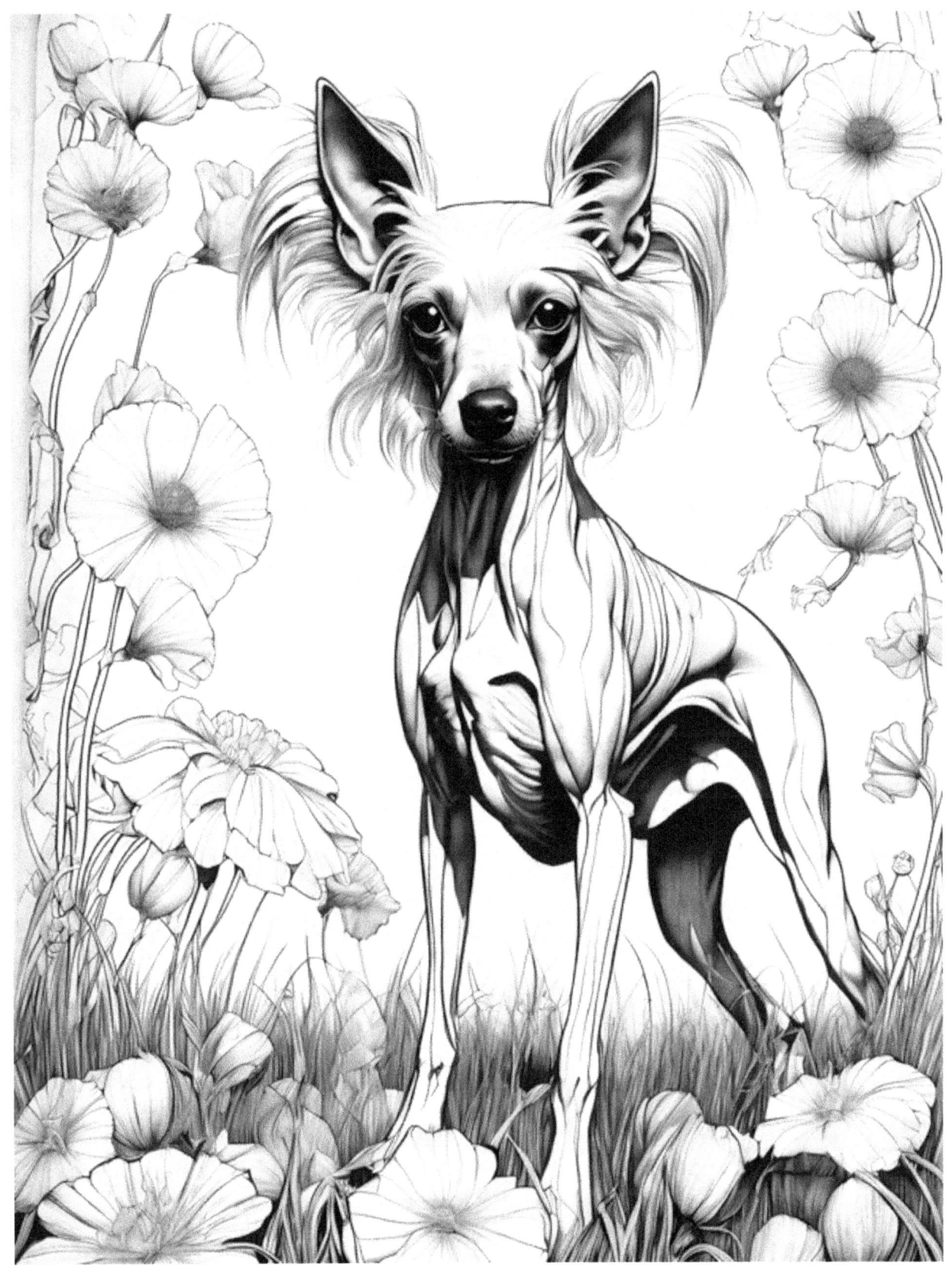

CHOW CHOW

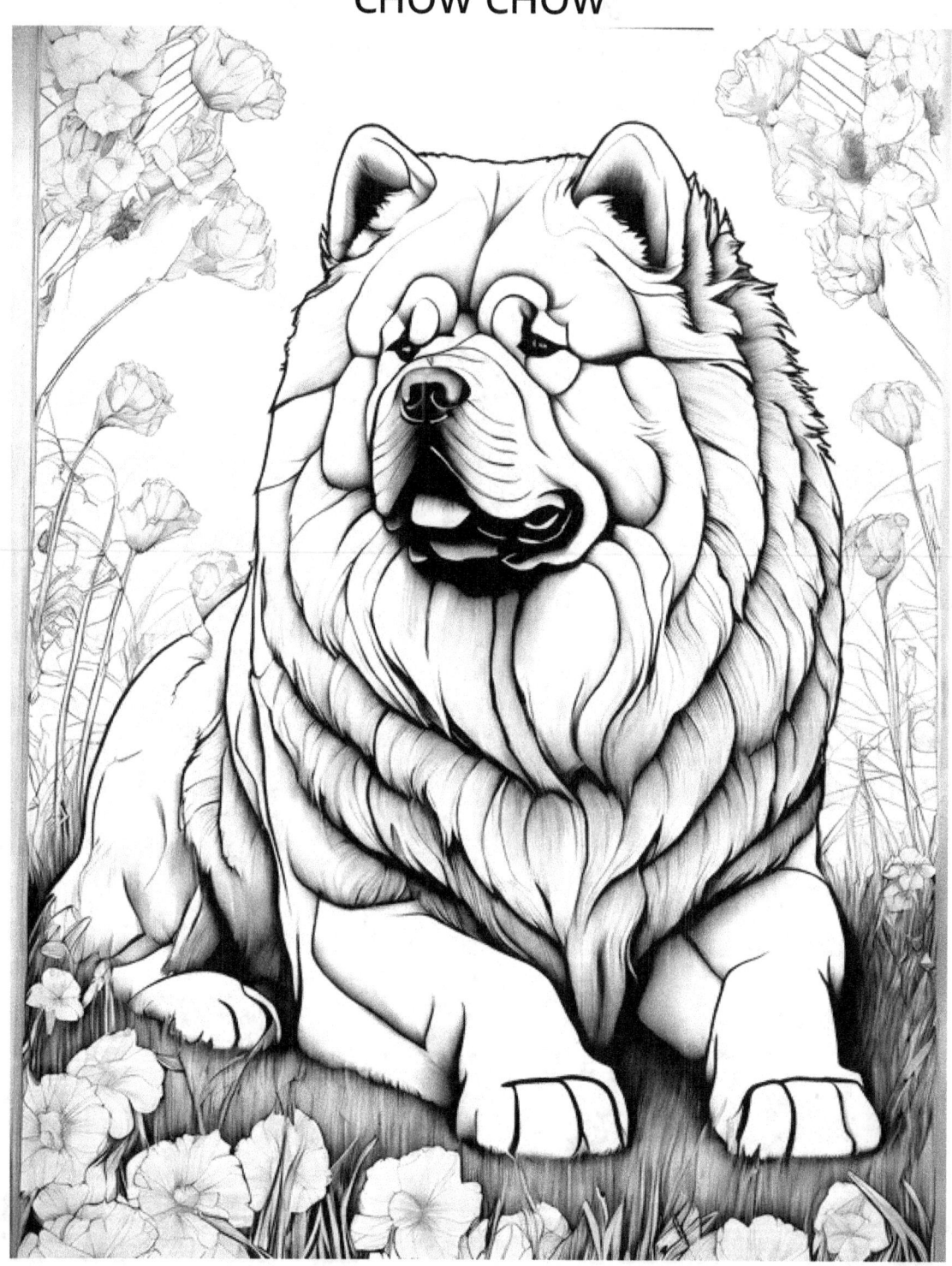

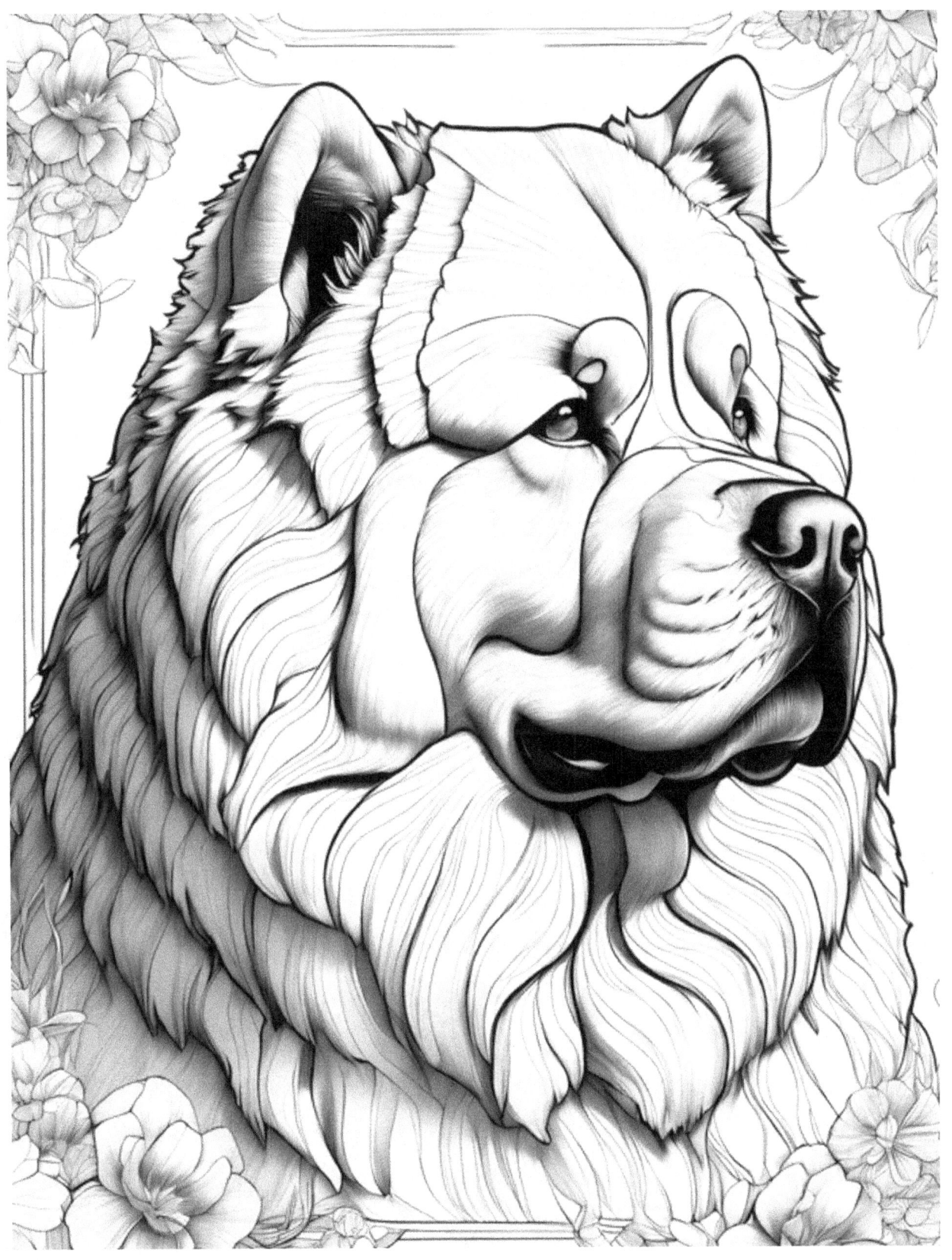

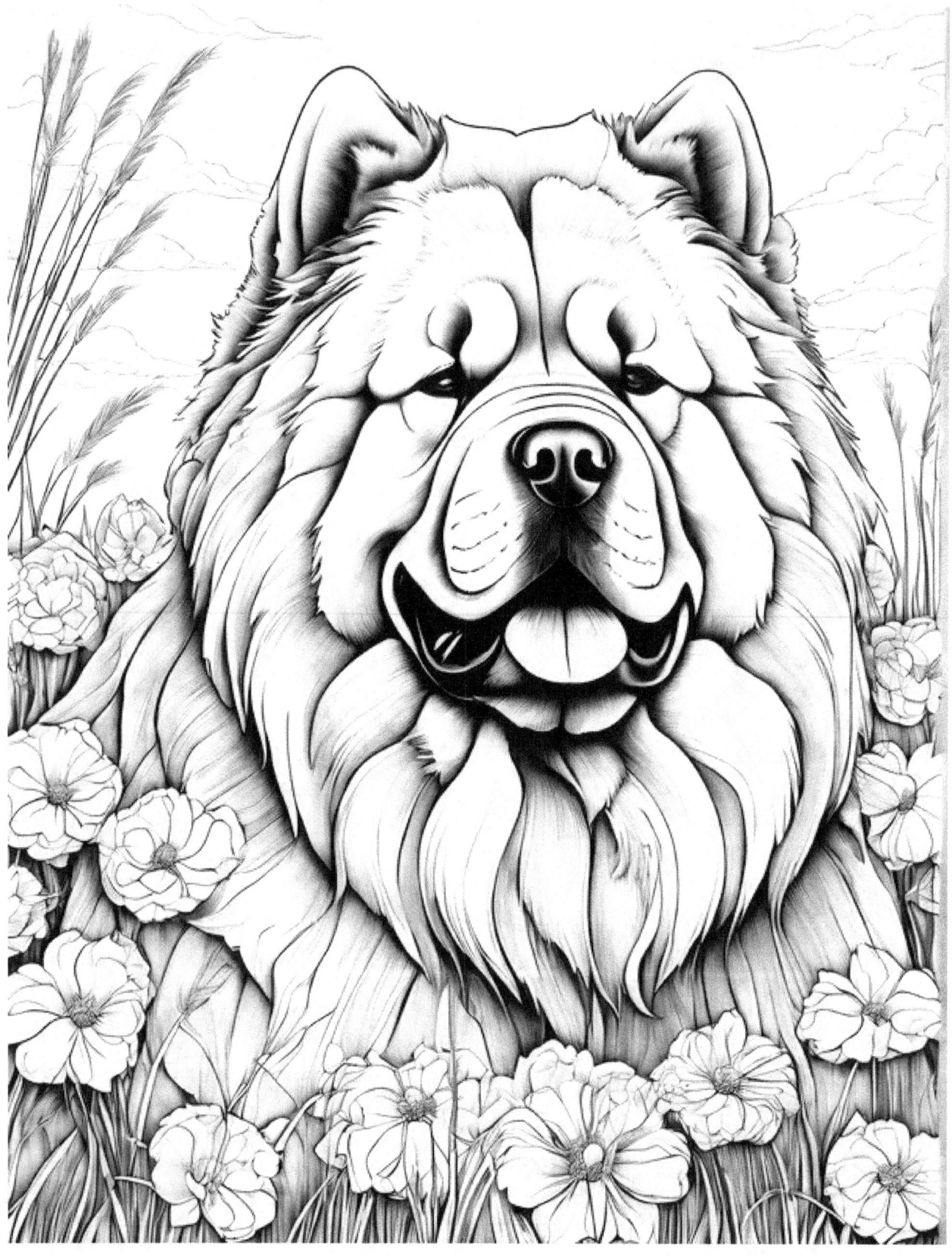

CIRNECO DELL'ETNA

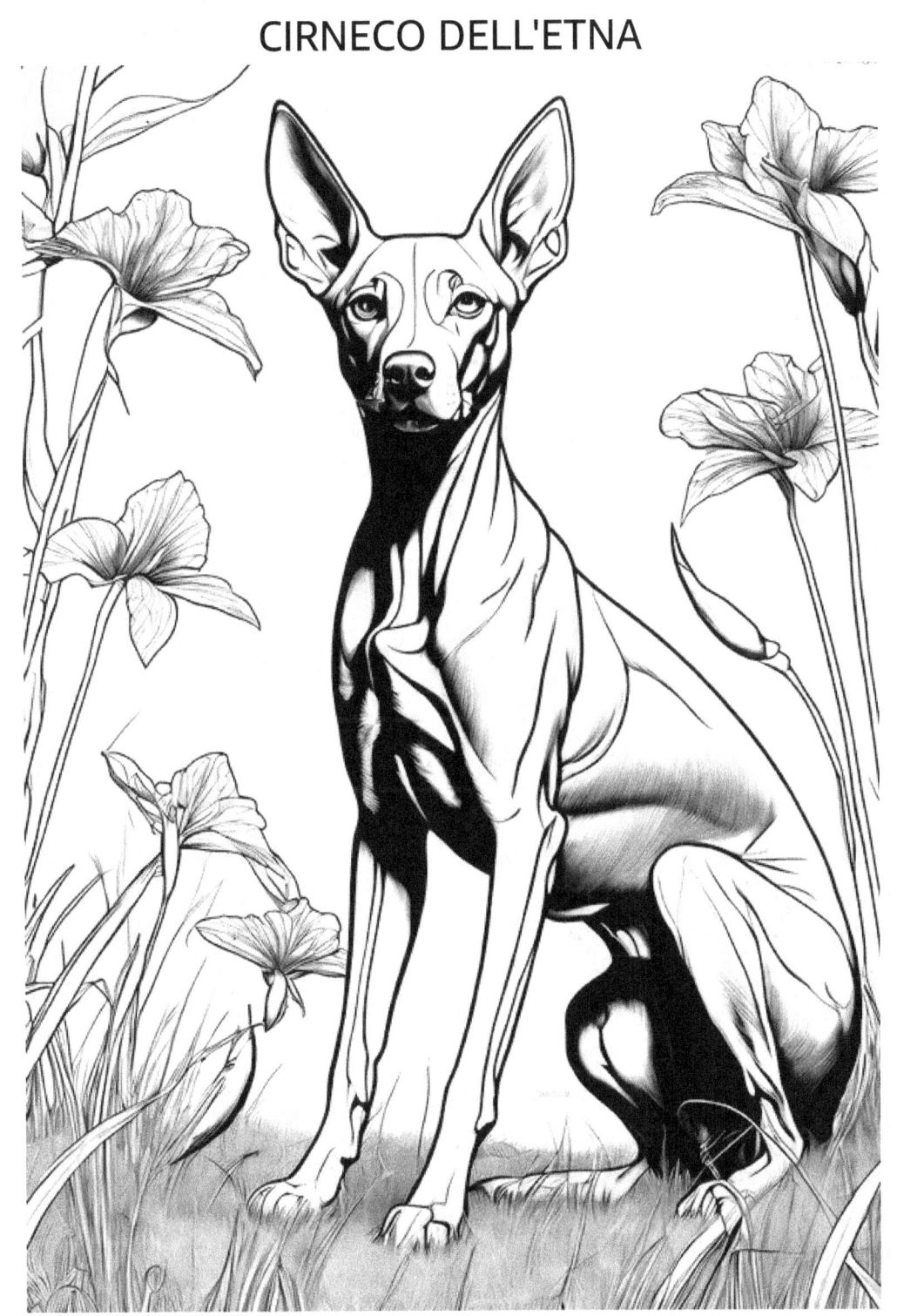

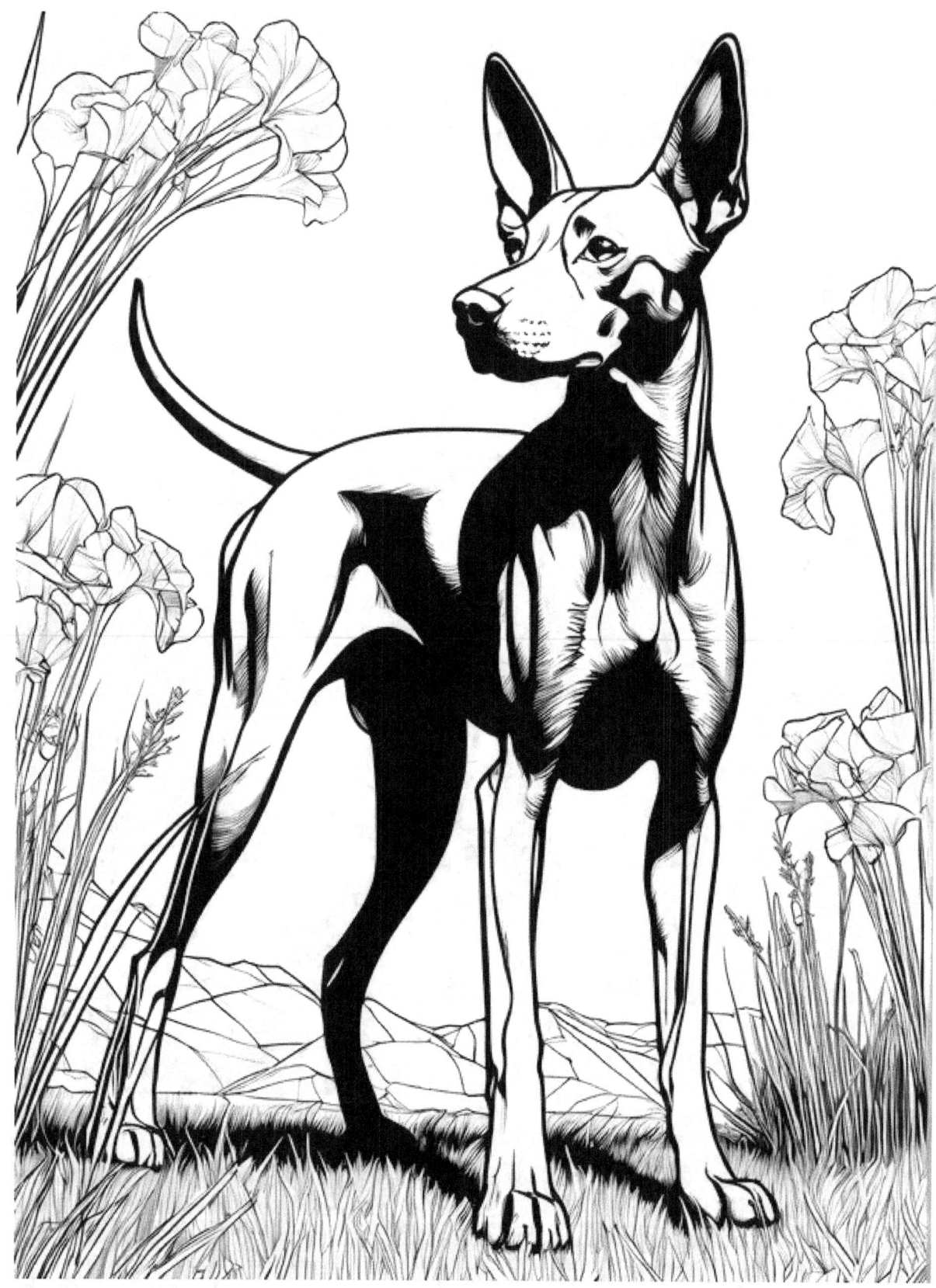

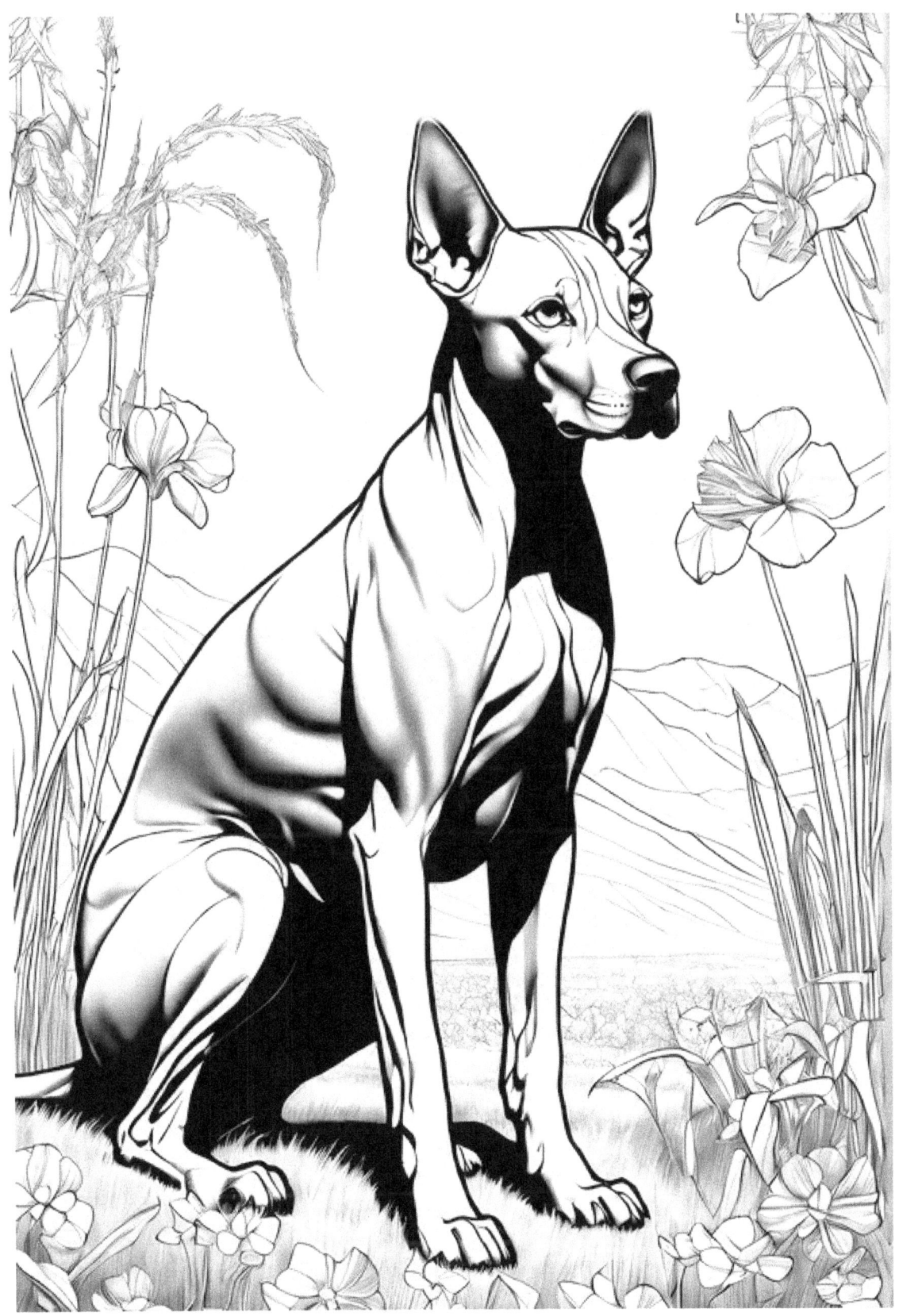

COCKER SPANIEL

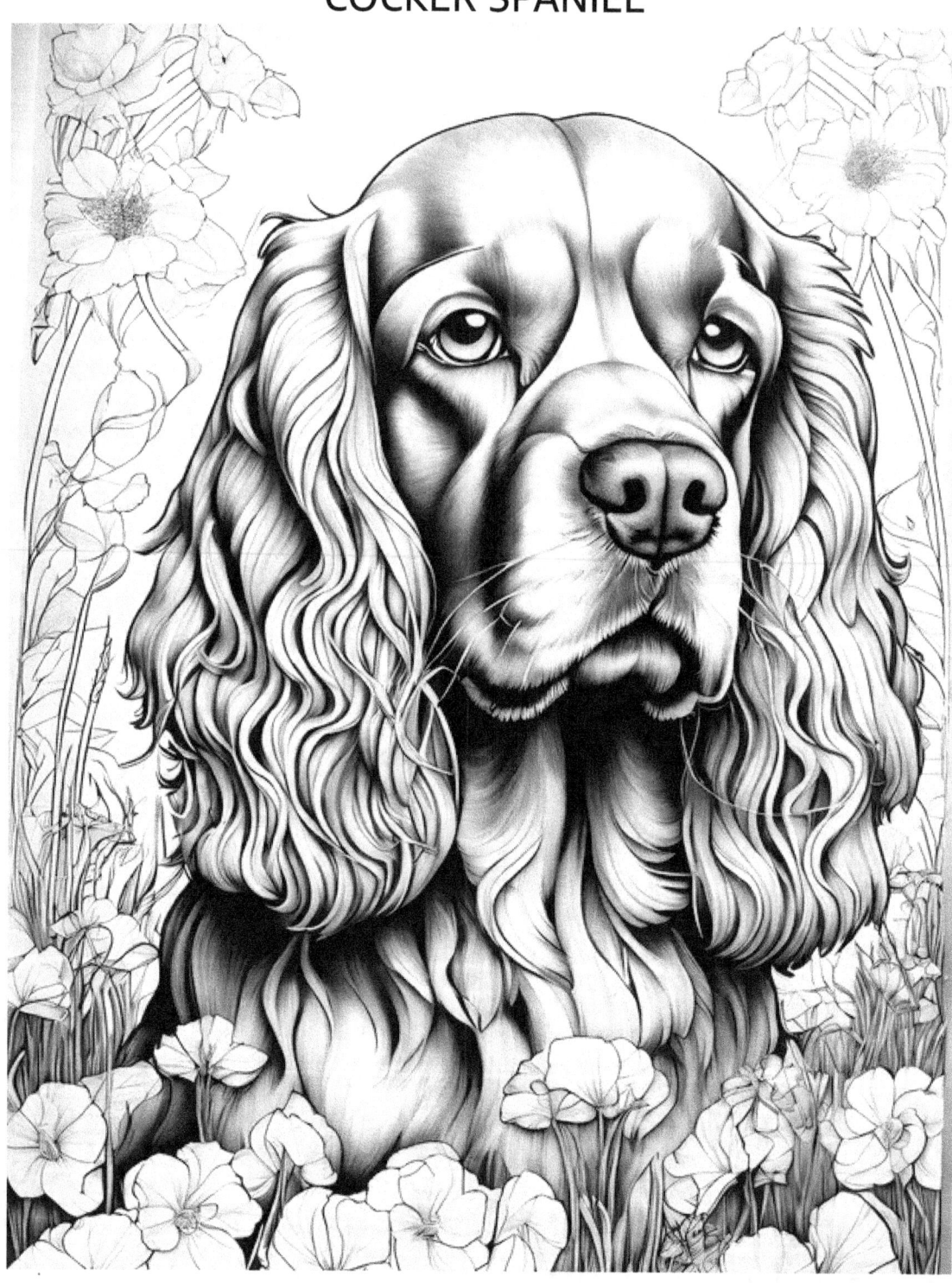

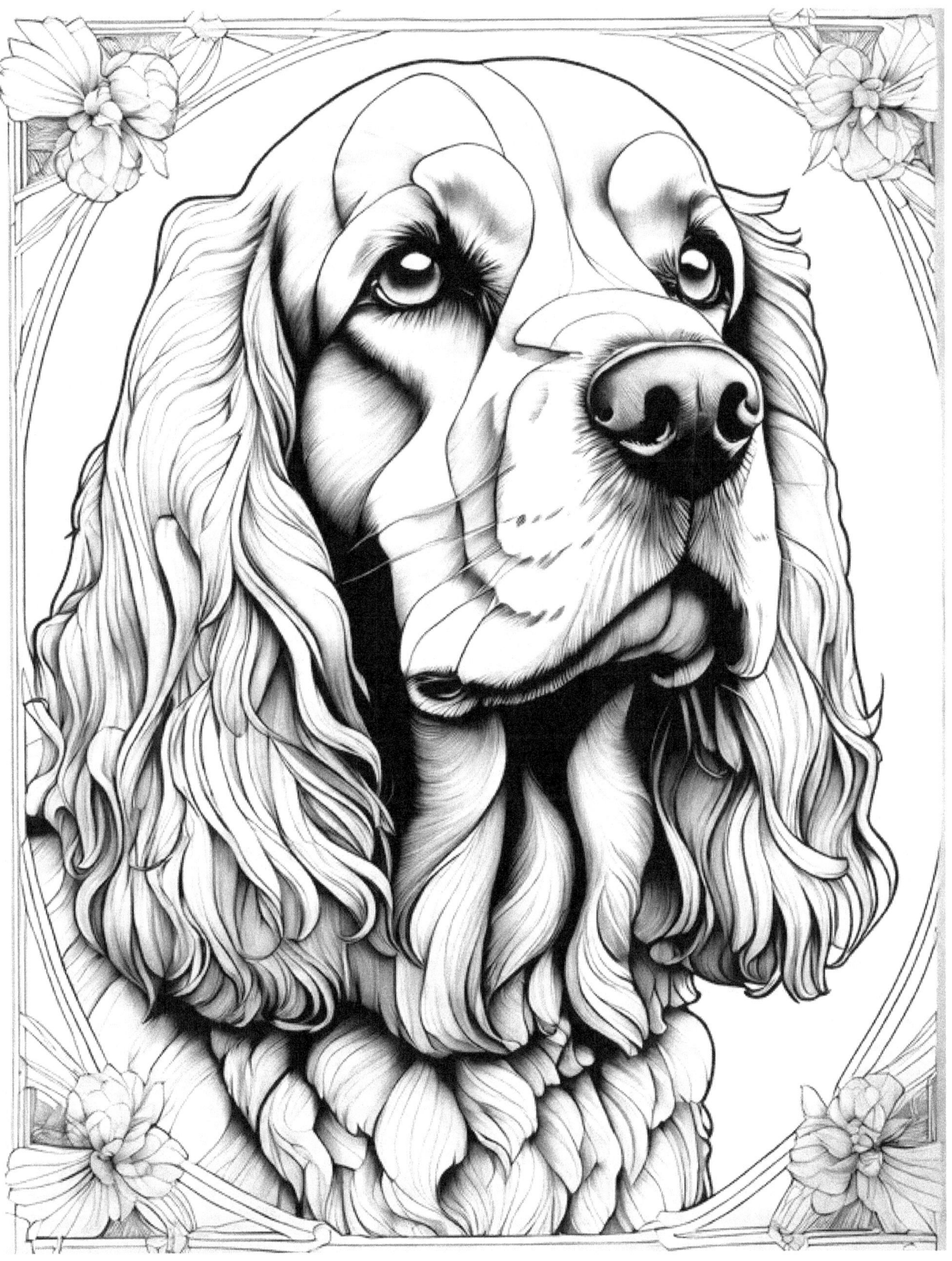

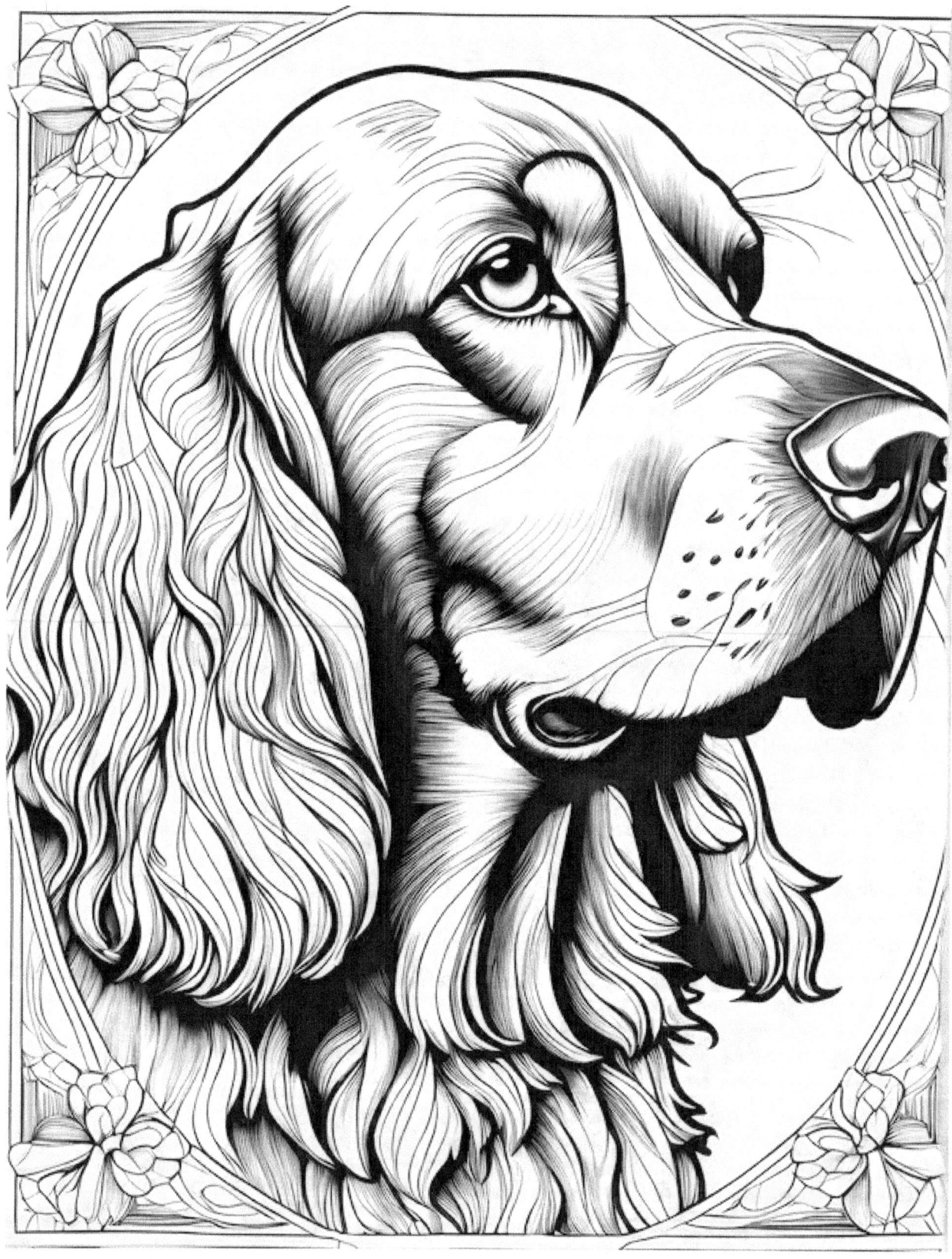

CORSO

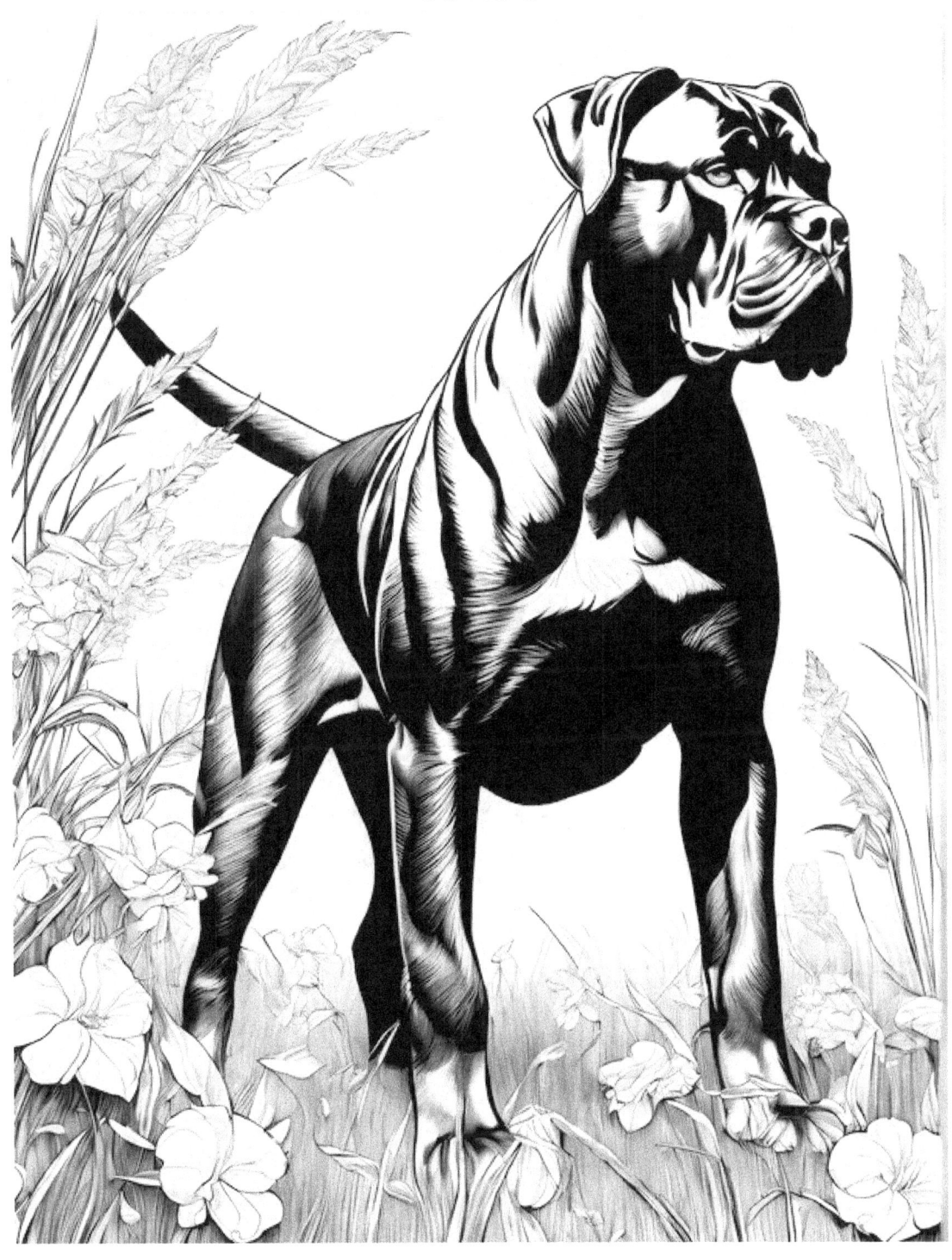

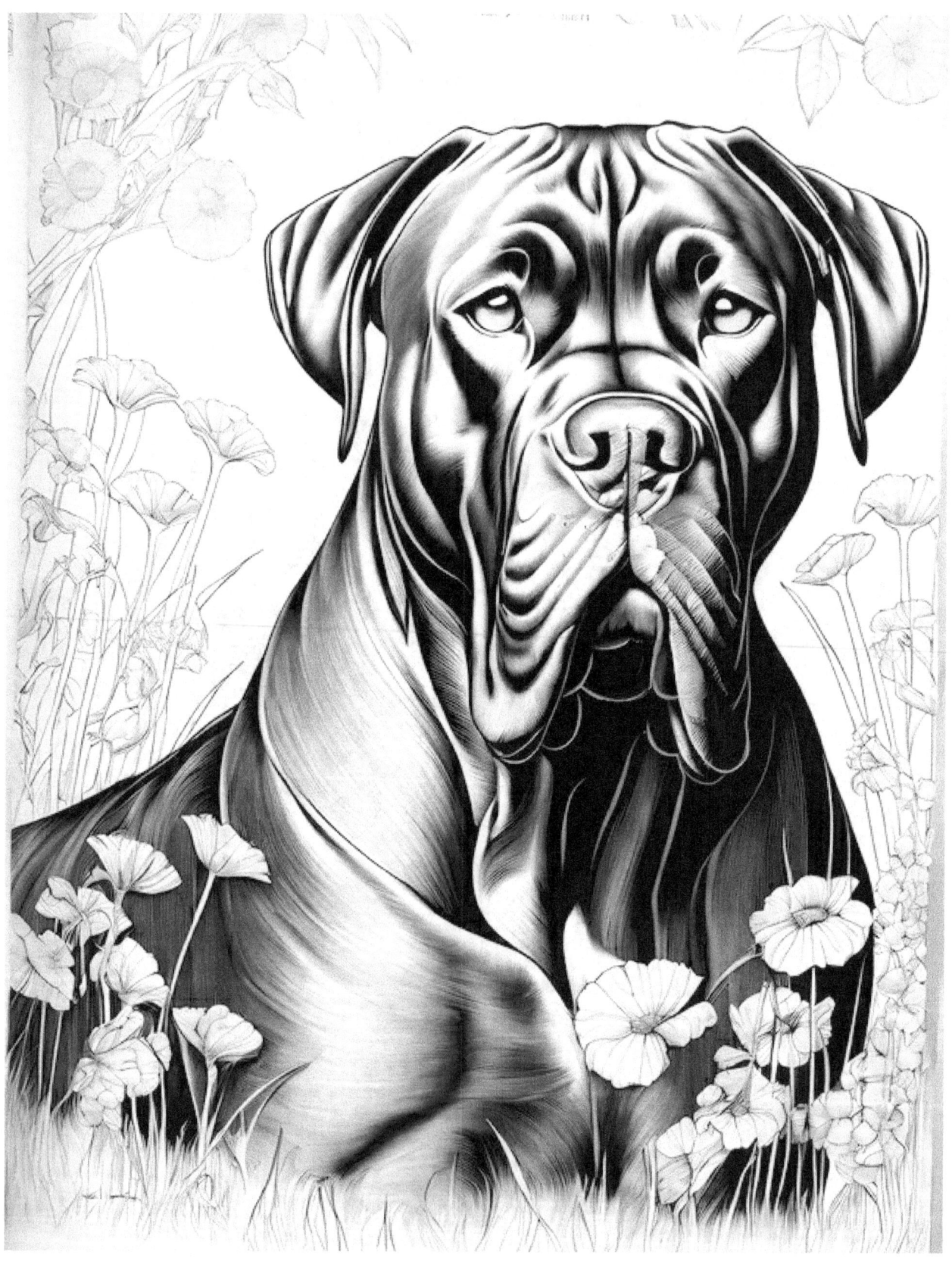

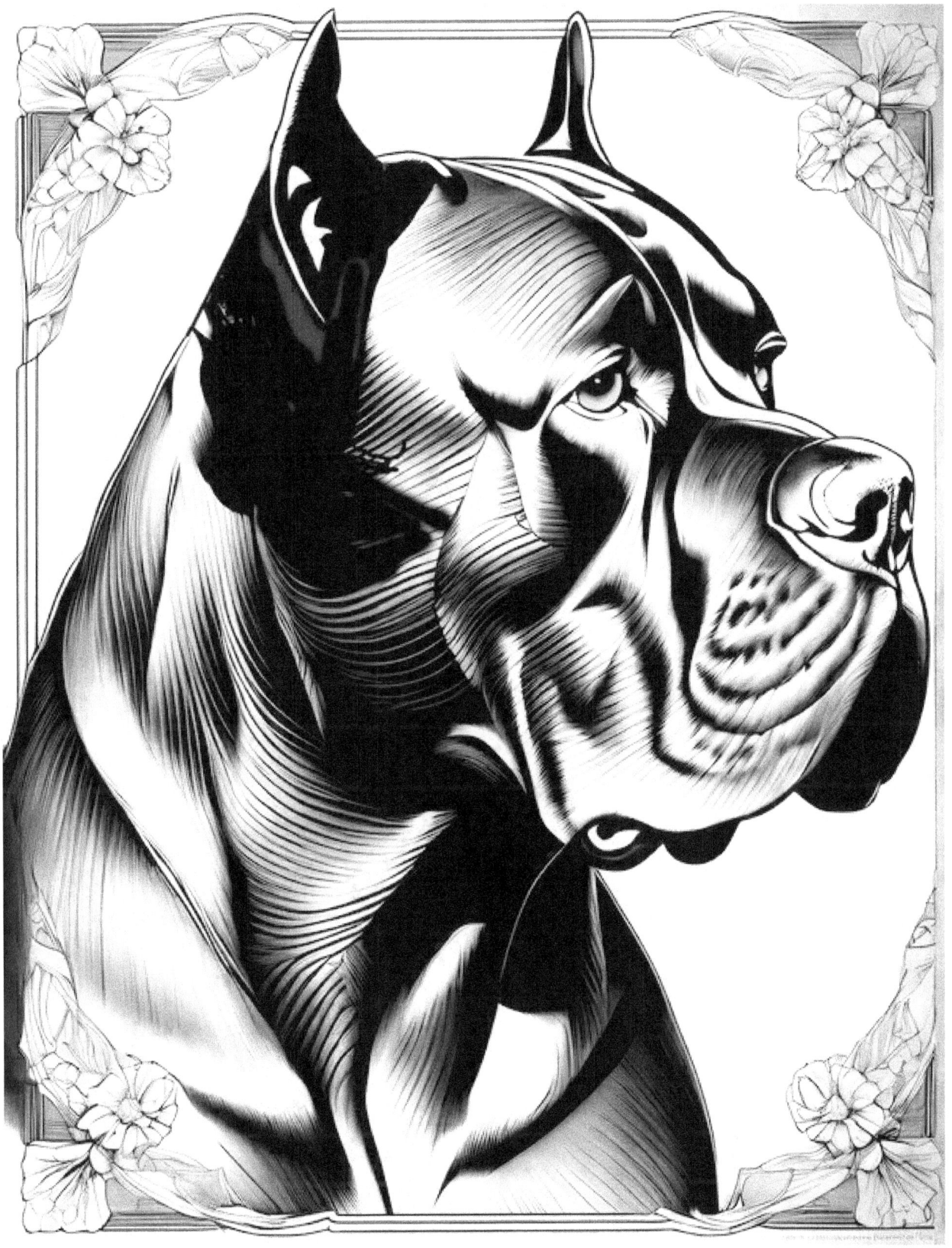

DACHSHUND

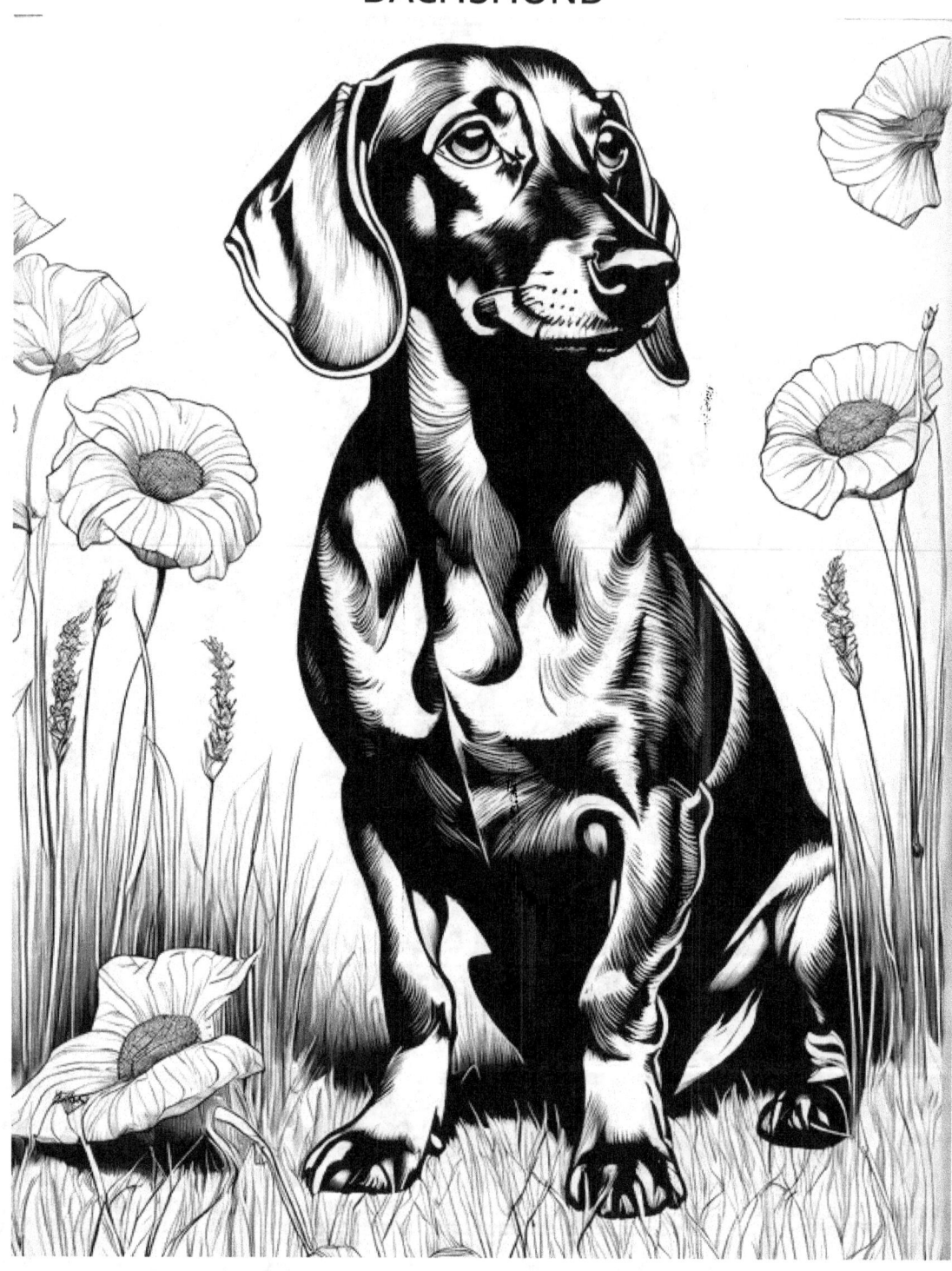

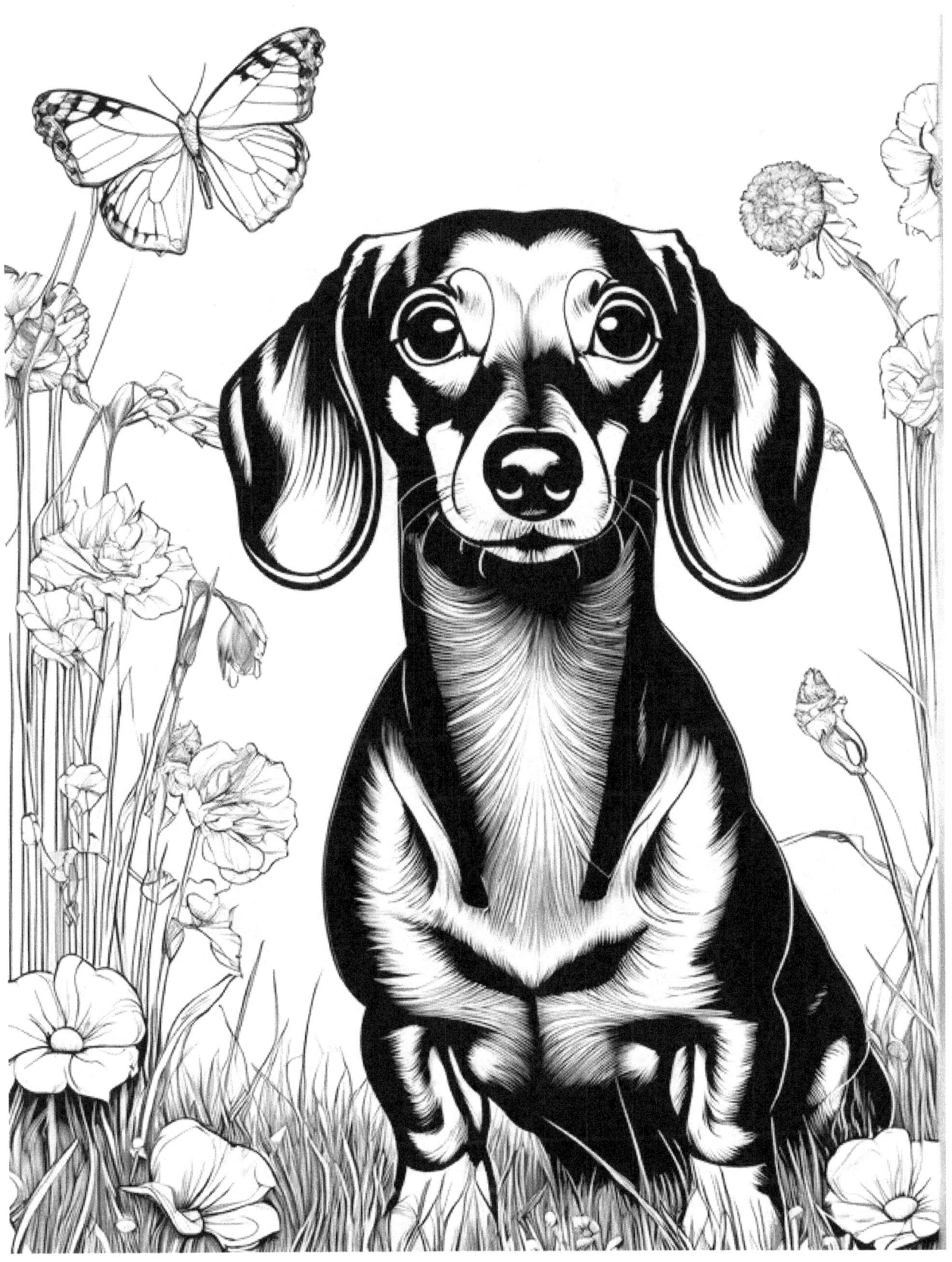

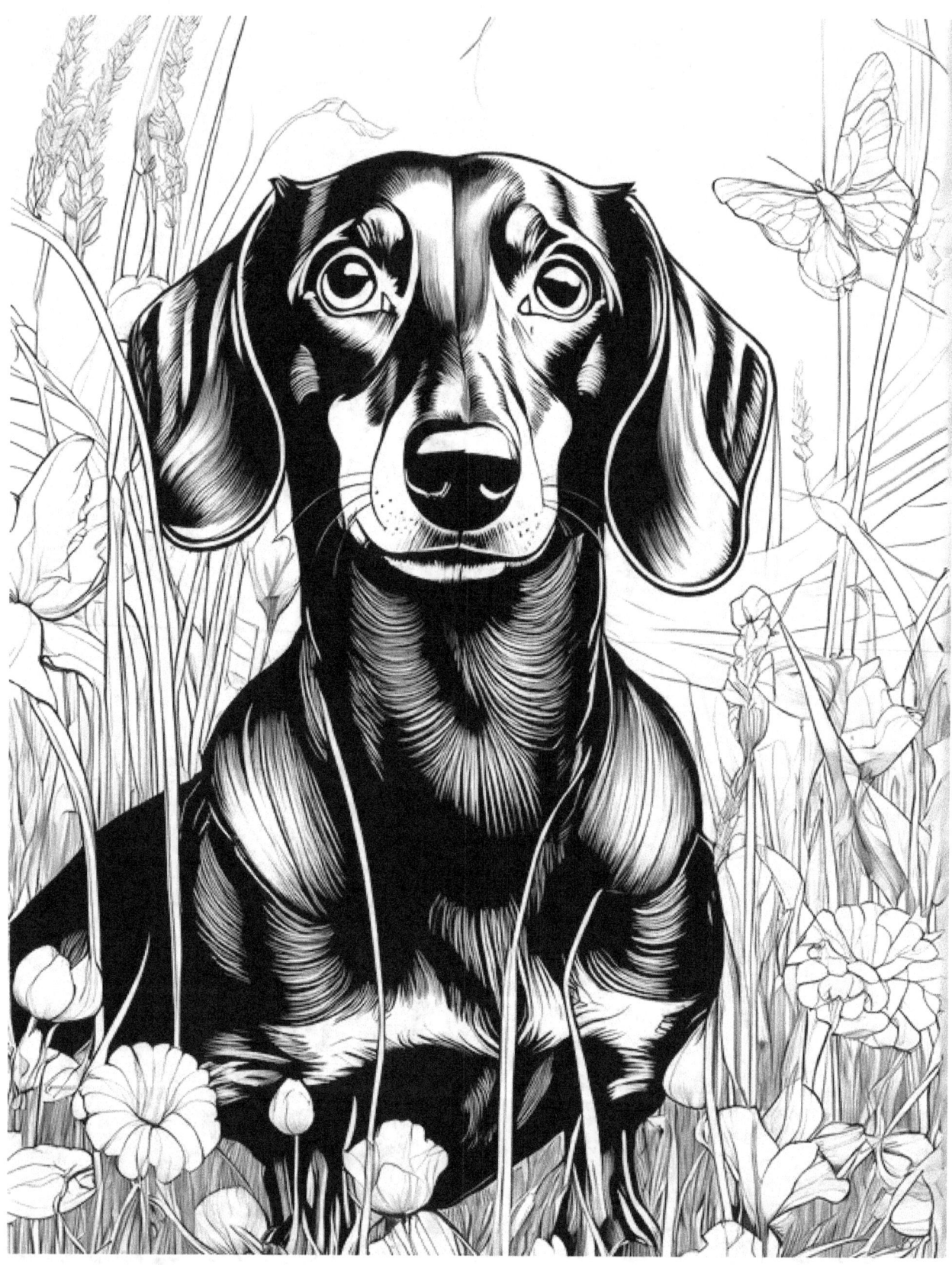

DANDIE DINMONT TERRIER

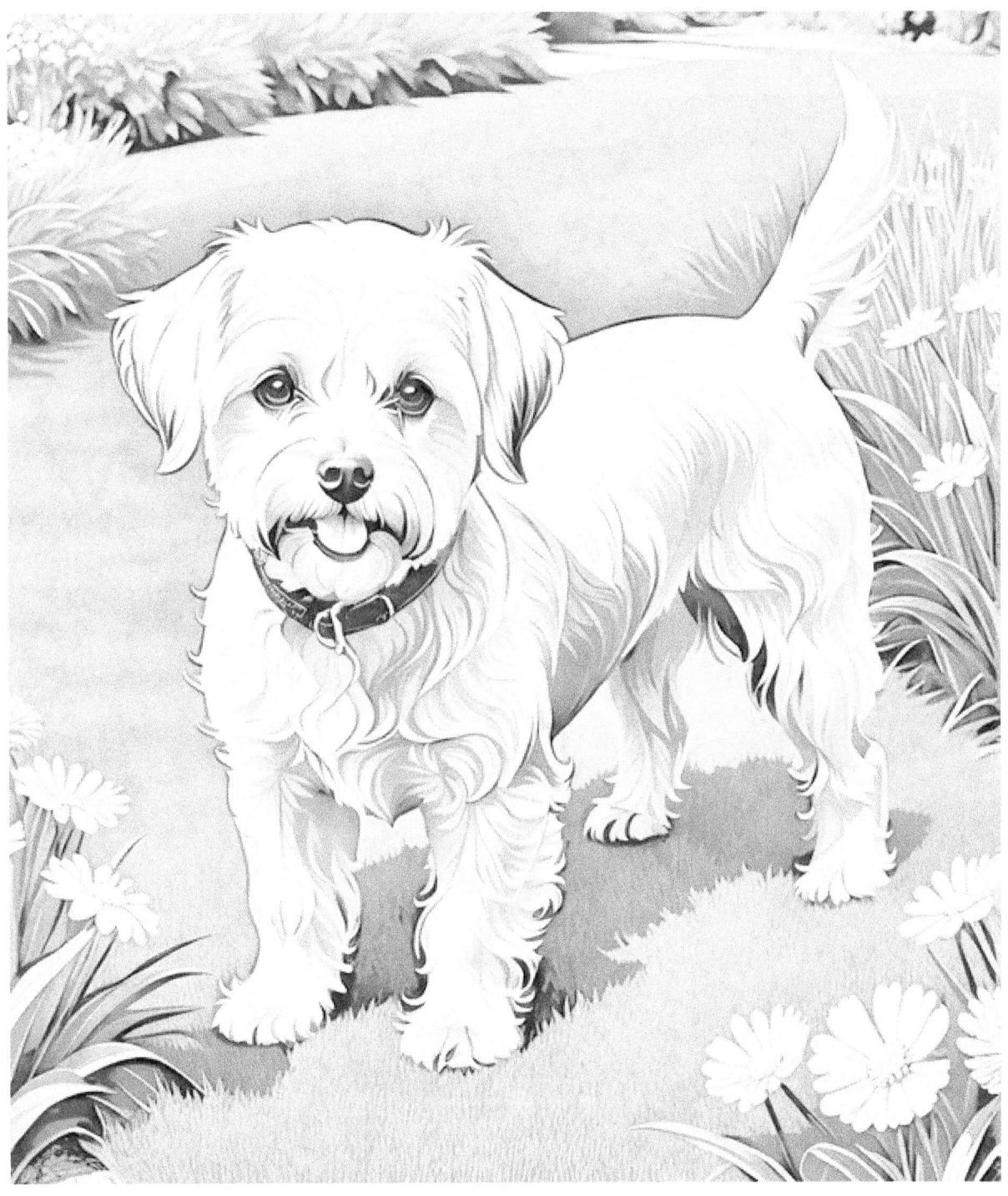

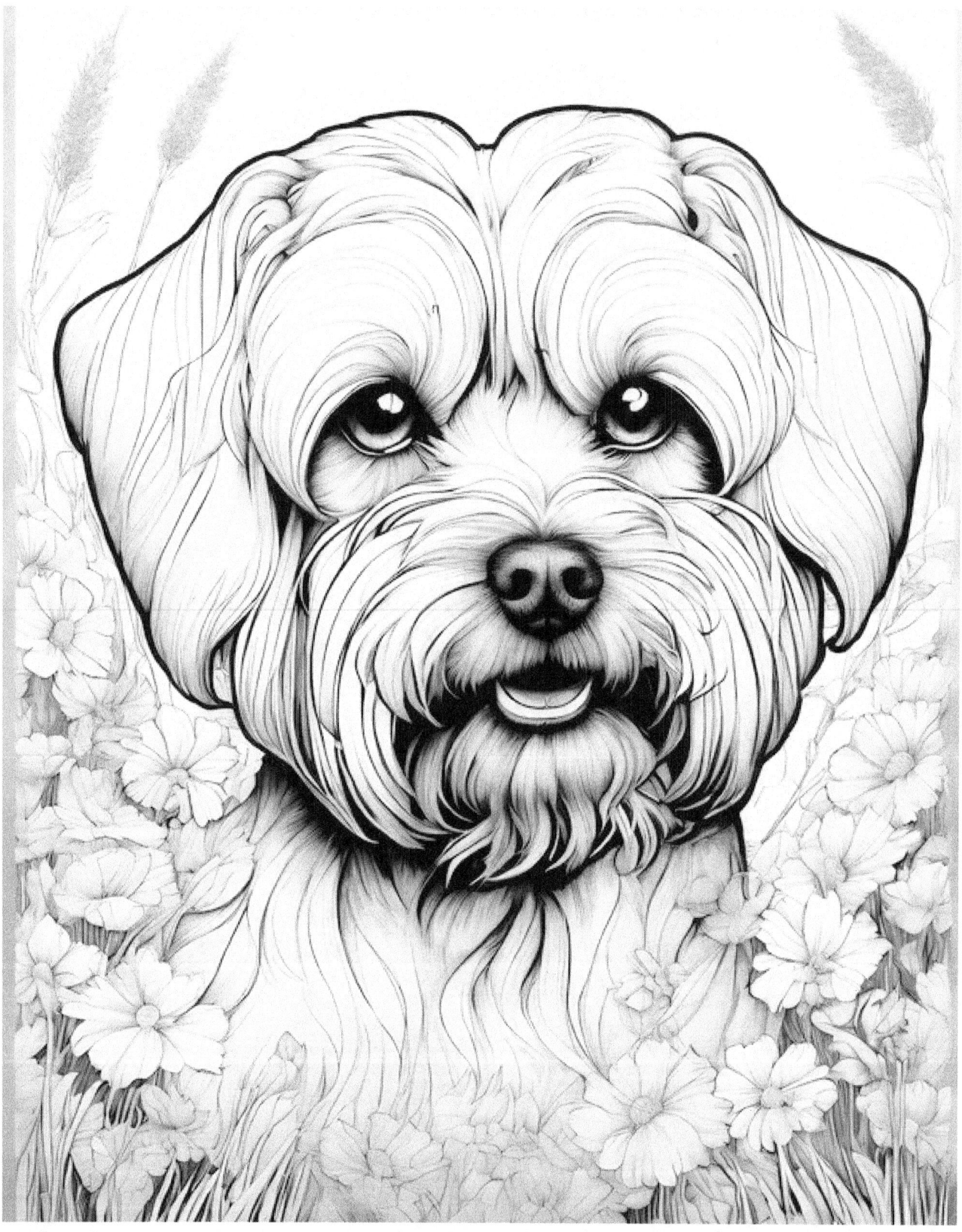

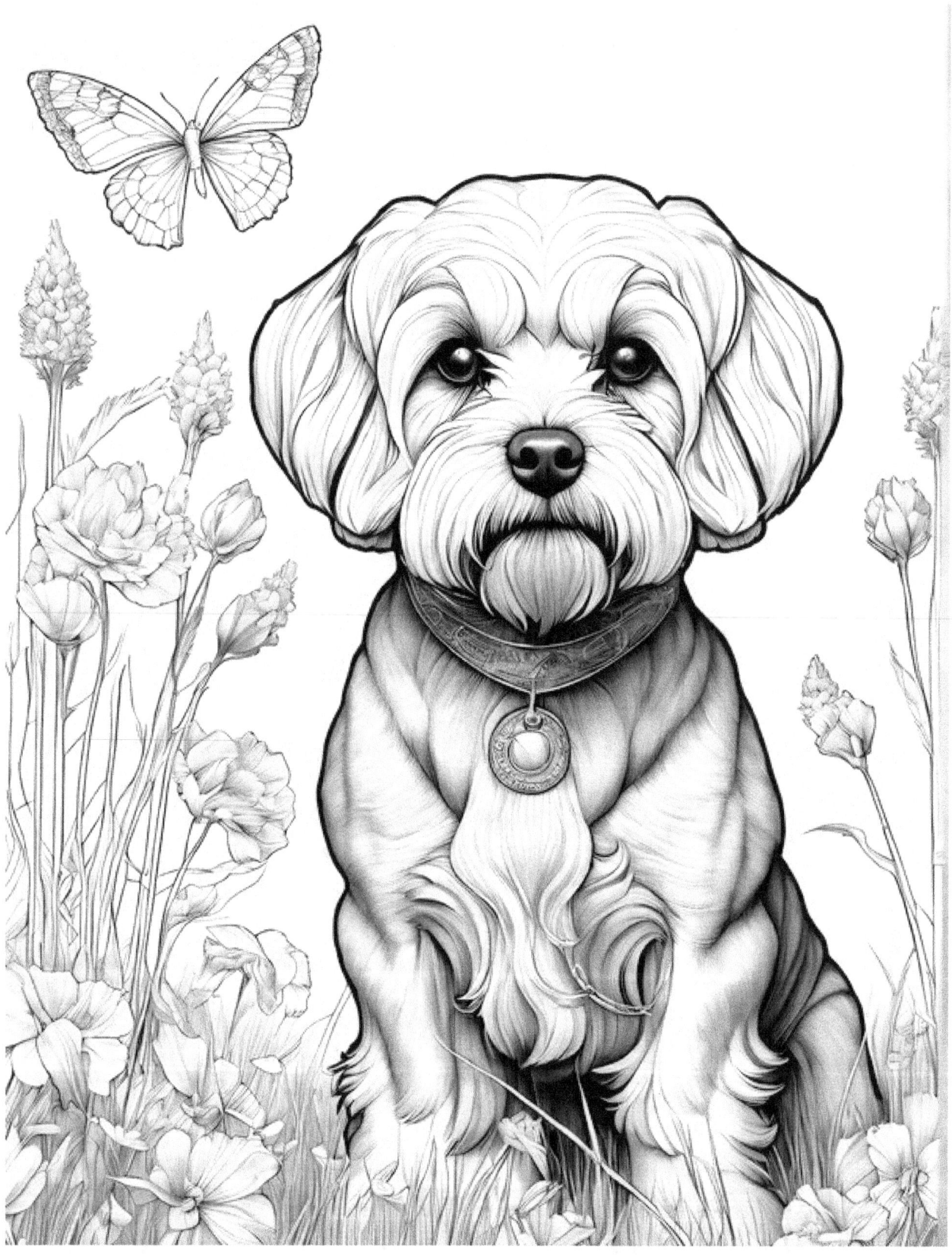

DOBERMAN

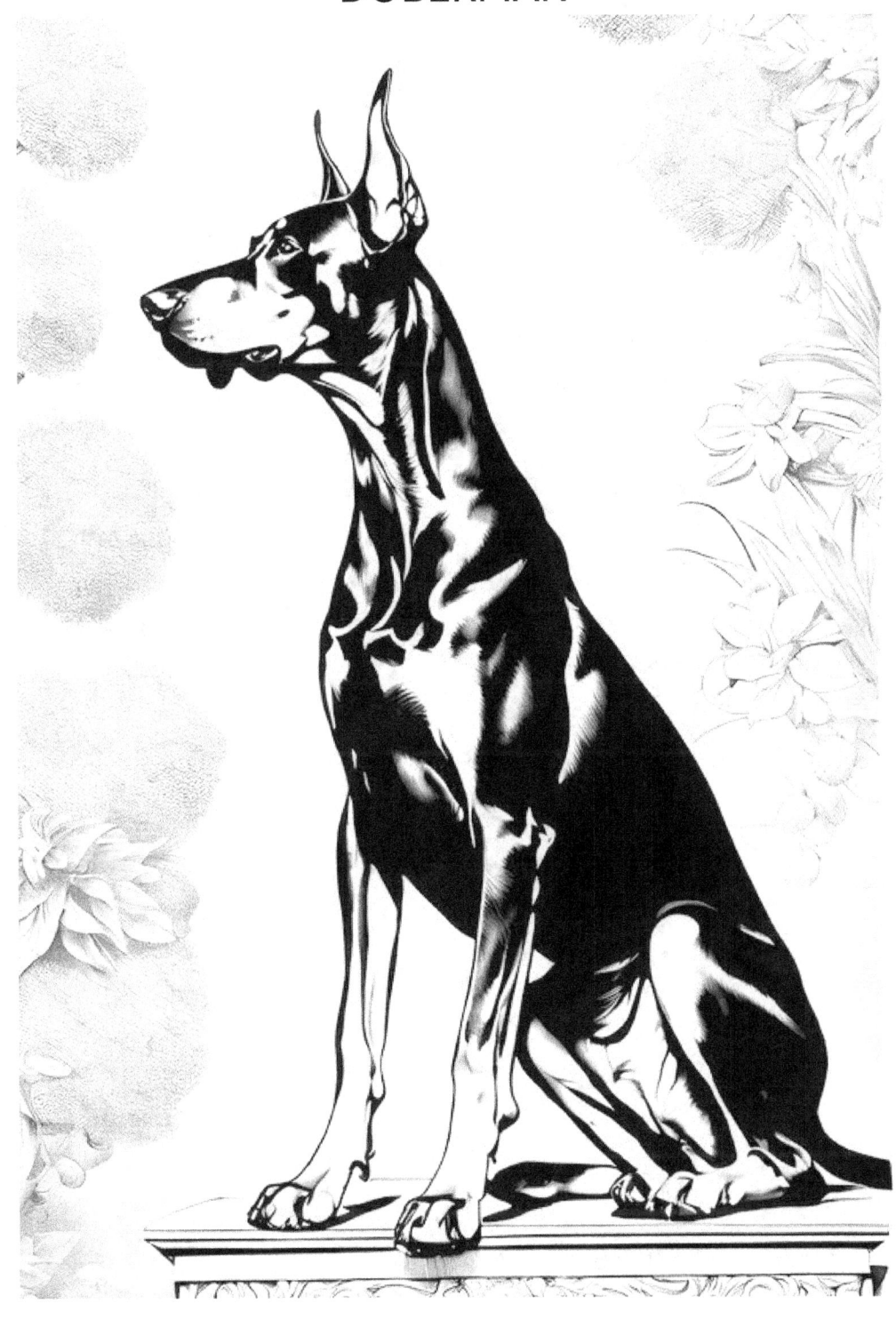

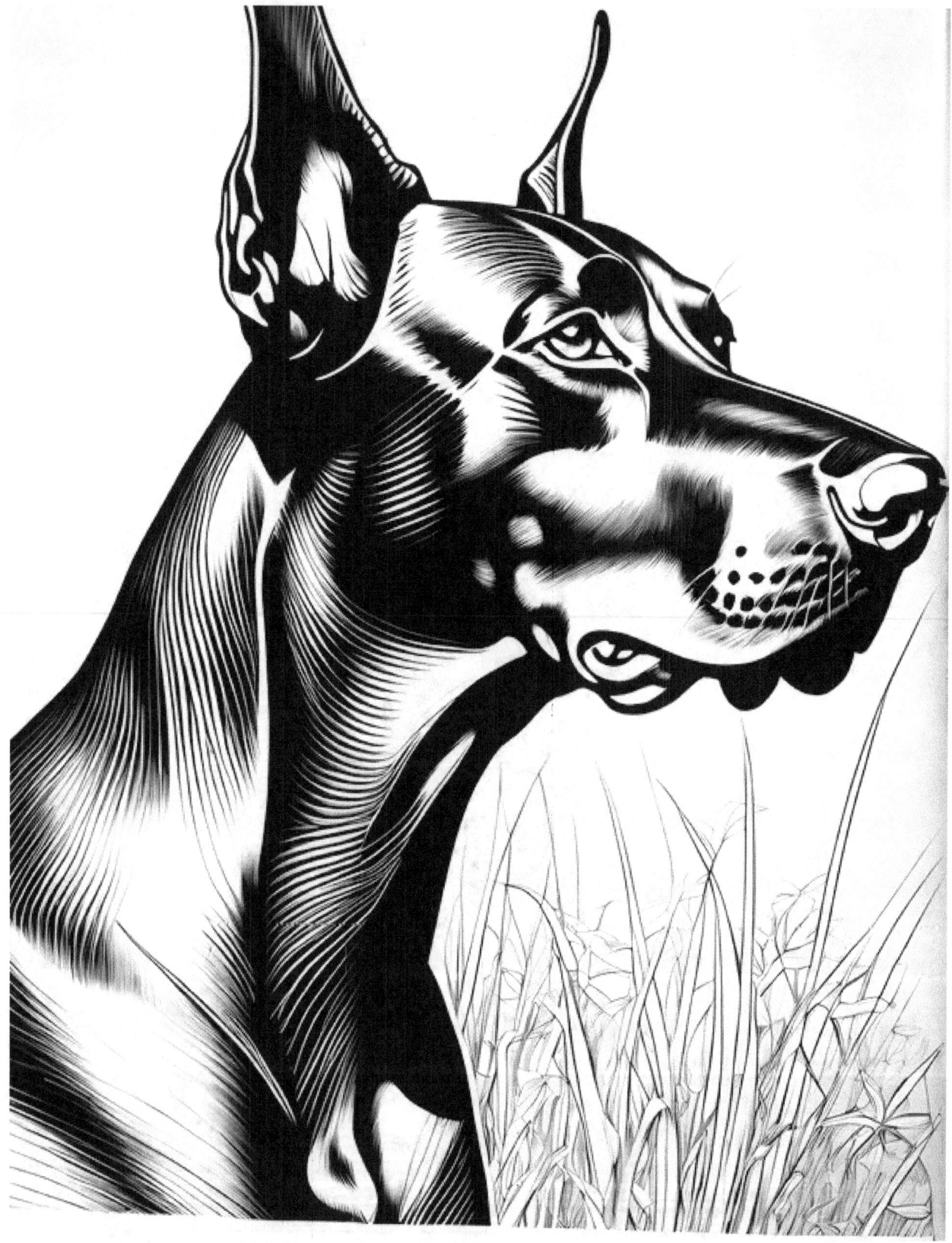

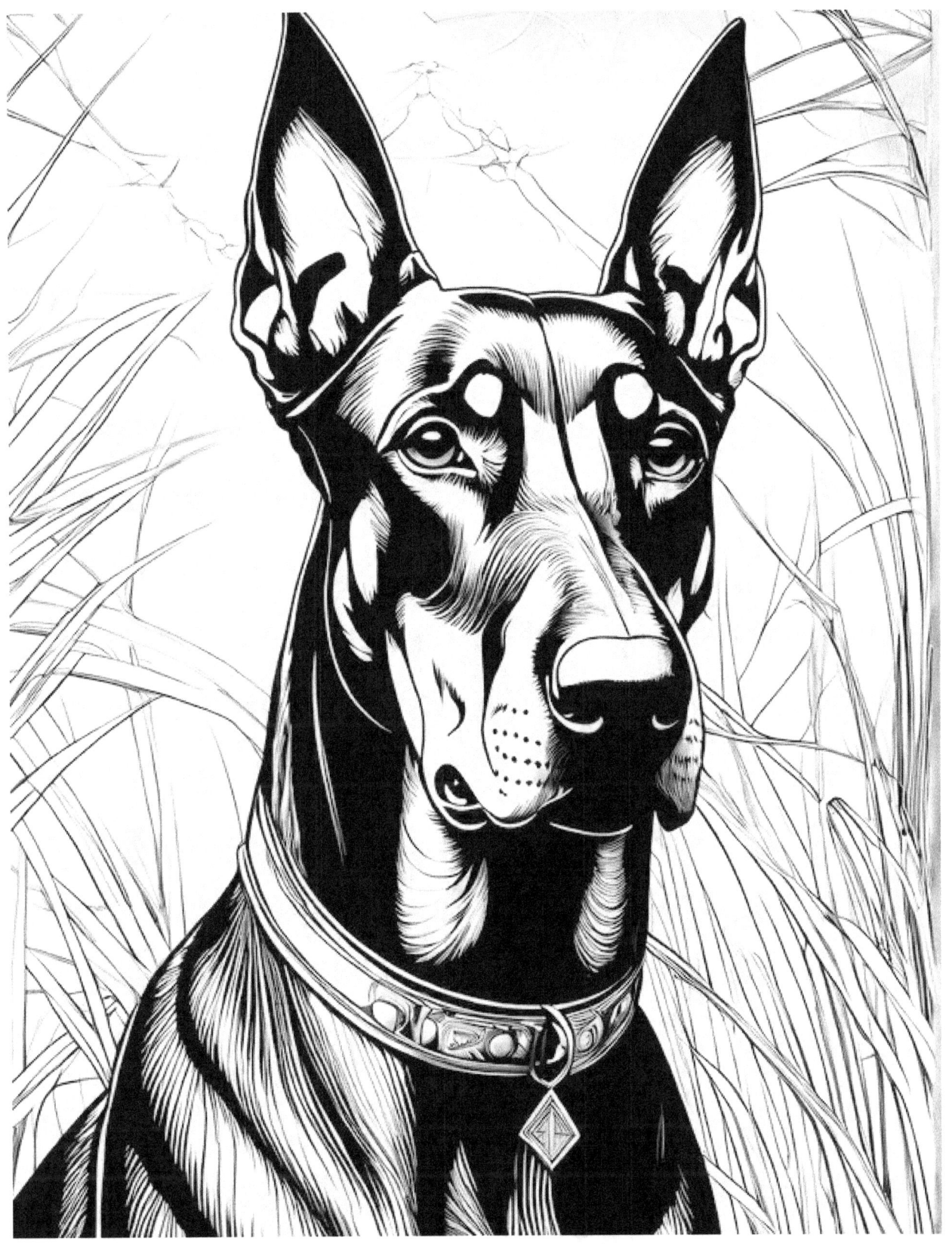

GOLDEN DOODLE

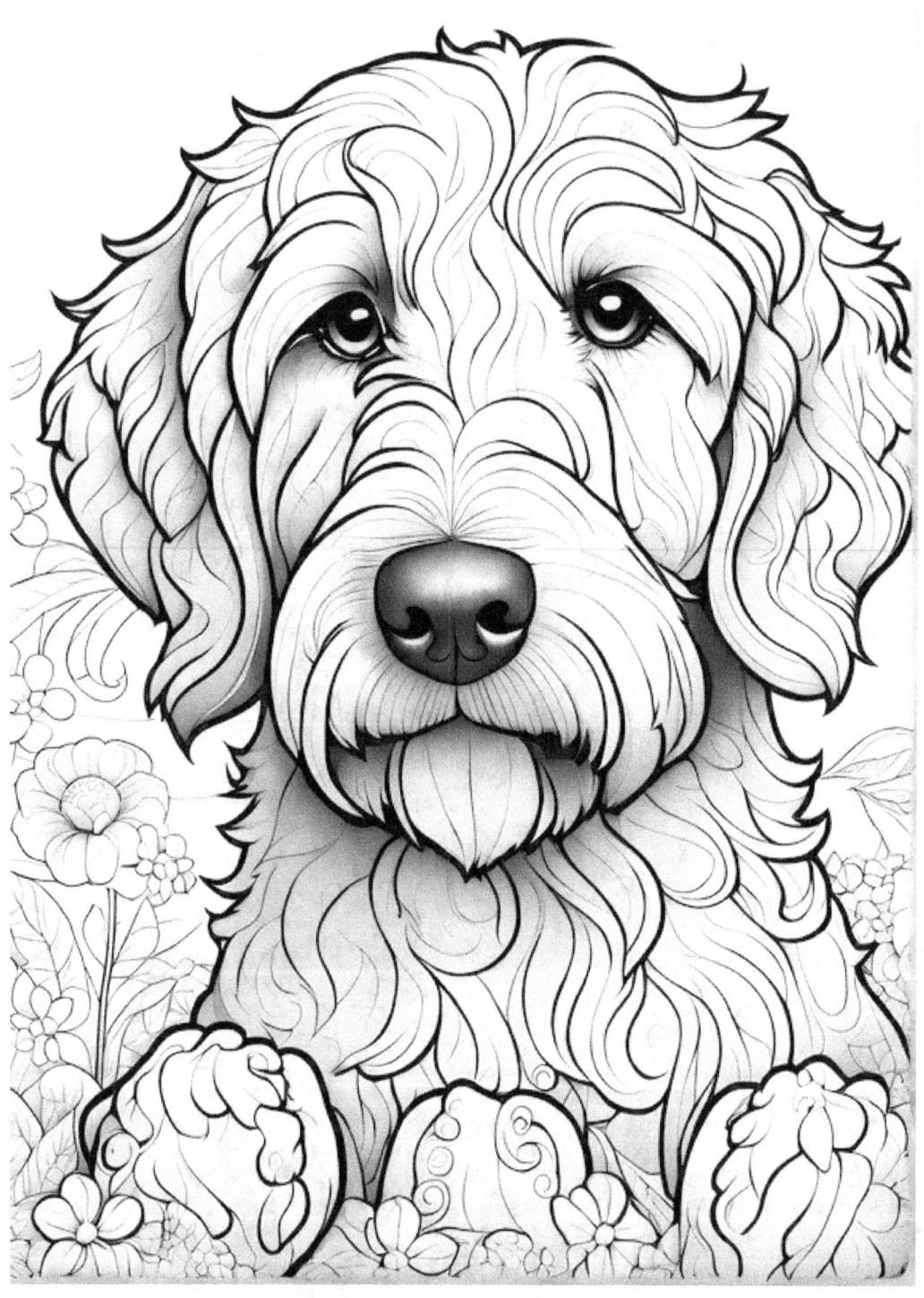

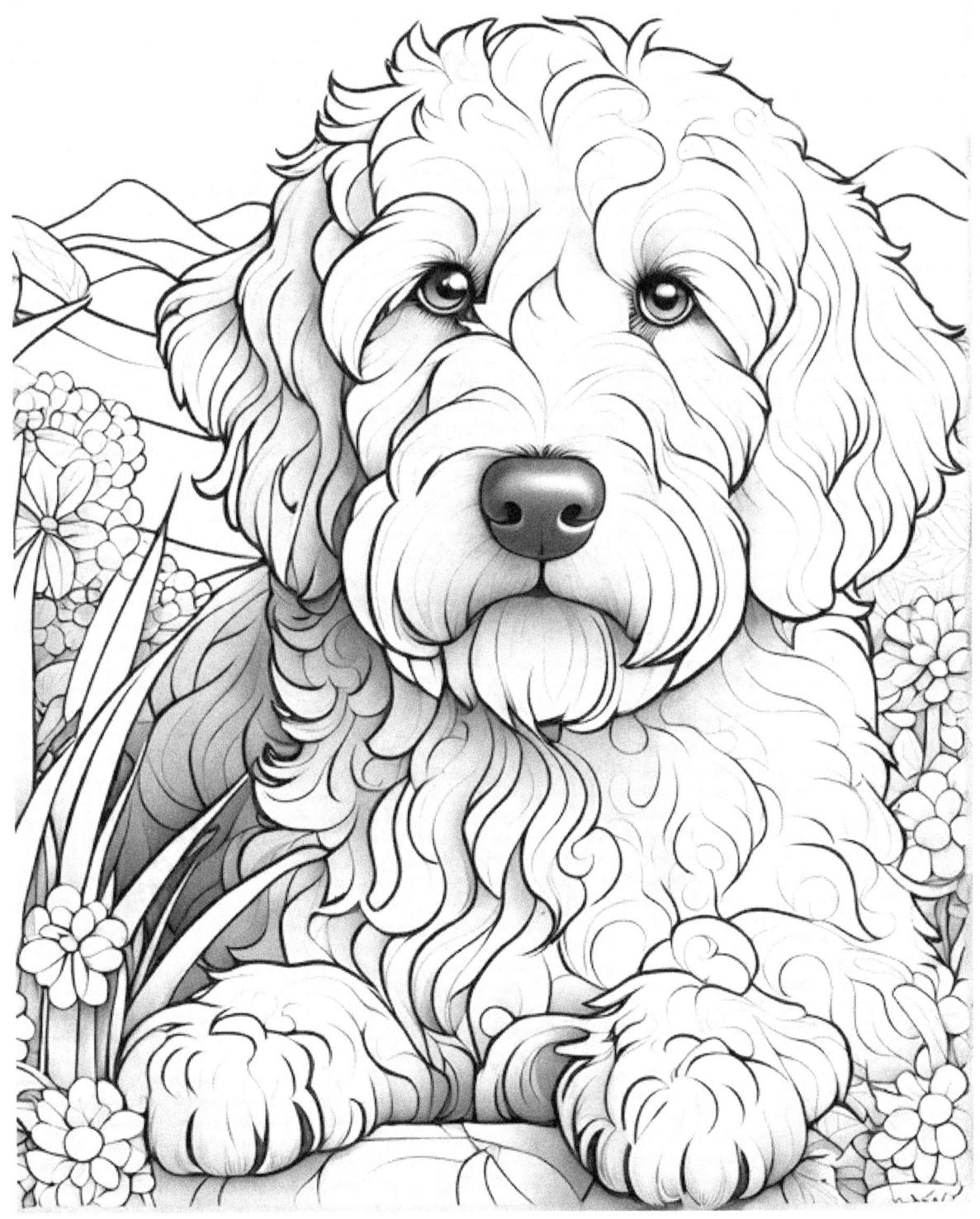

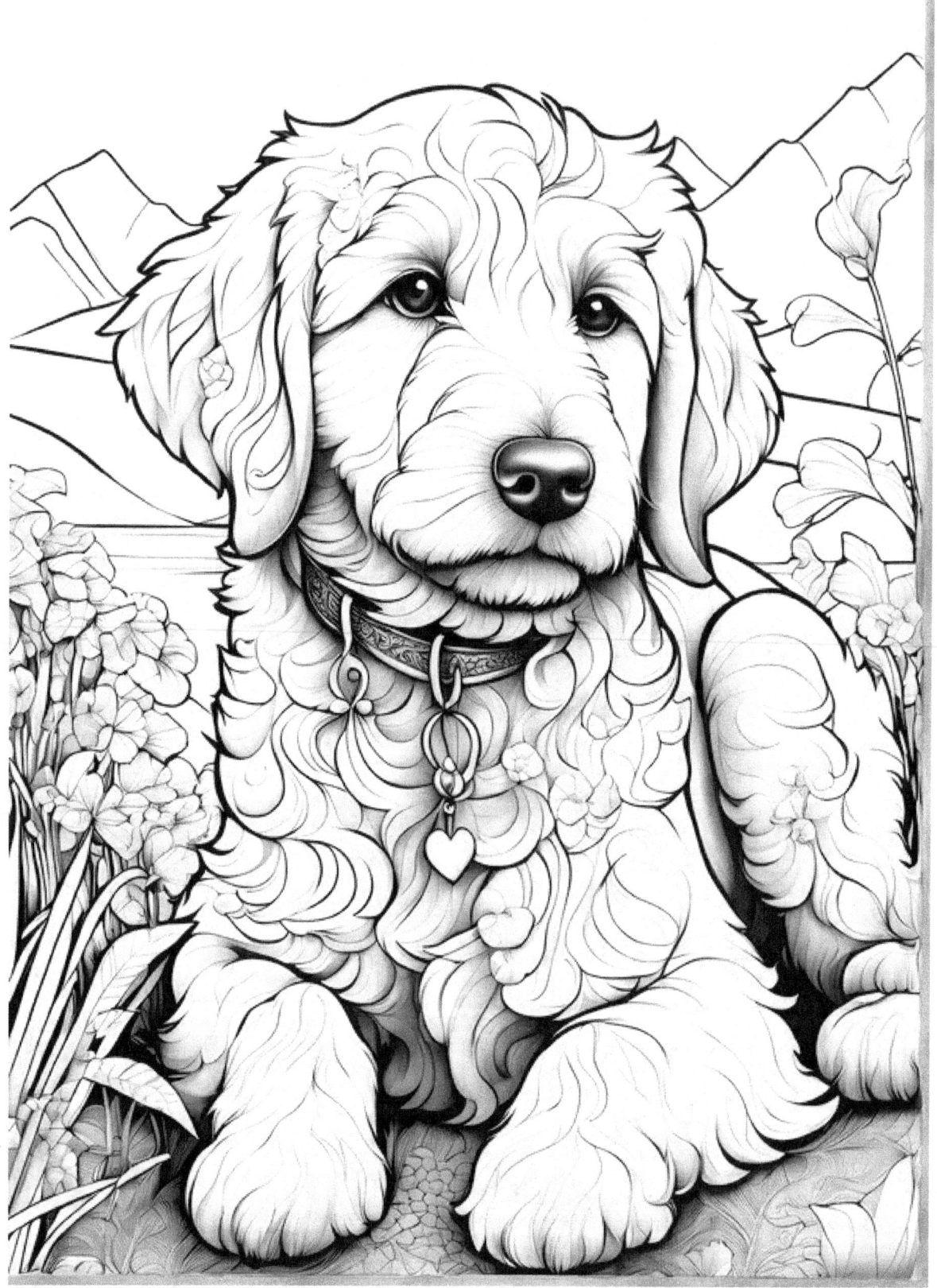

GOLDEN RETRIVE

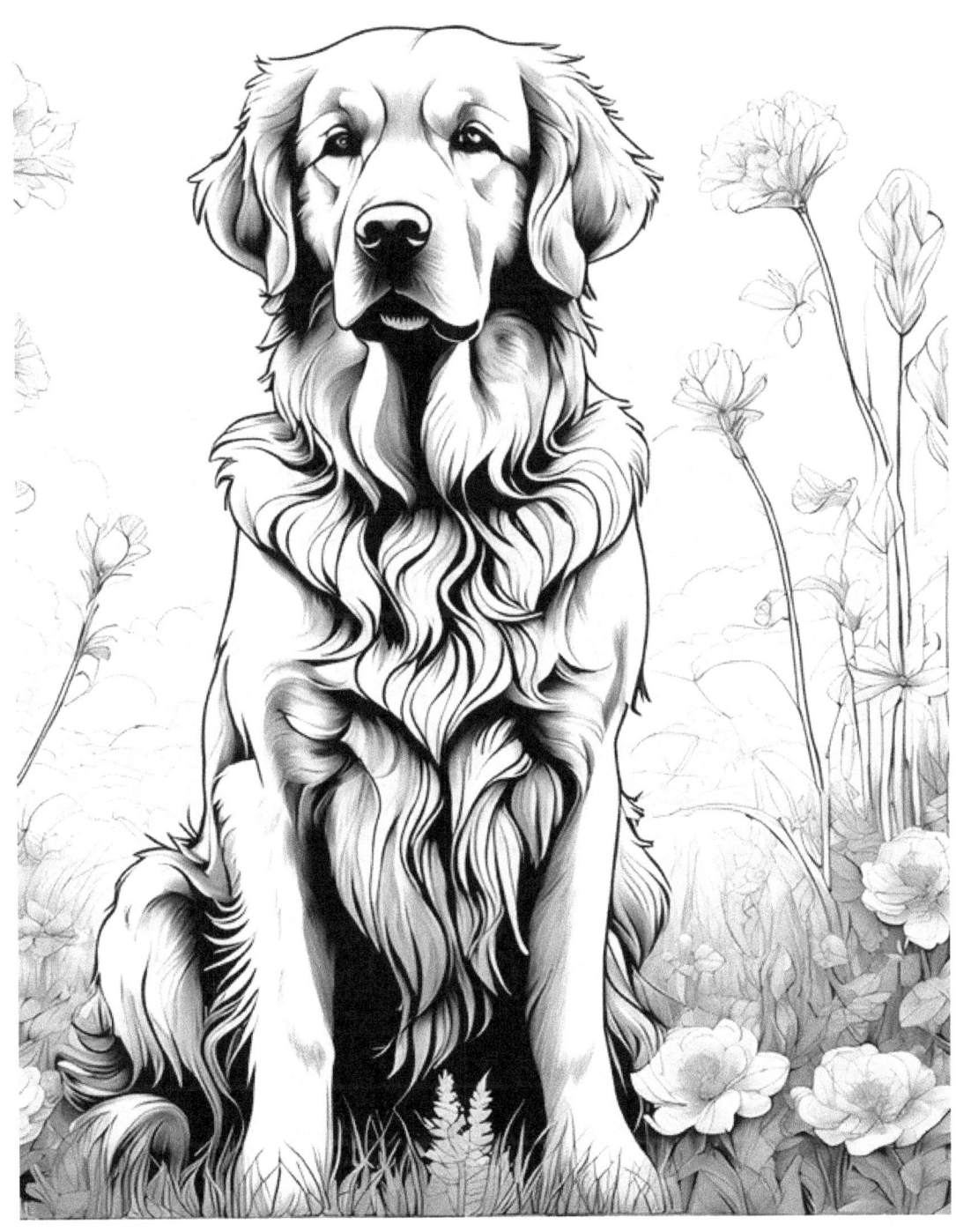

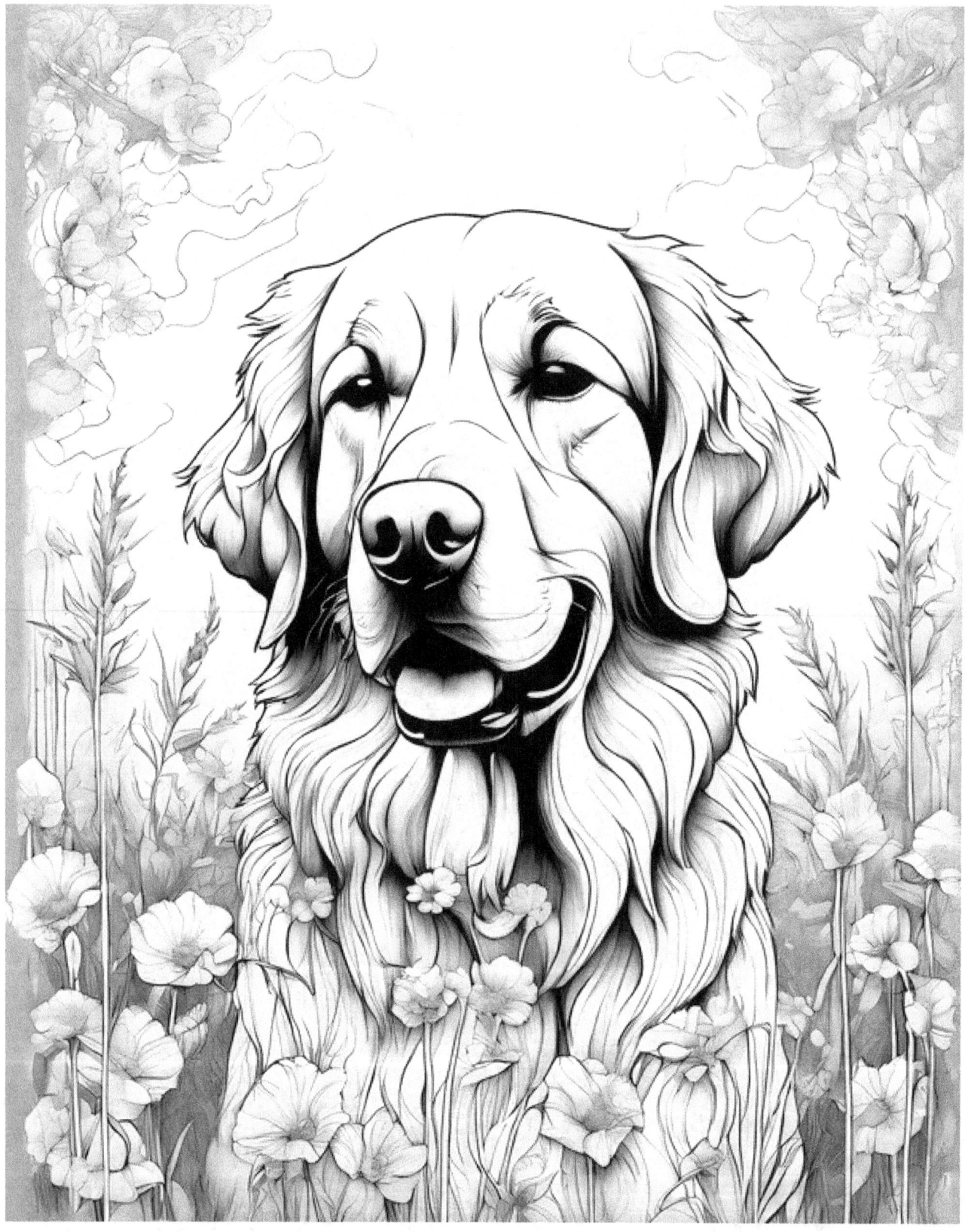

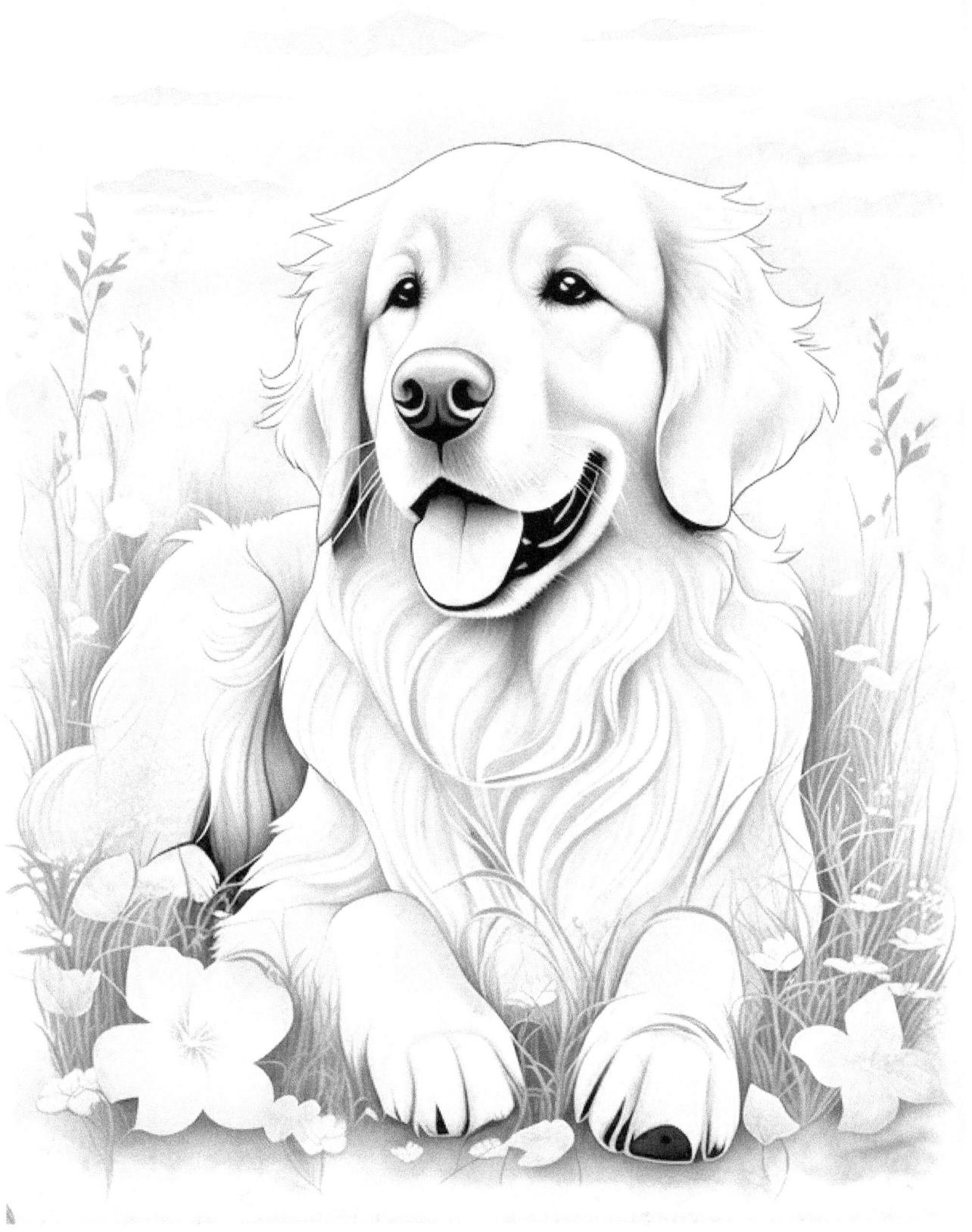

IRISH WOLFHOUND

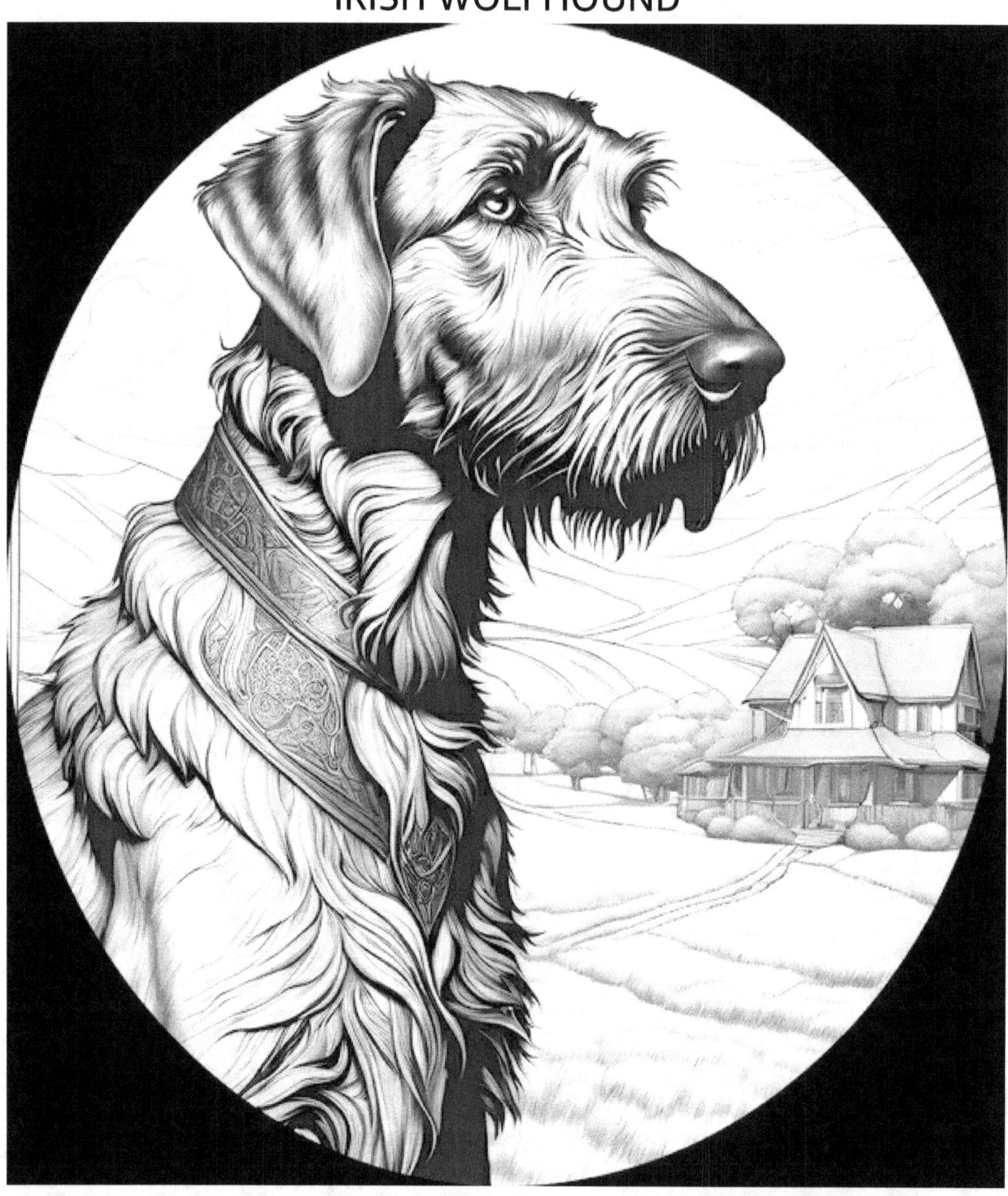

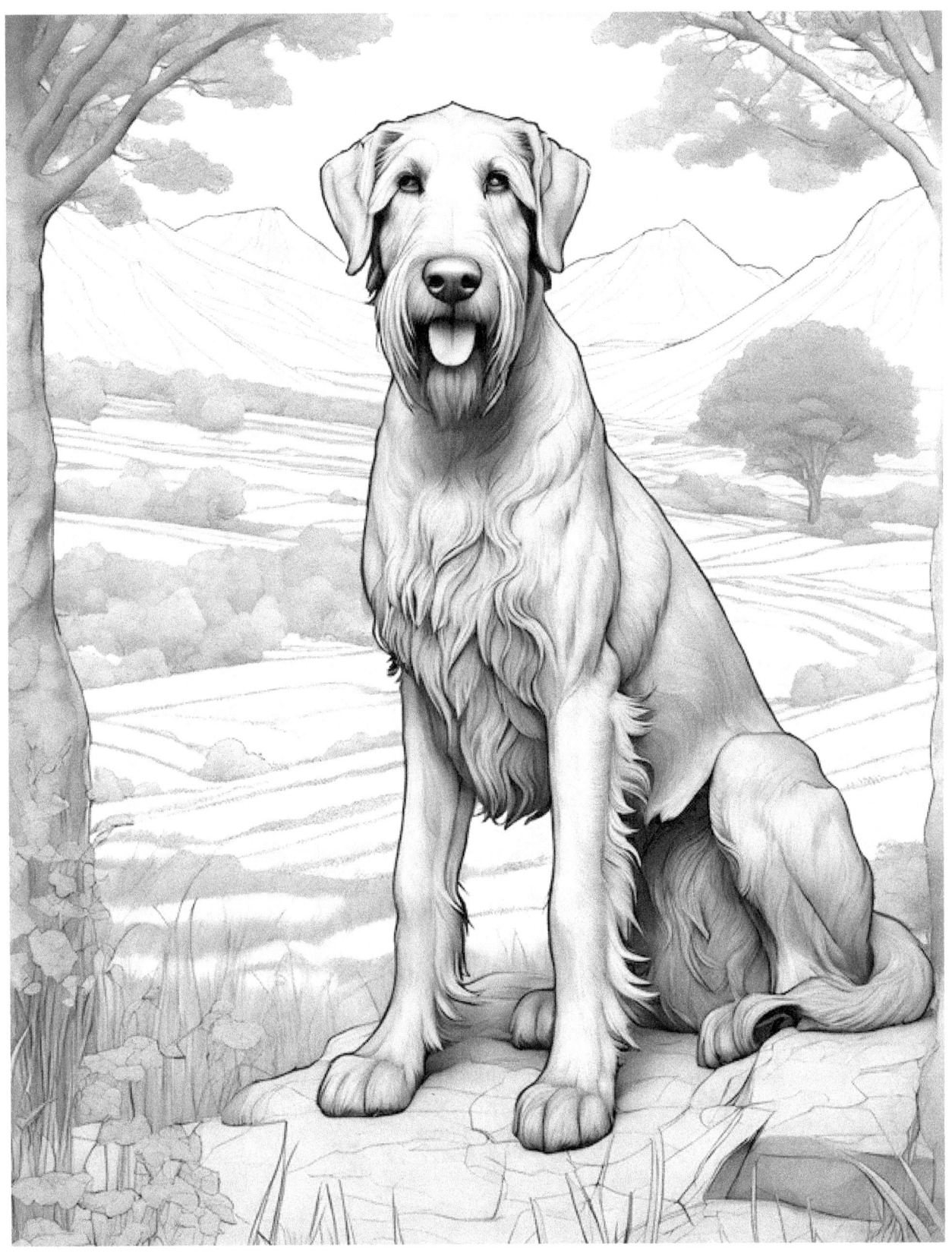

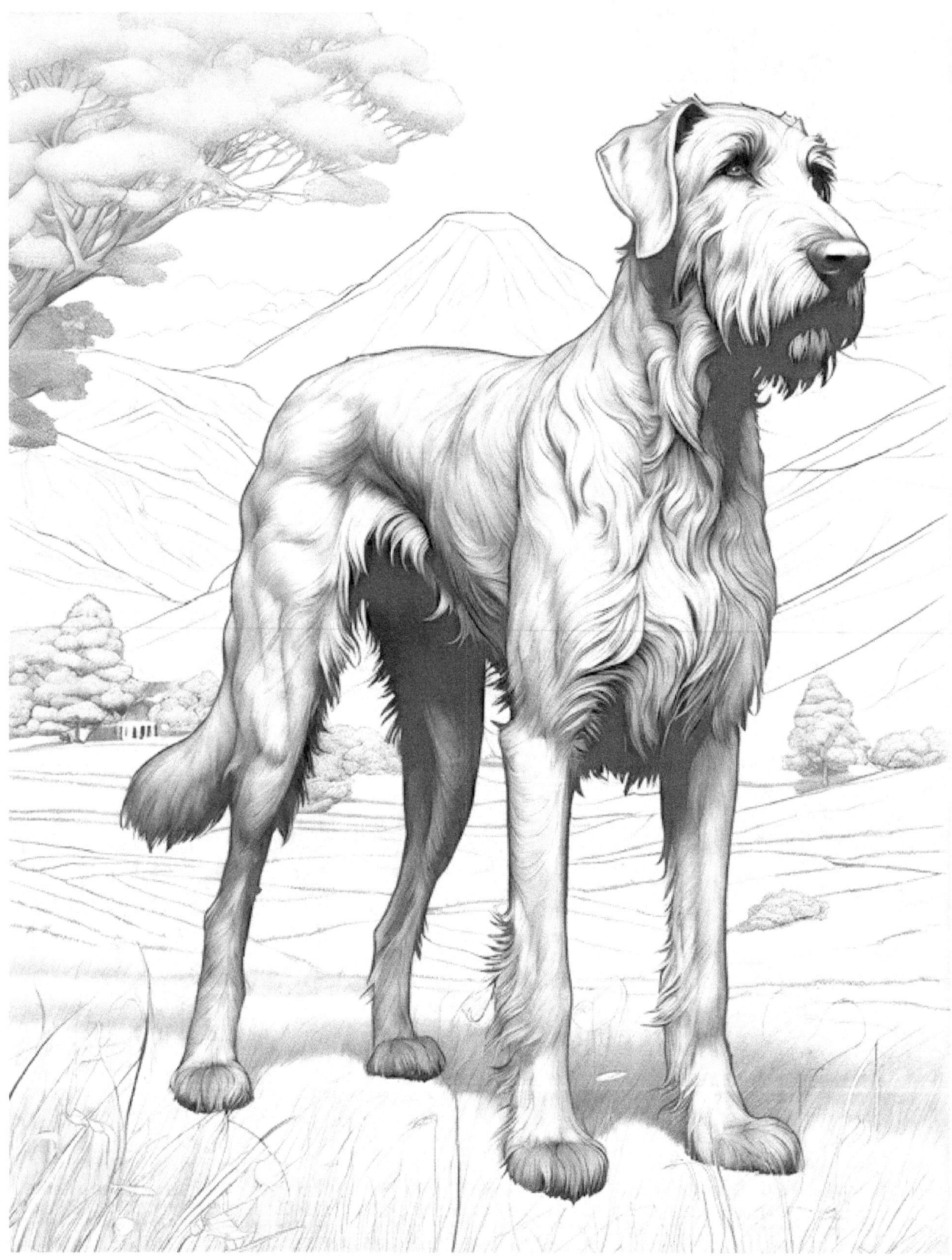

JACK RUSSEL

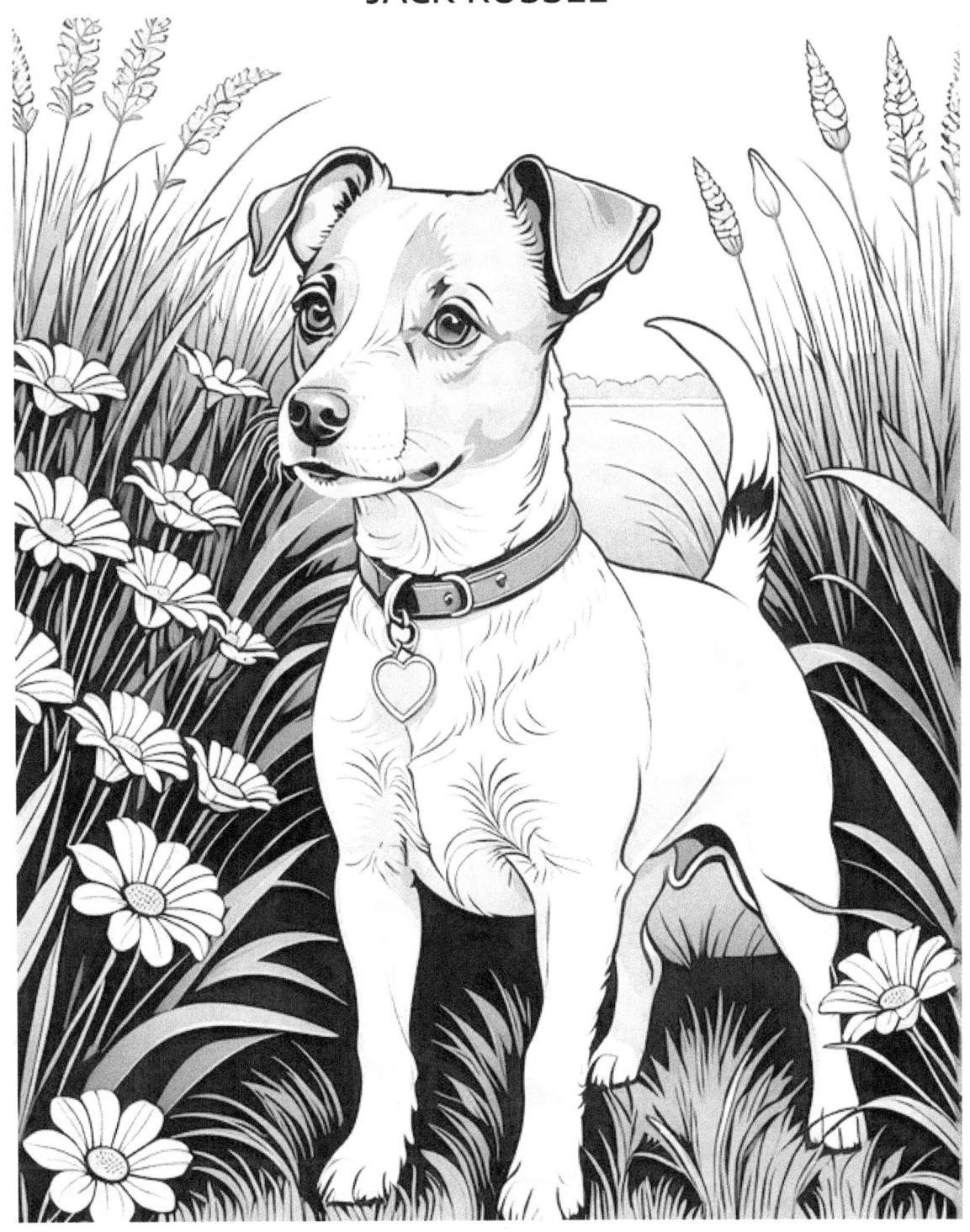

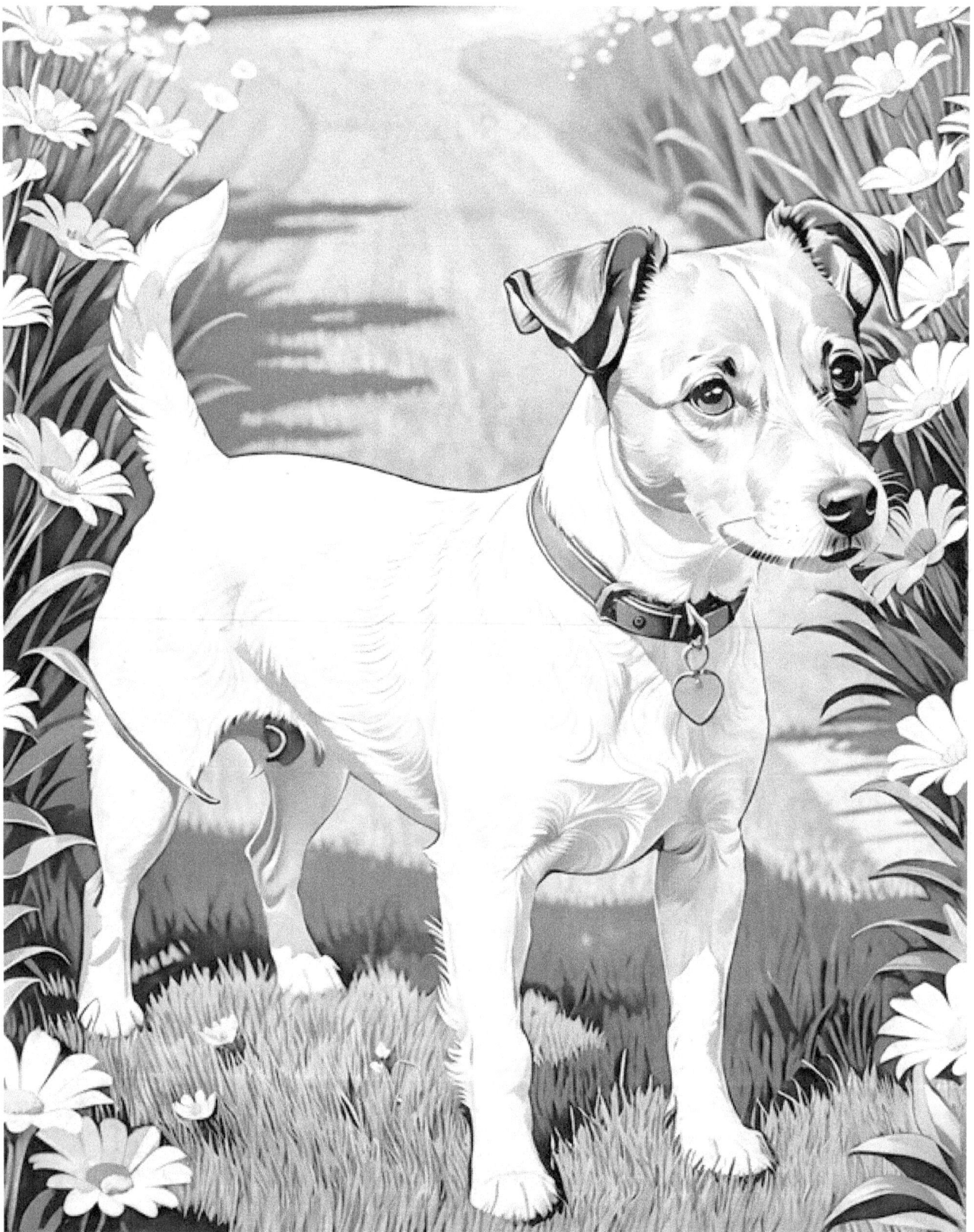

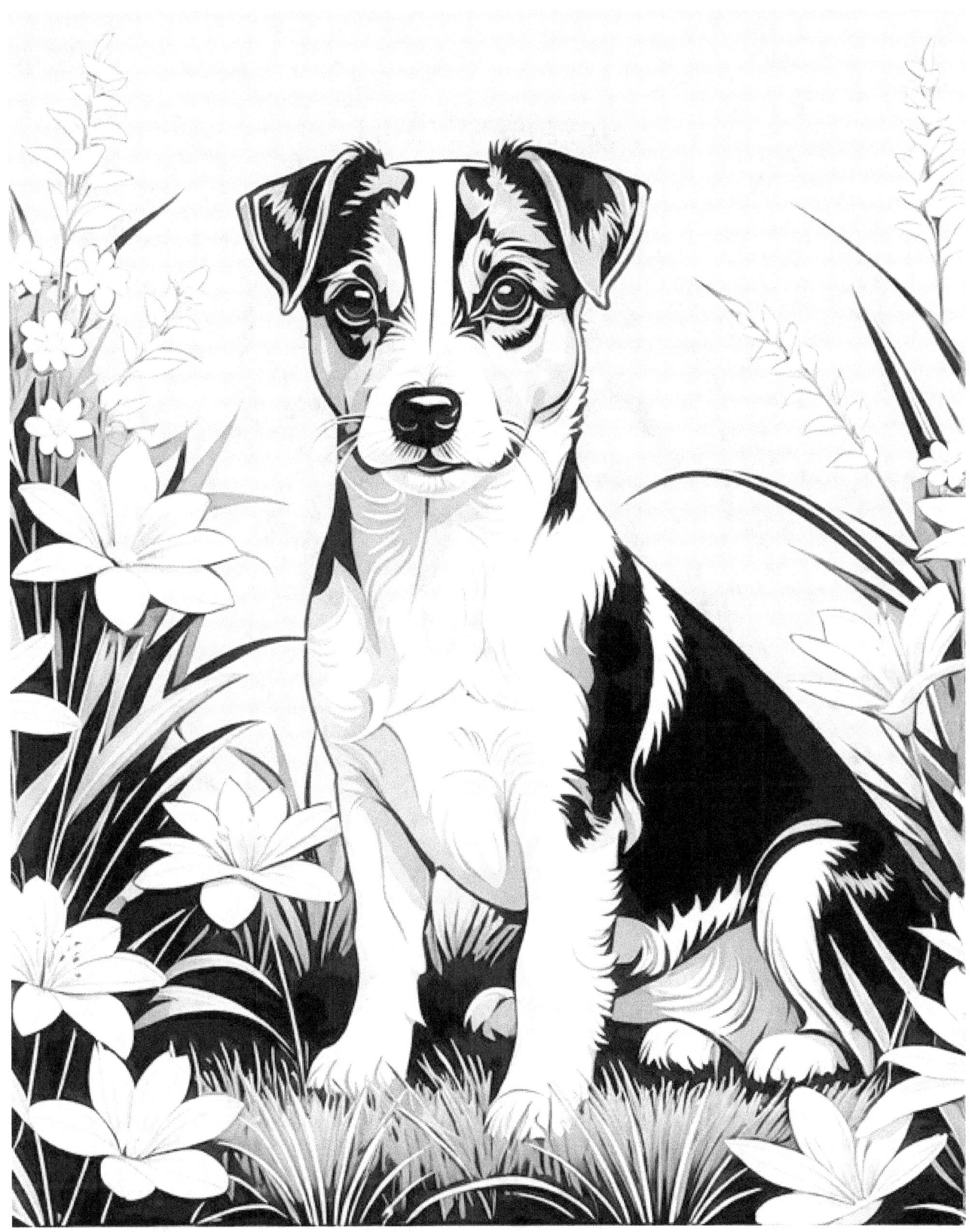

JAPANESE CHIN

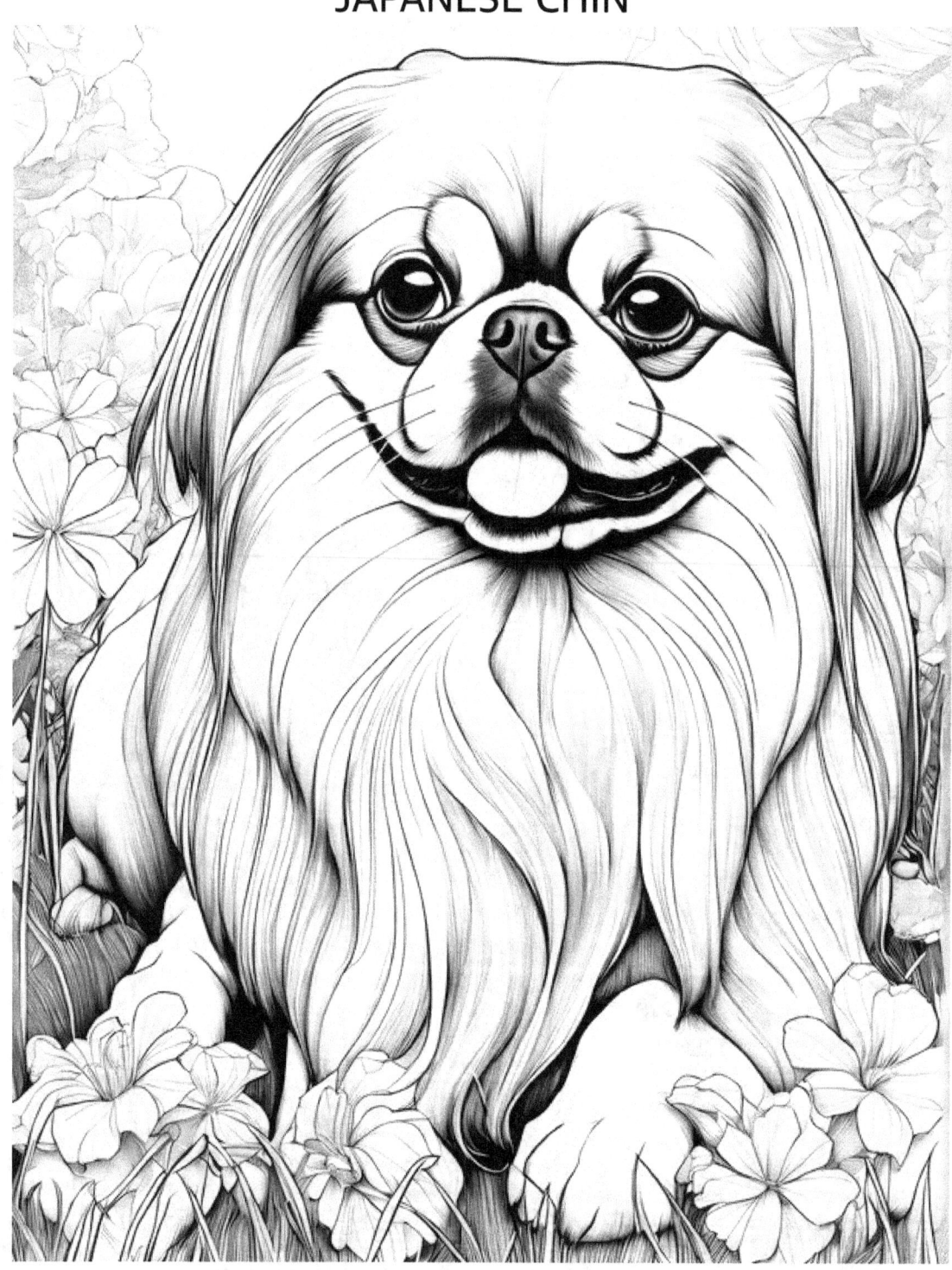

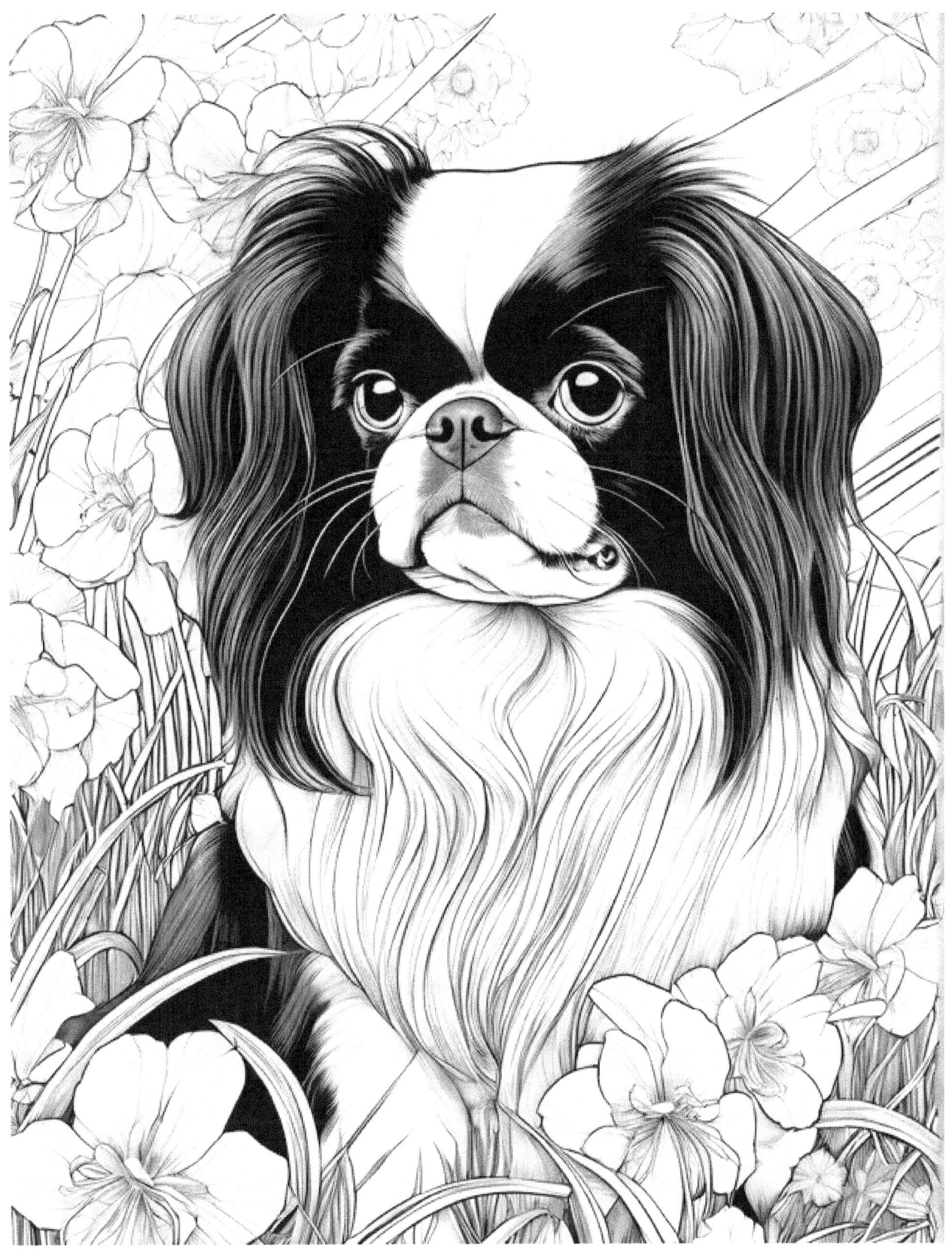

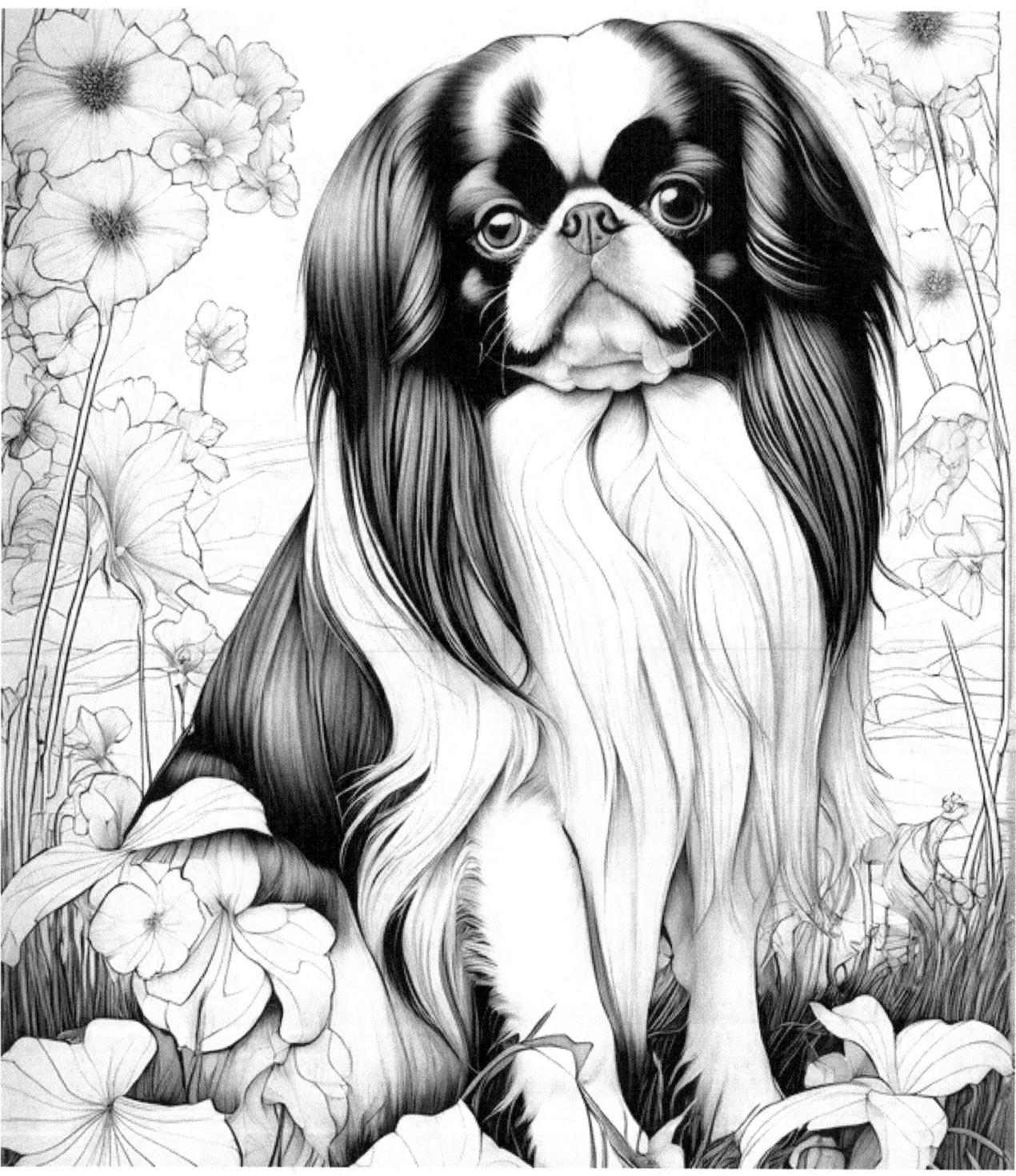

KOMONDOR

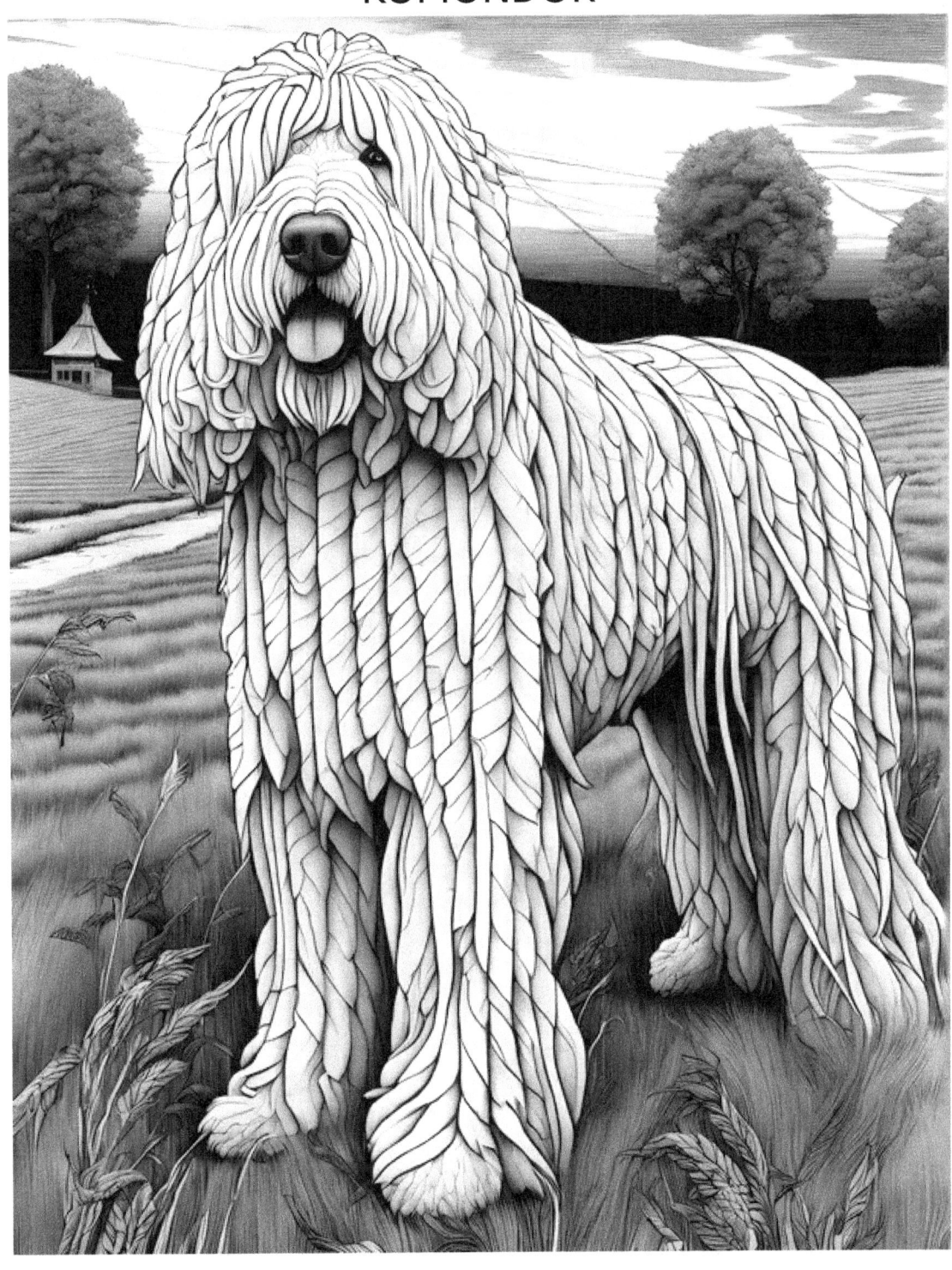

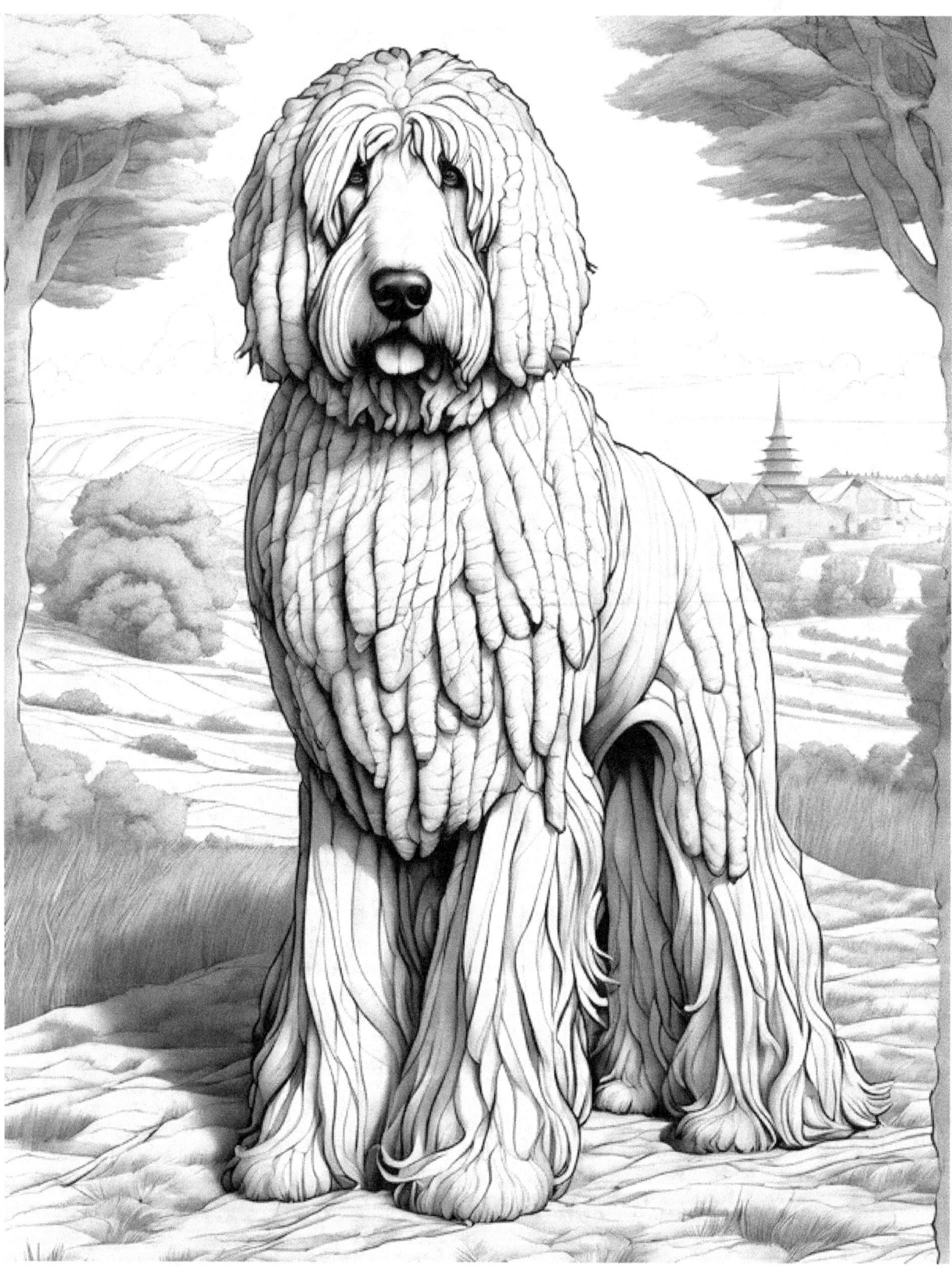

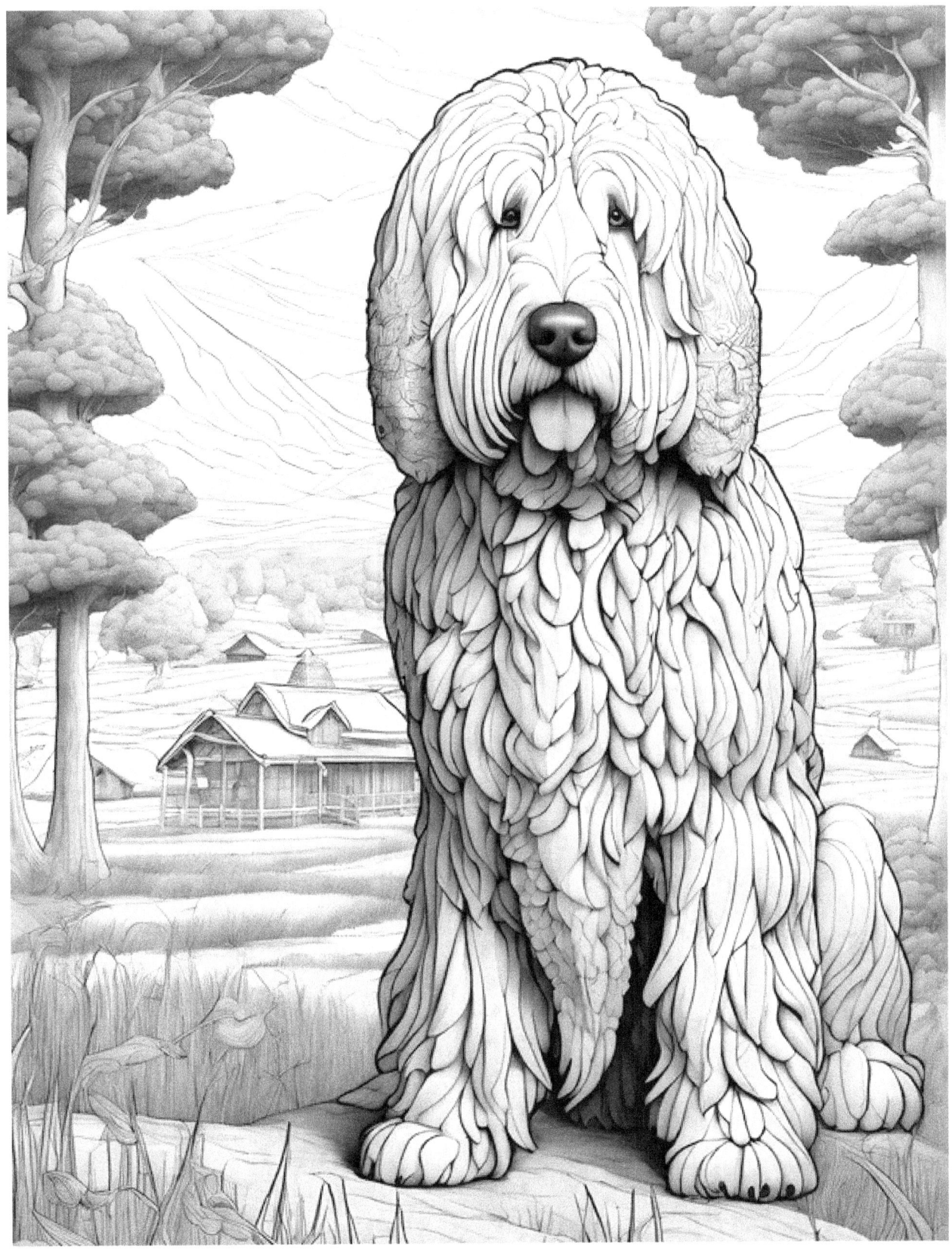

LABRADOR

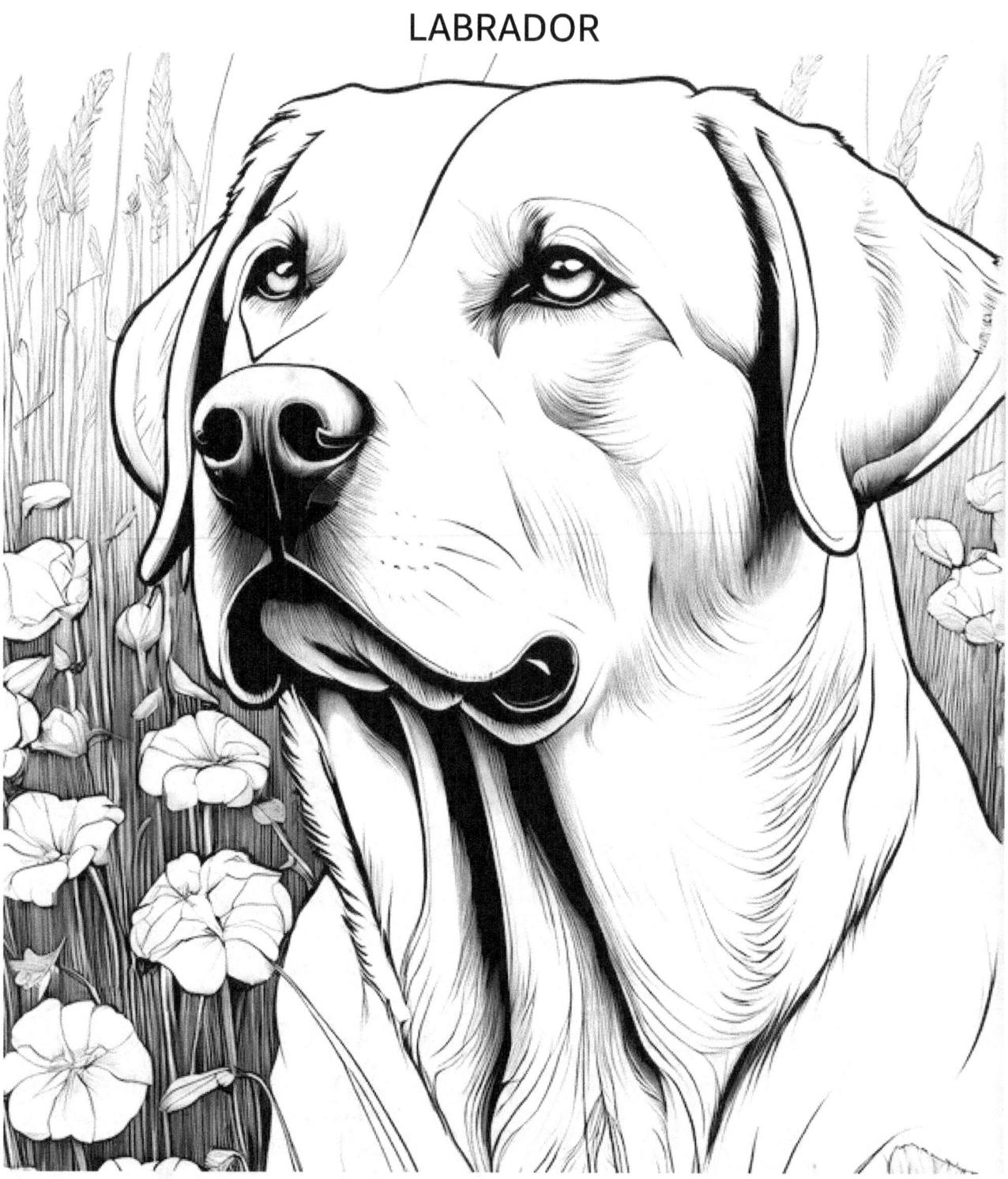

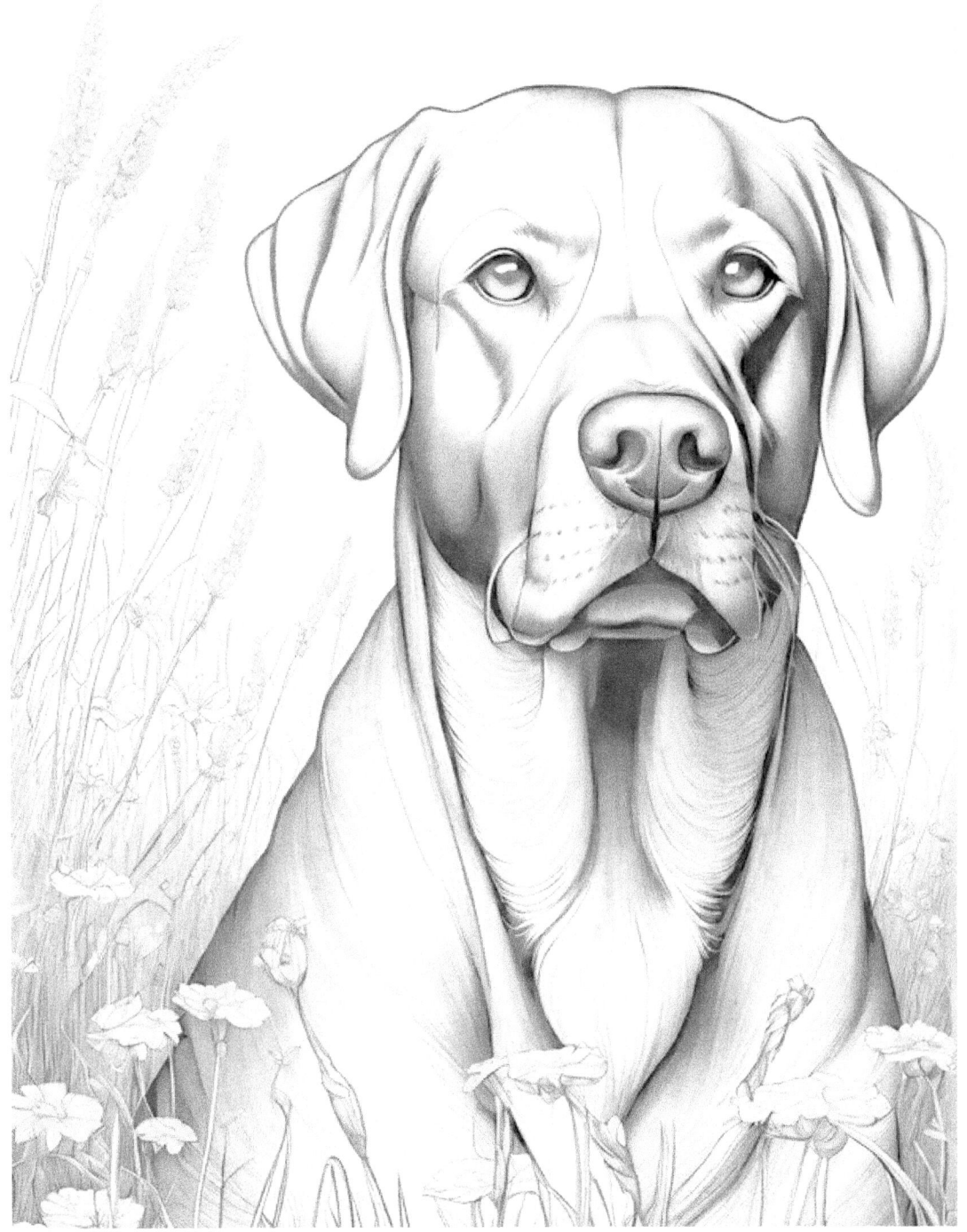

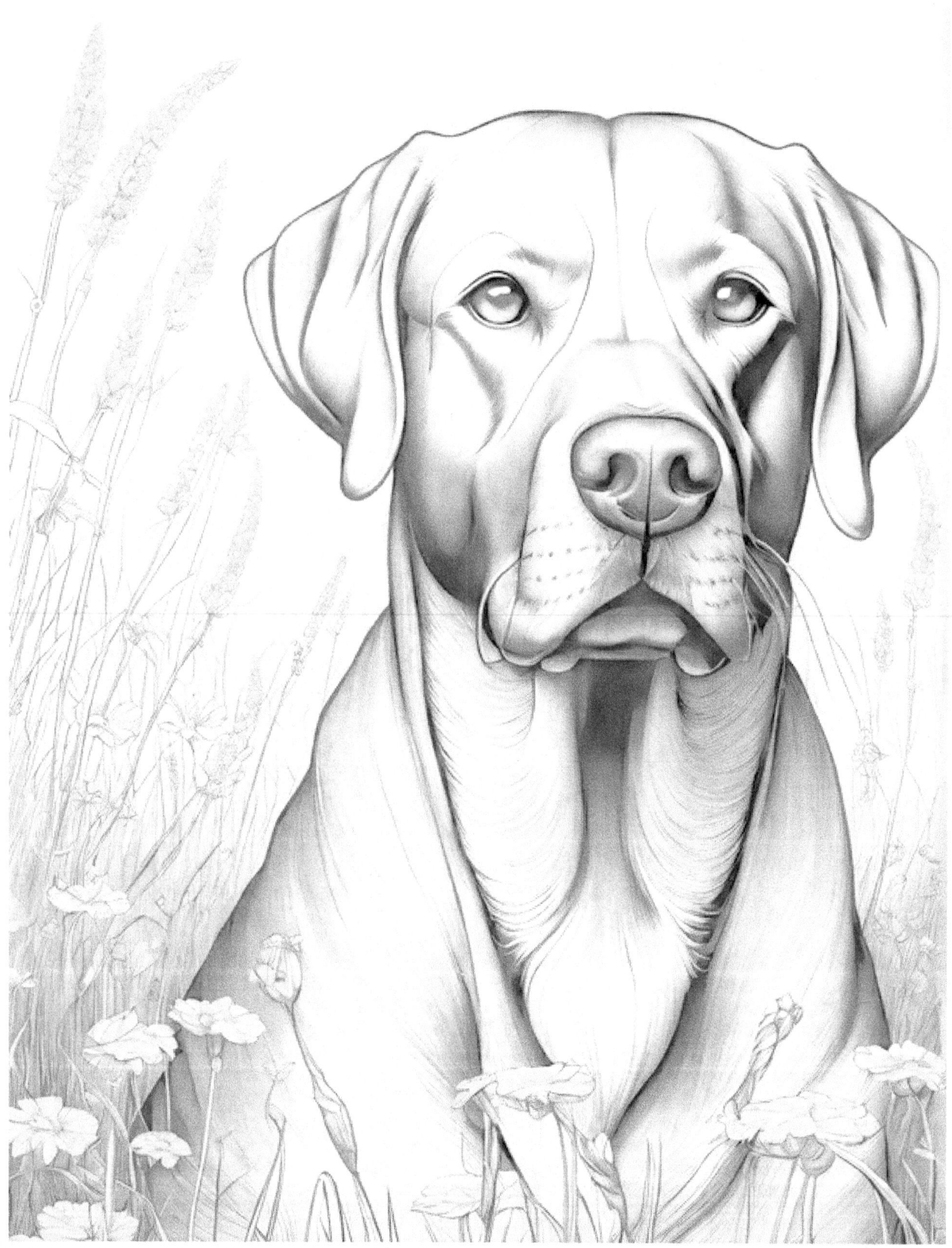

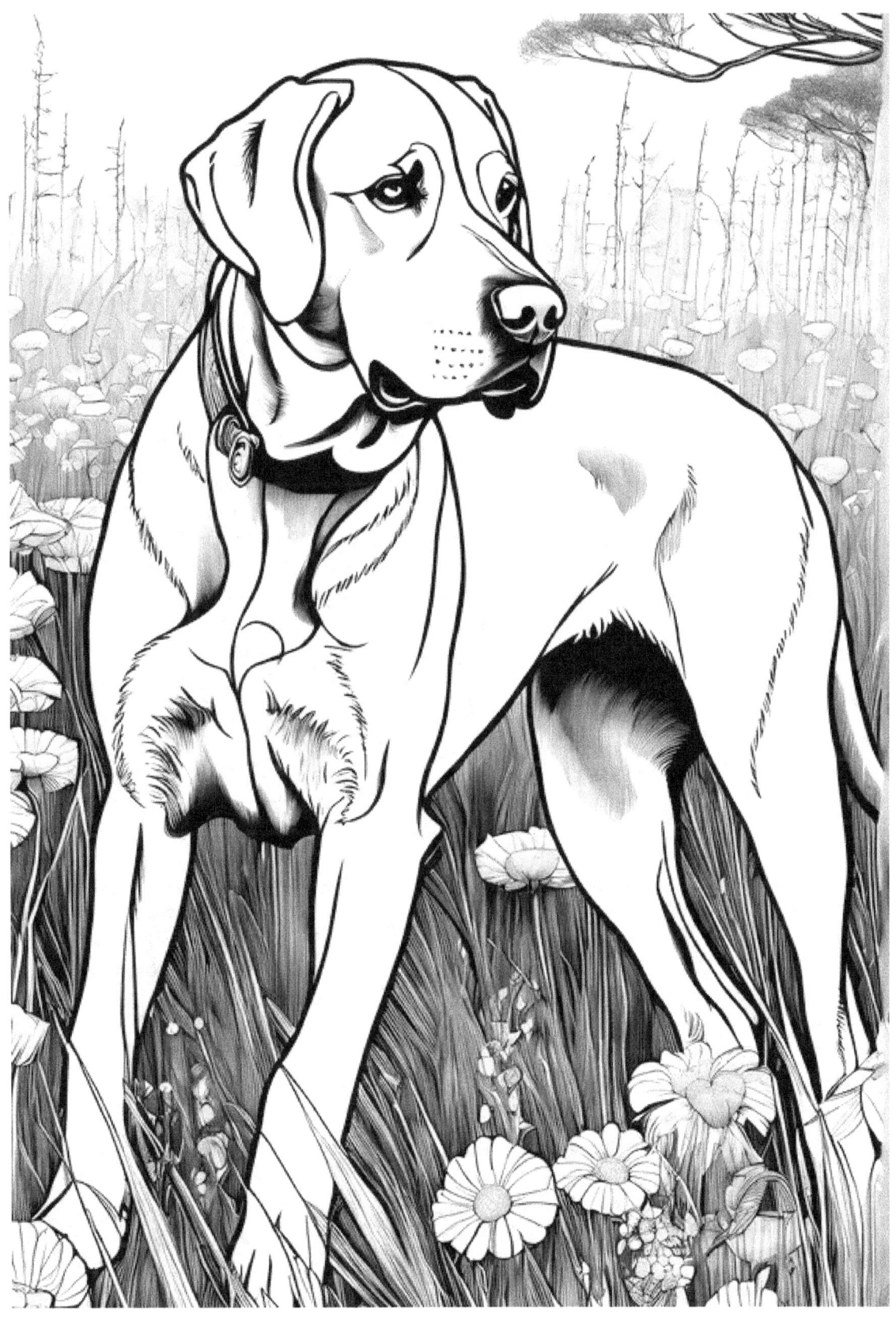

LEONBERG

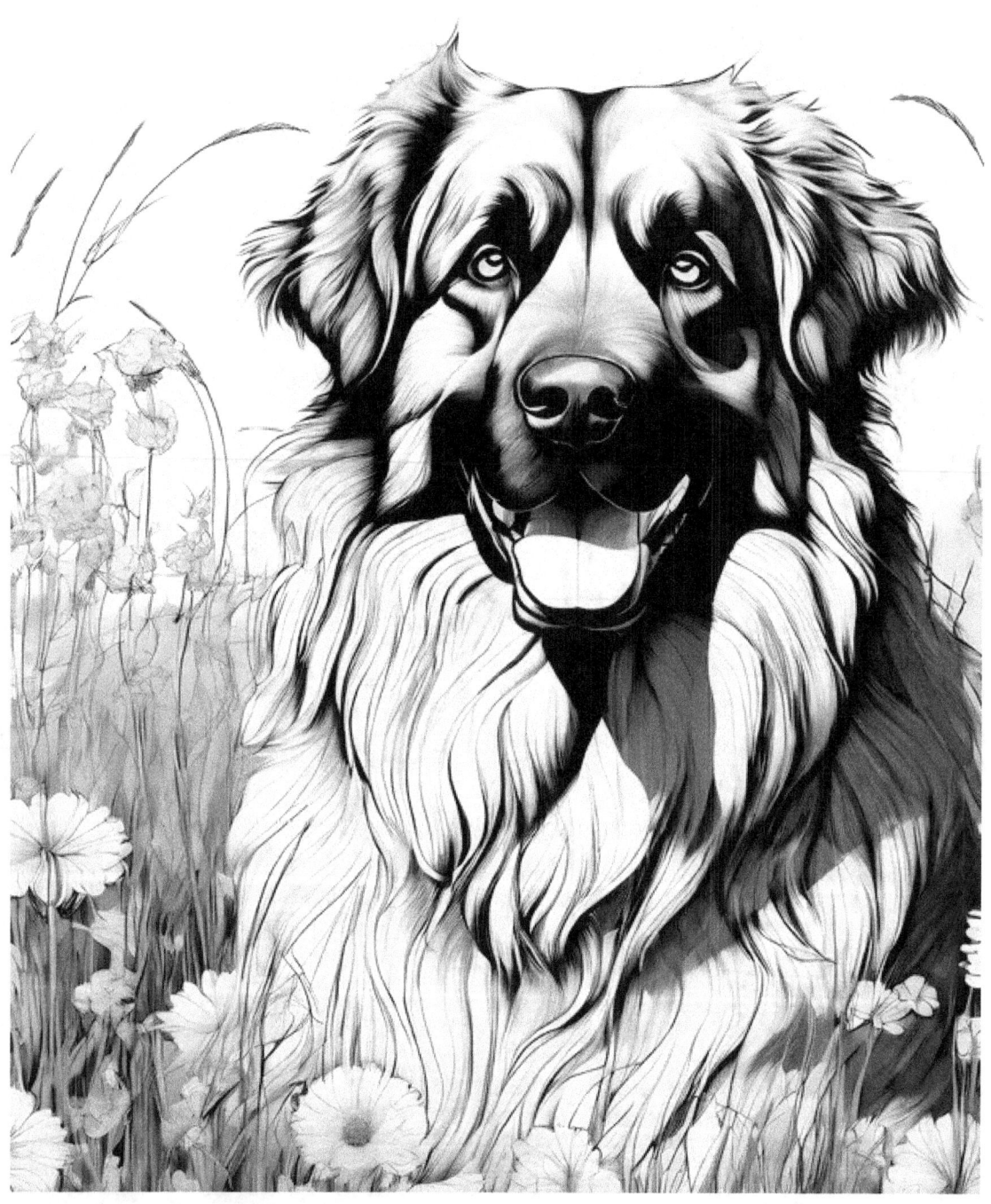

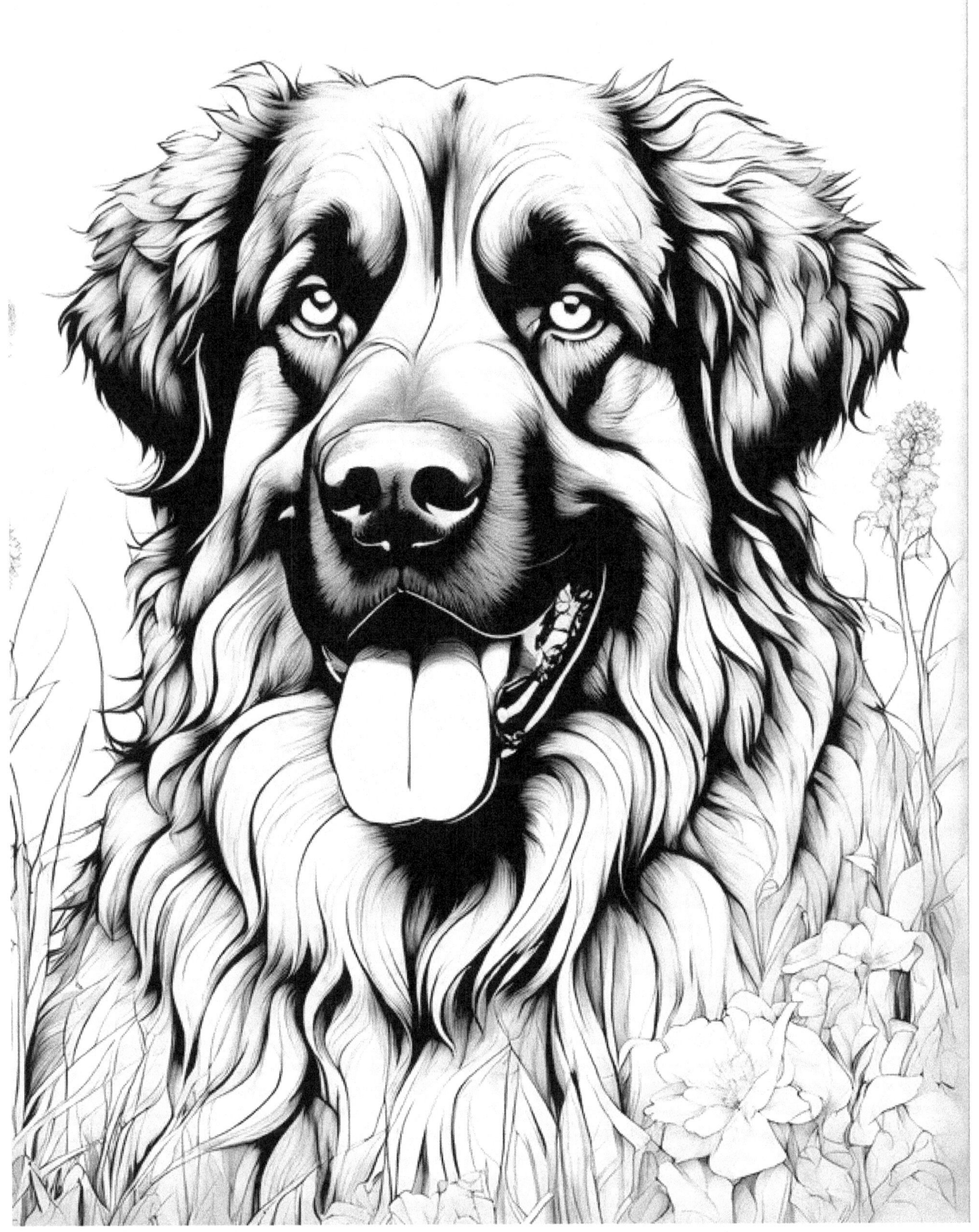

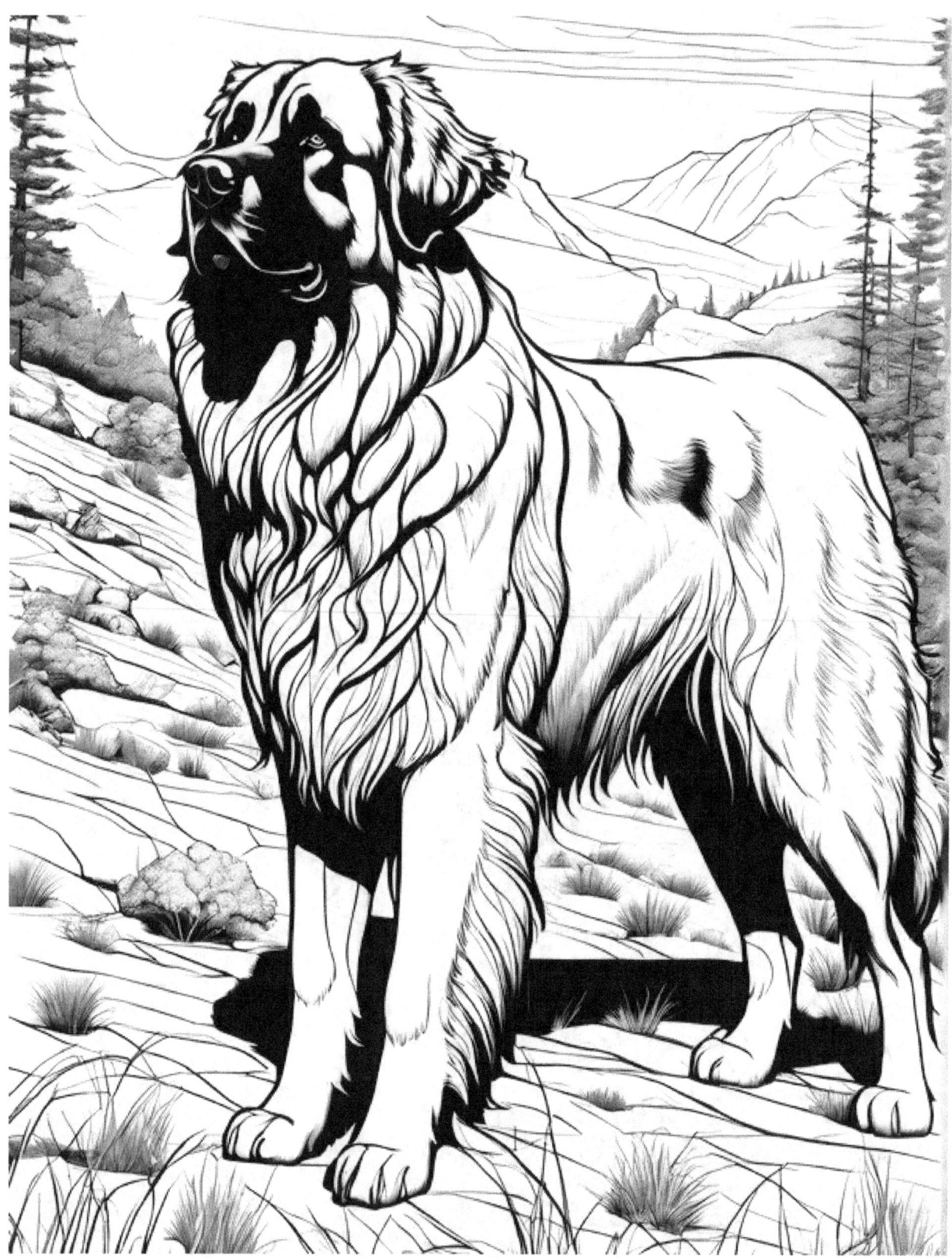

MIXER BREED

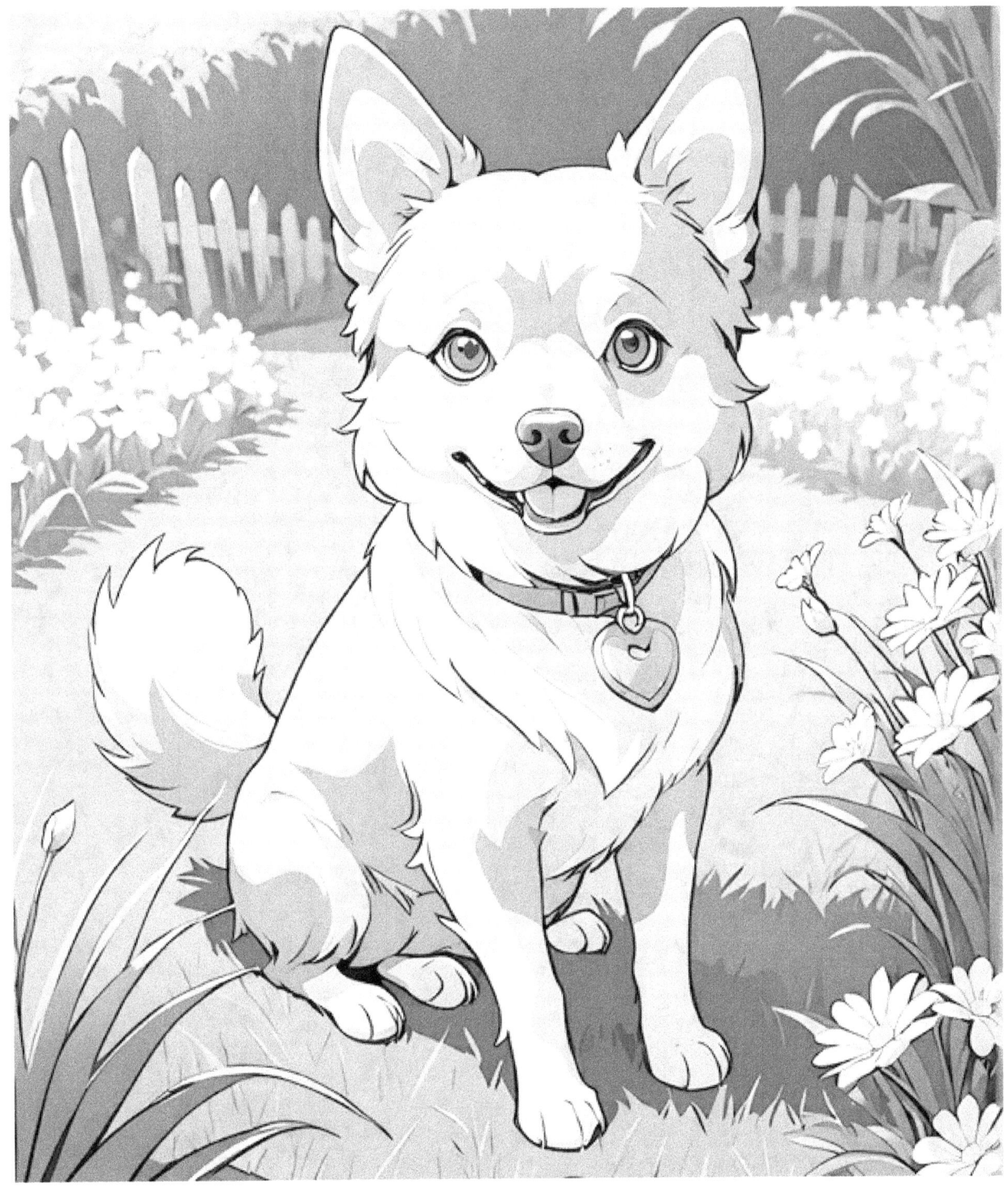

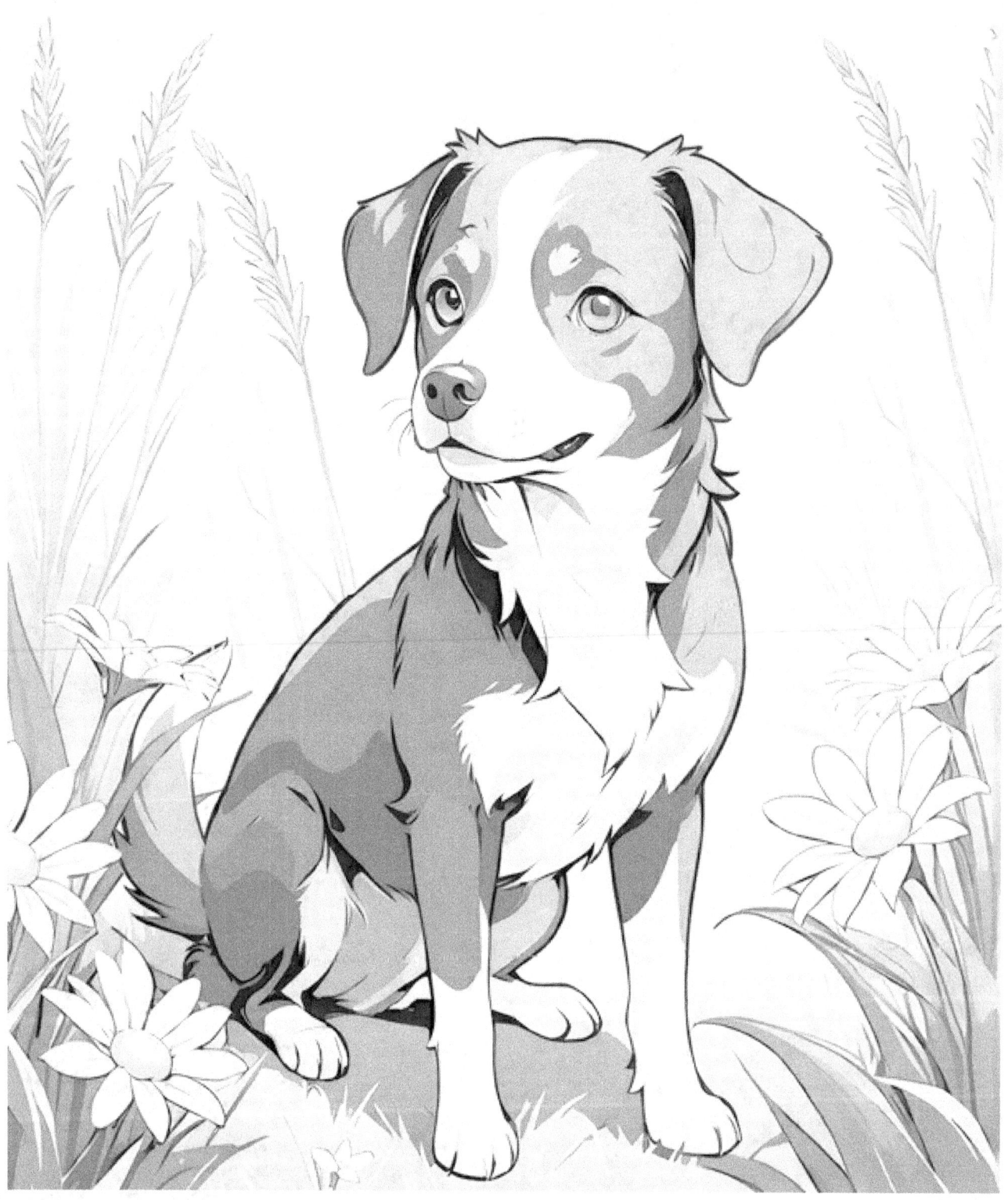

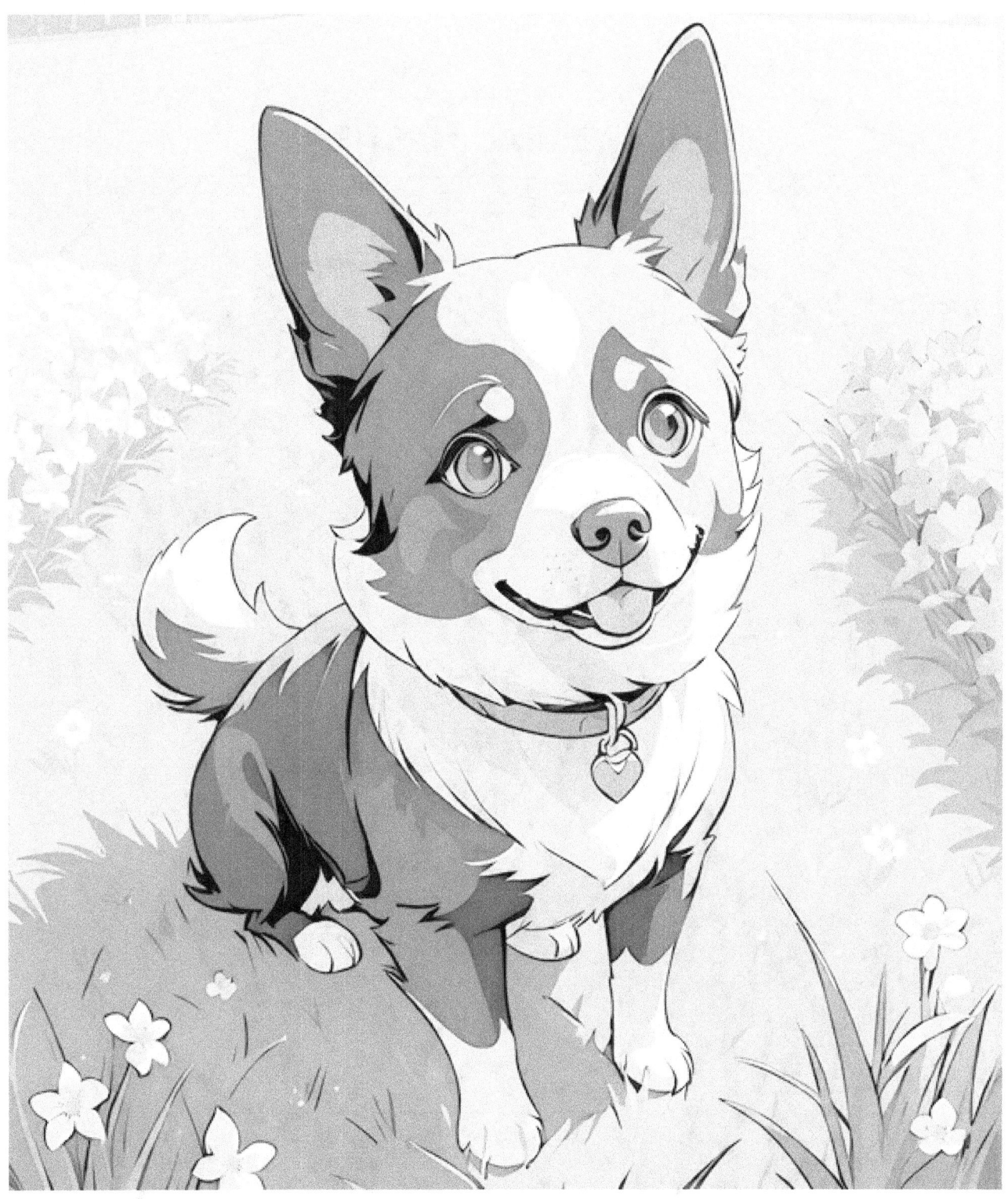

NEAPOLITAN MASTIFF

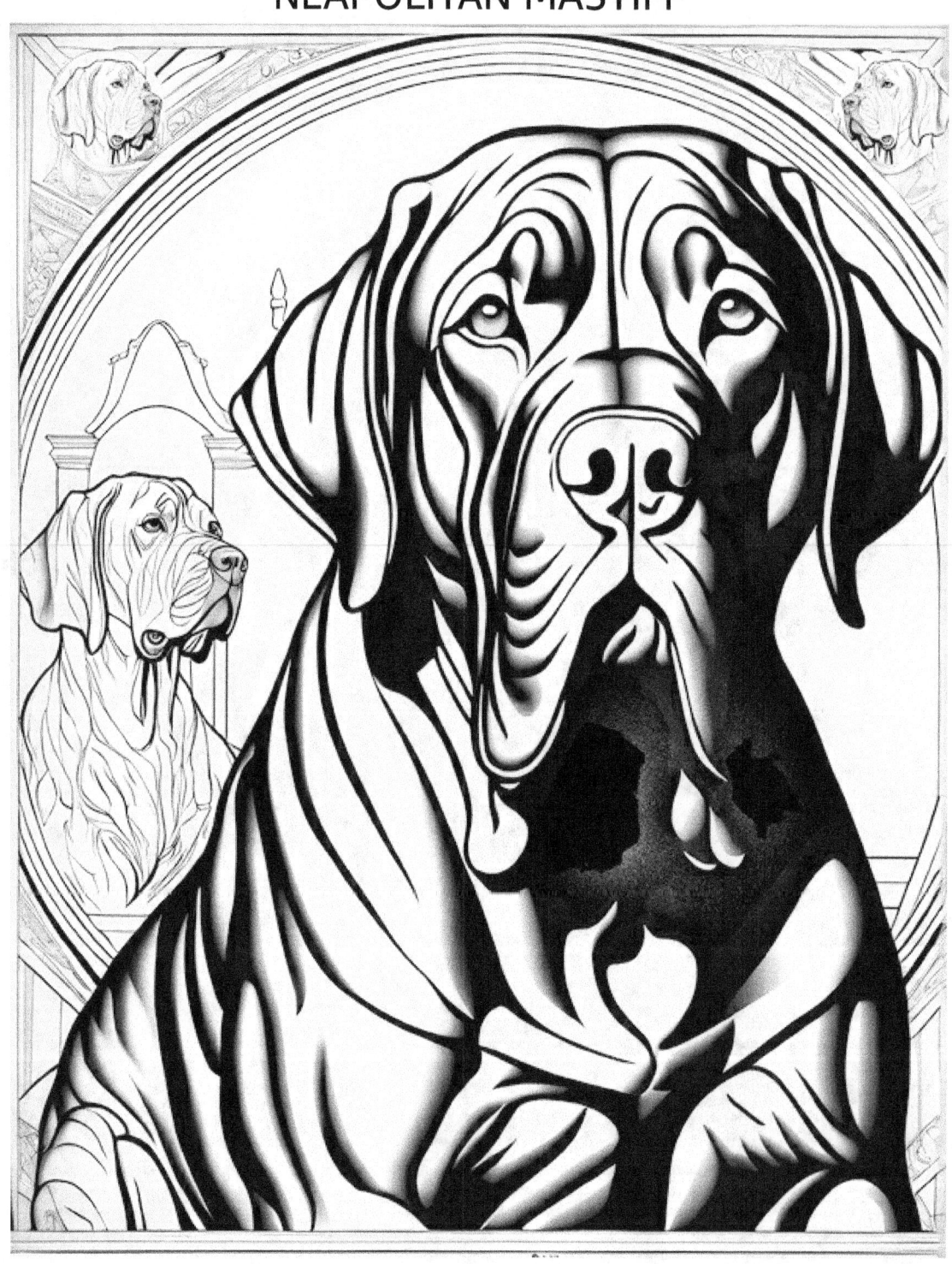

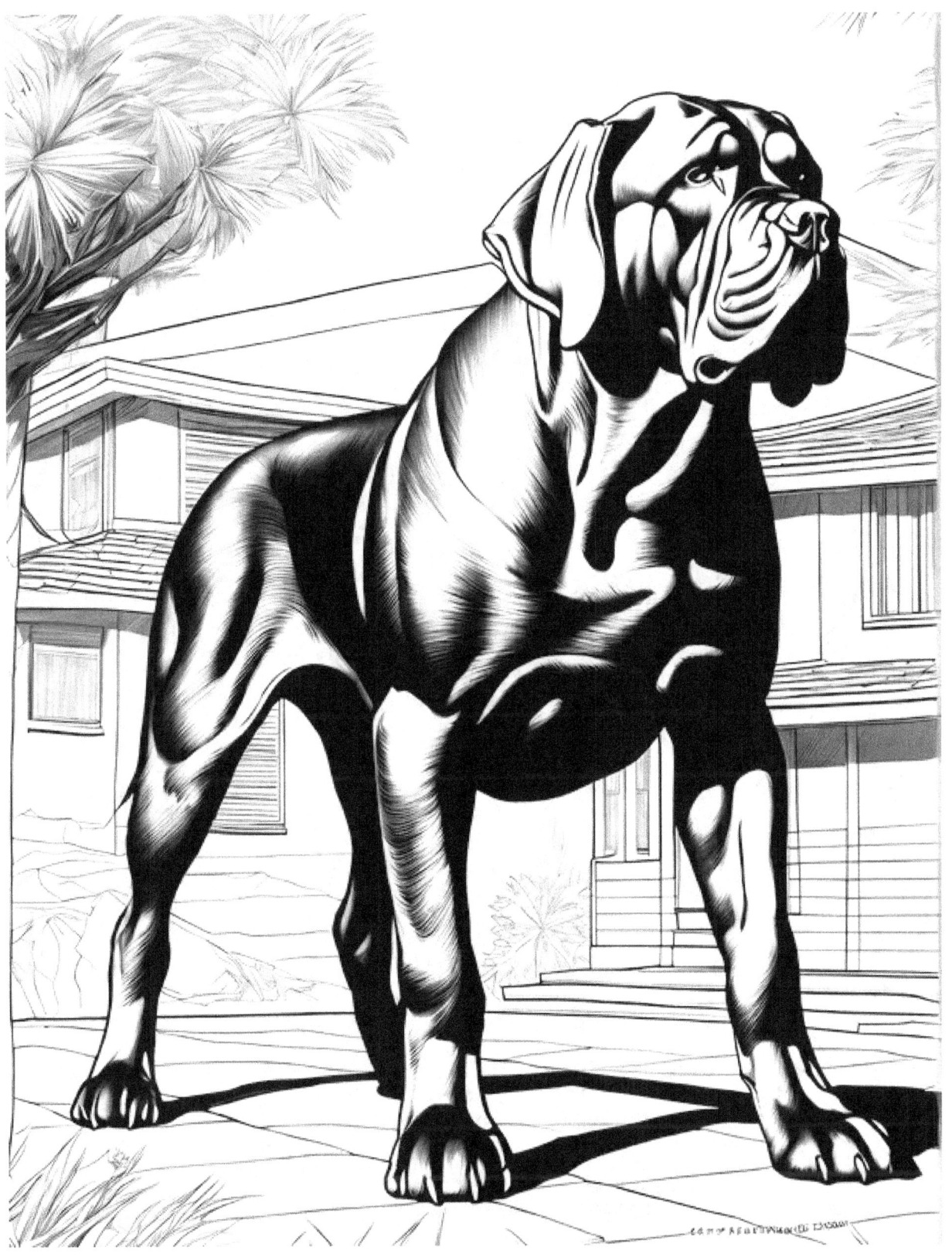

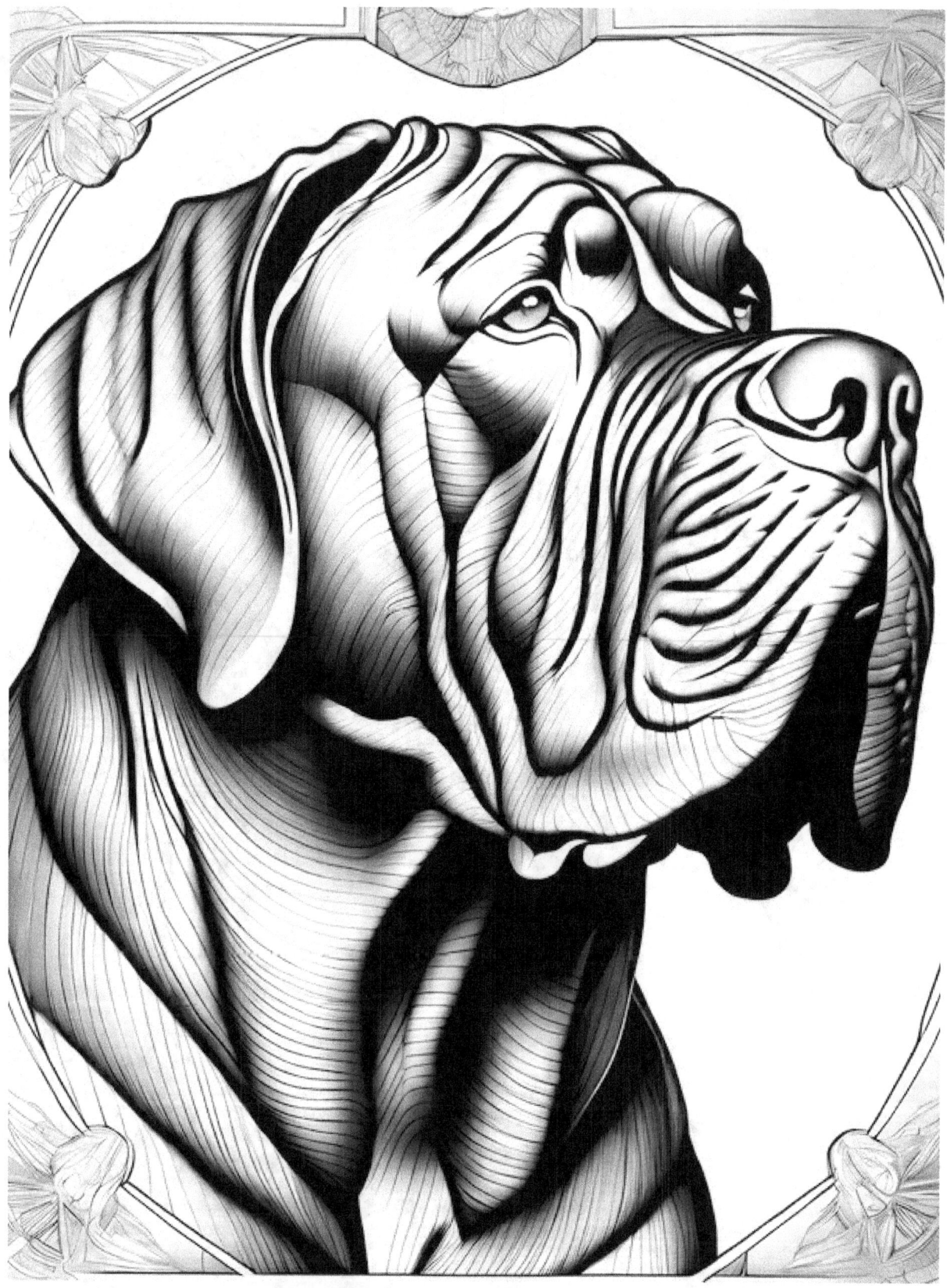

NORWEGIAN LUNDEHUND

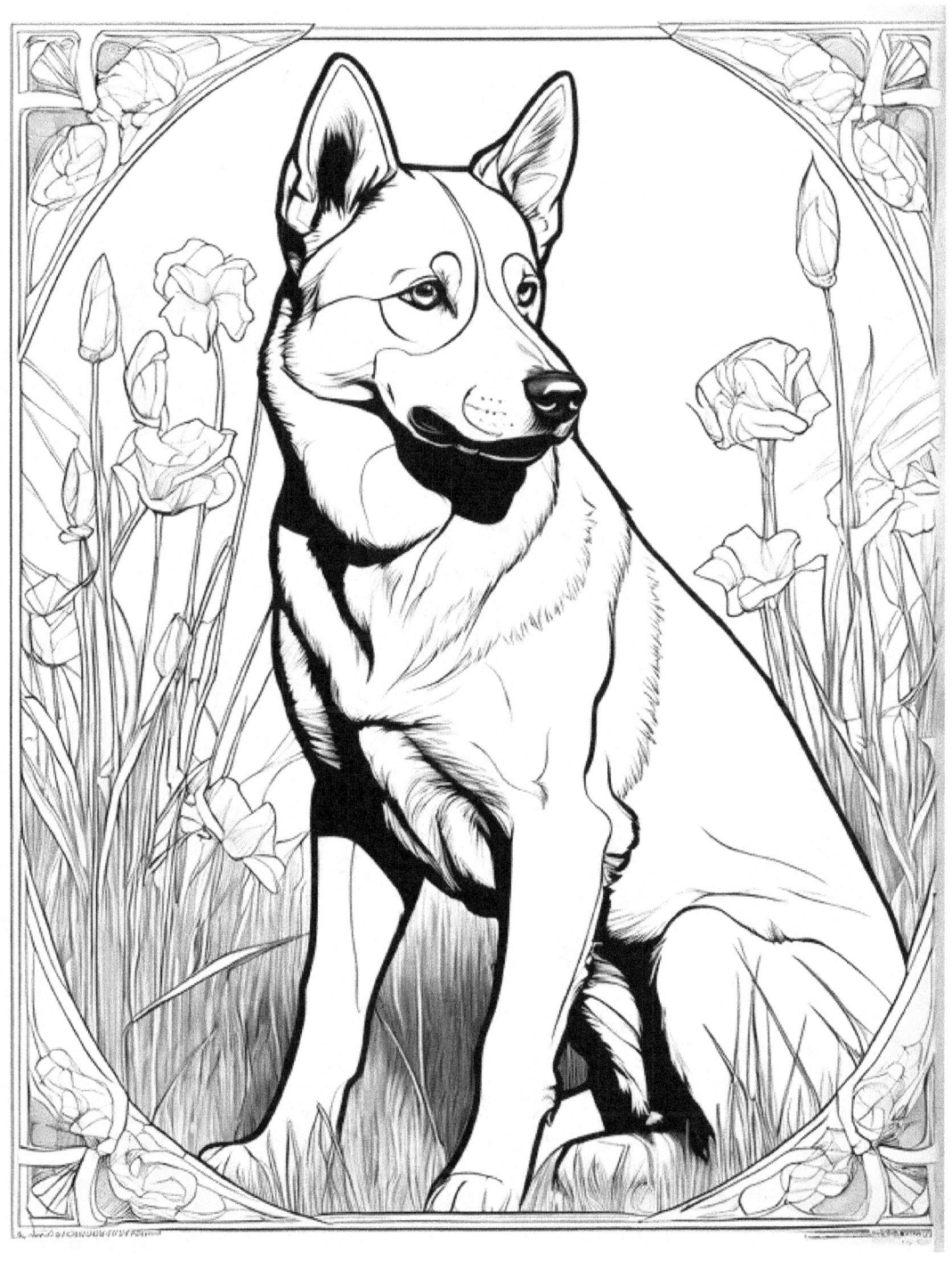

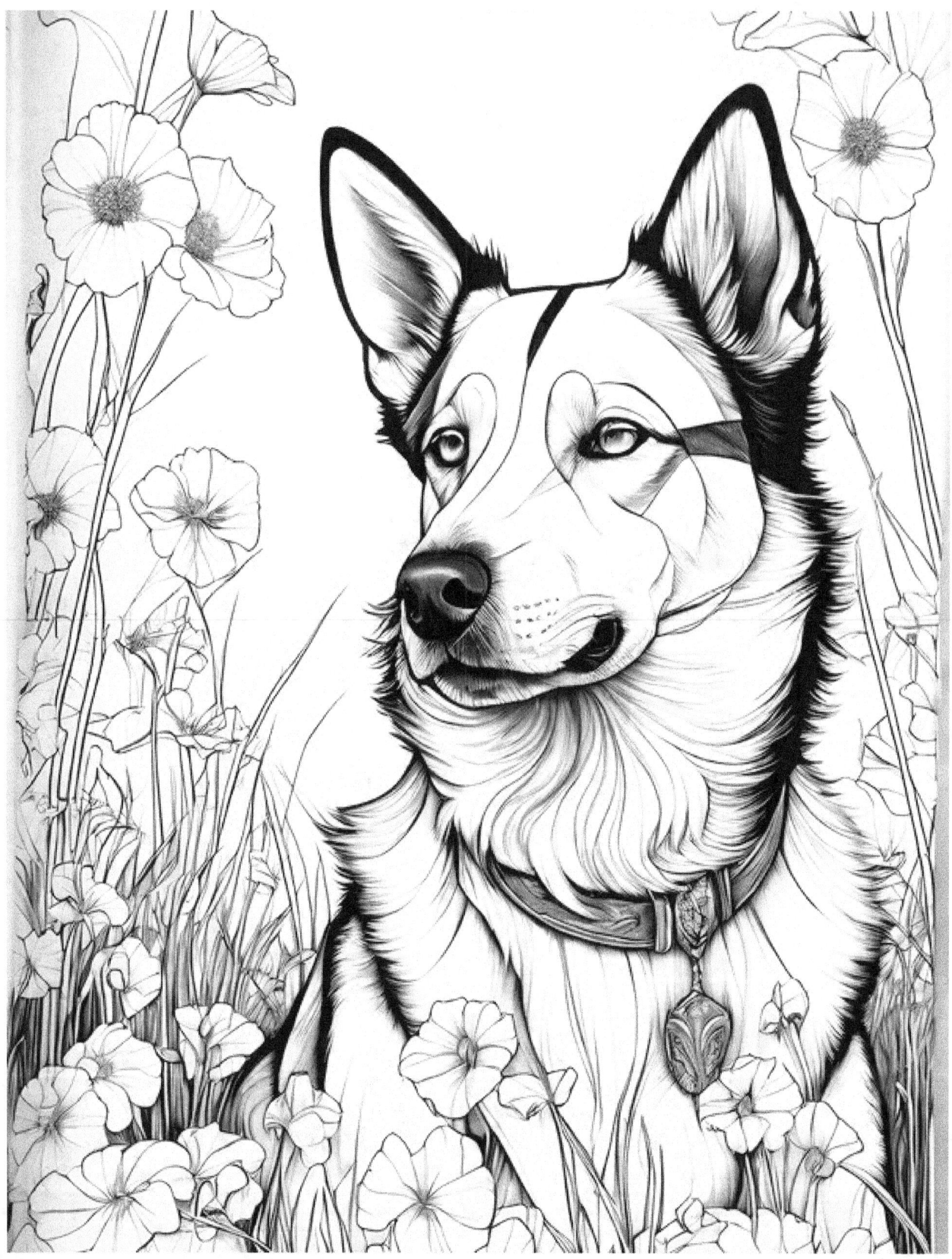

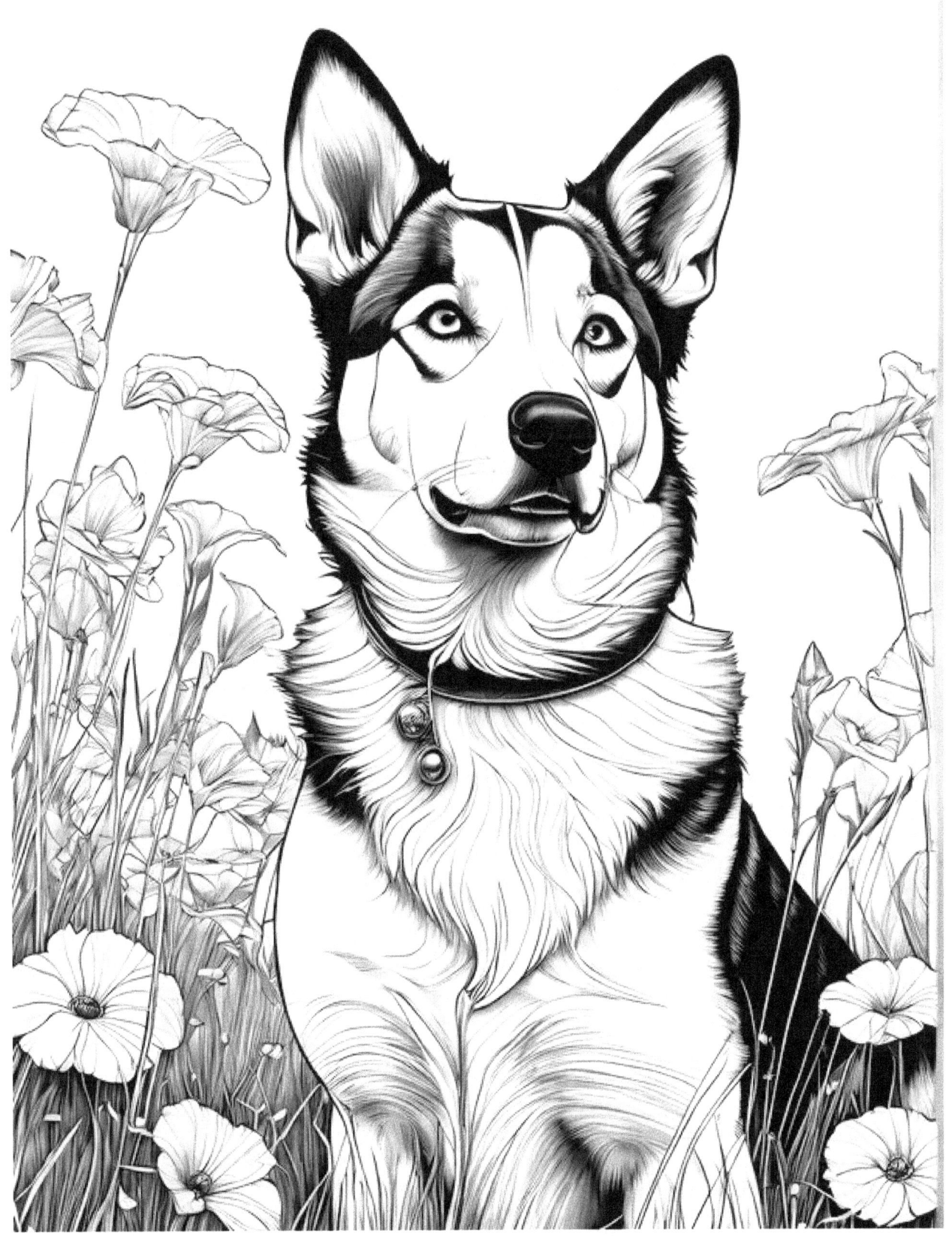

ROBERTO BARONDI

PEKINGESE

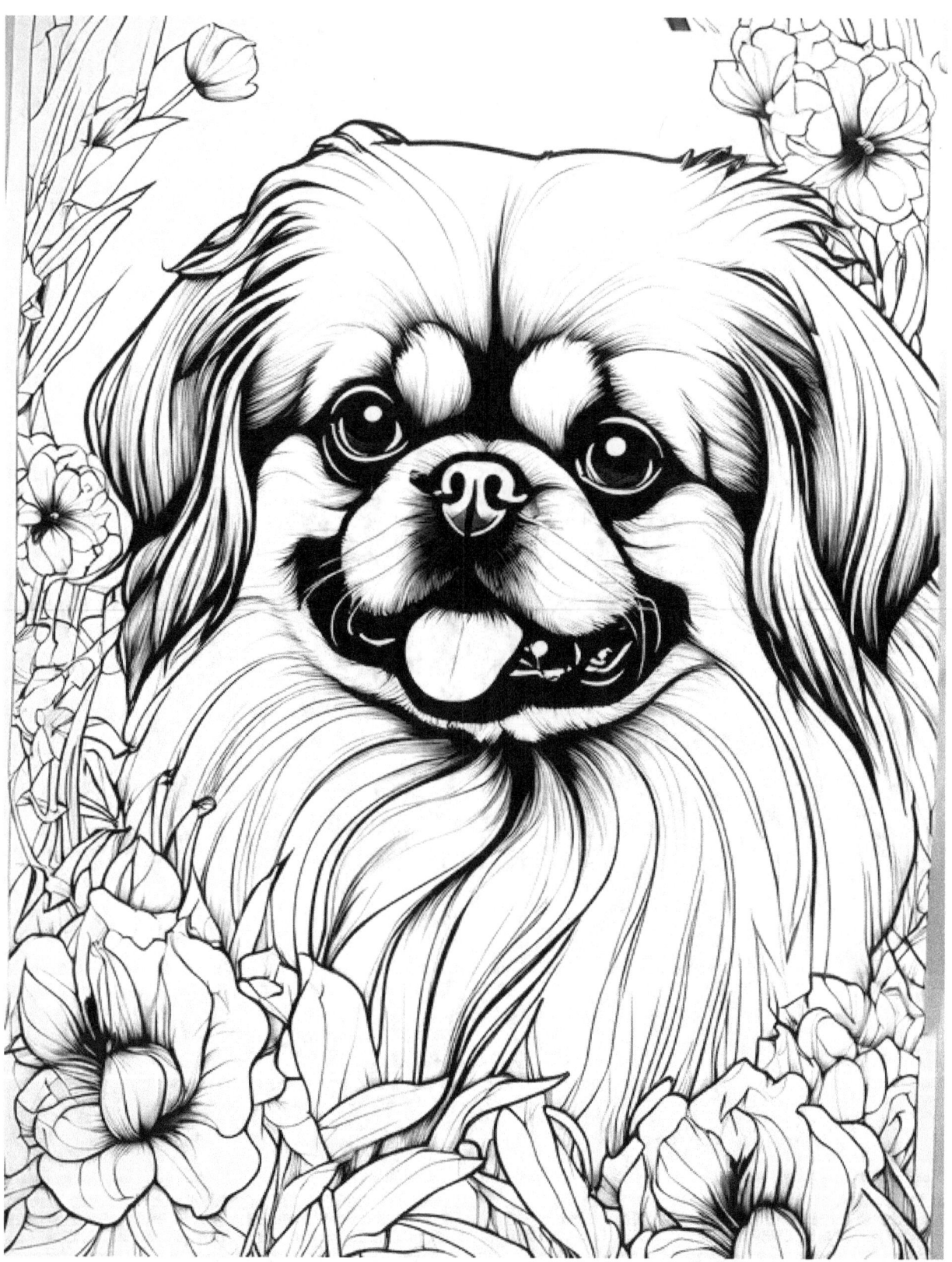

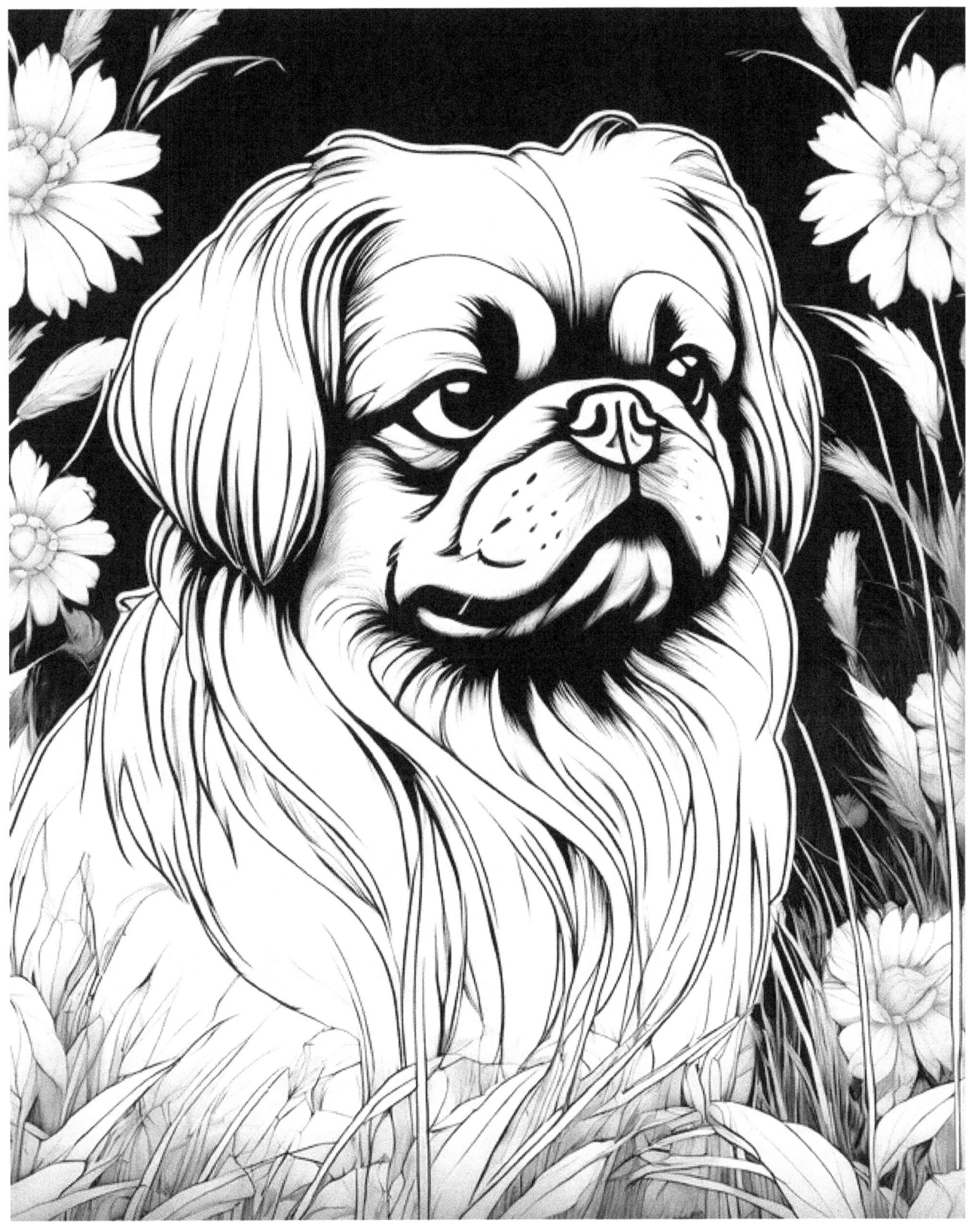

POMERANIAN

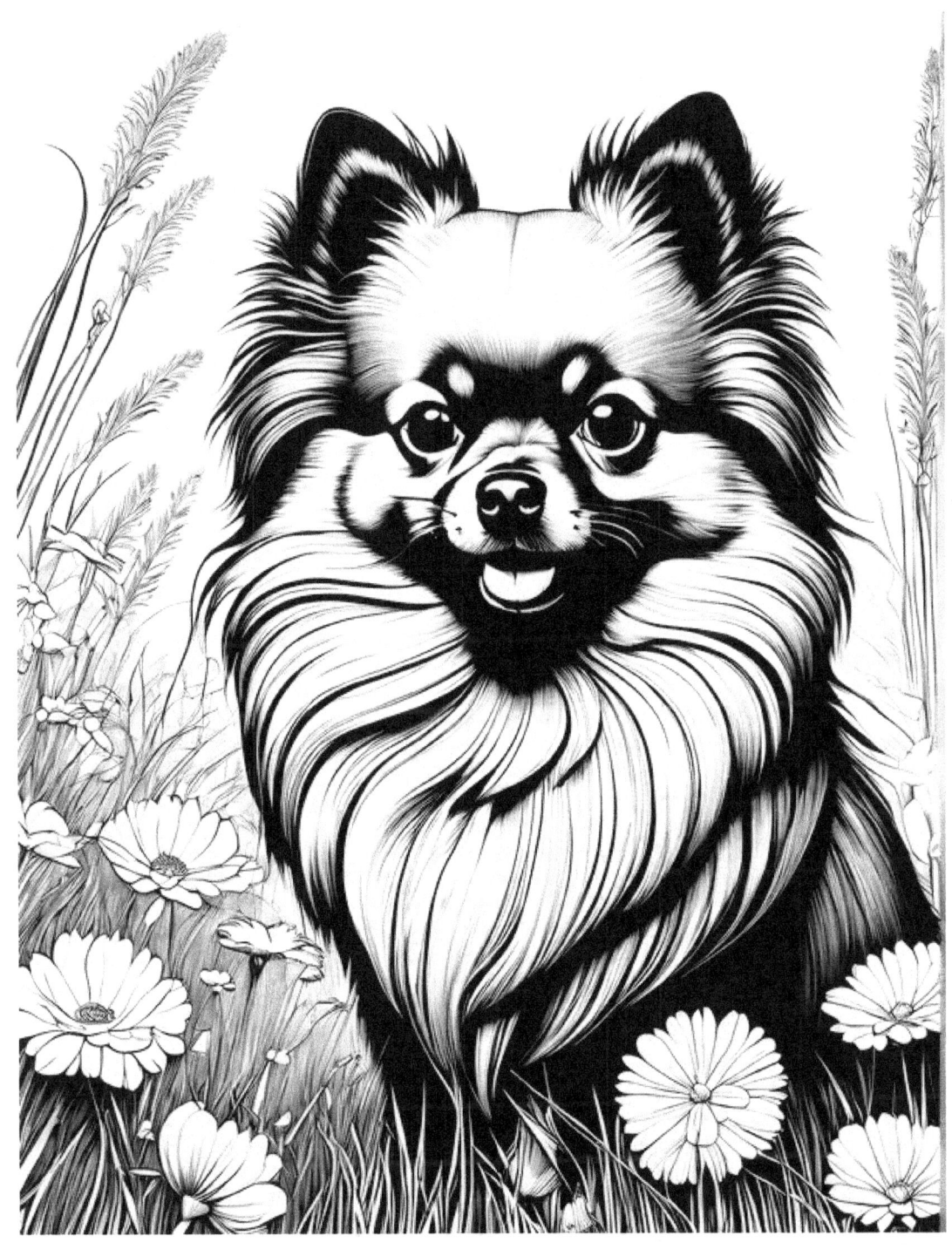

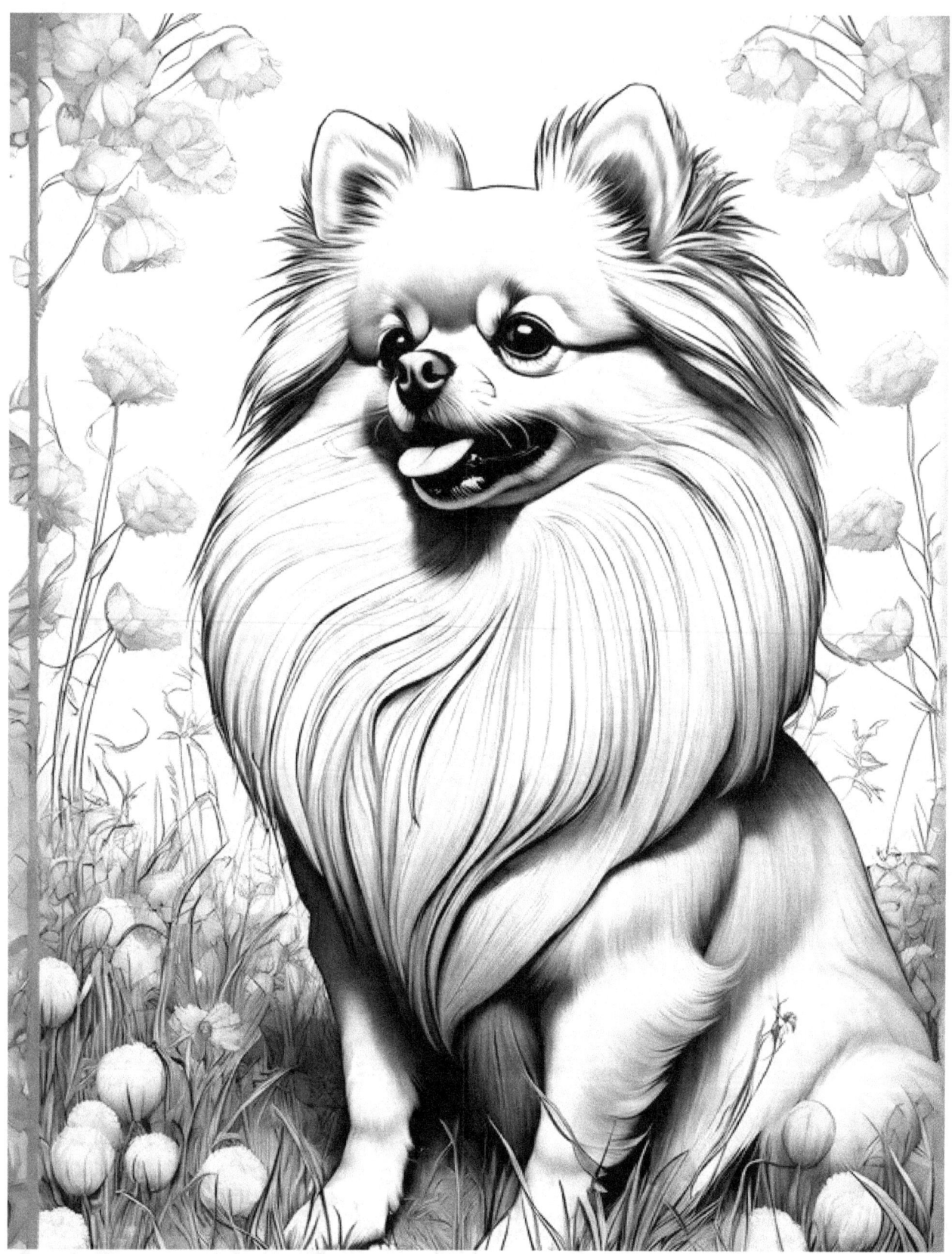

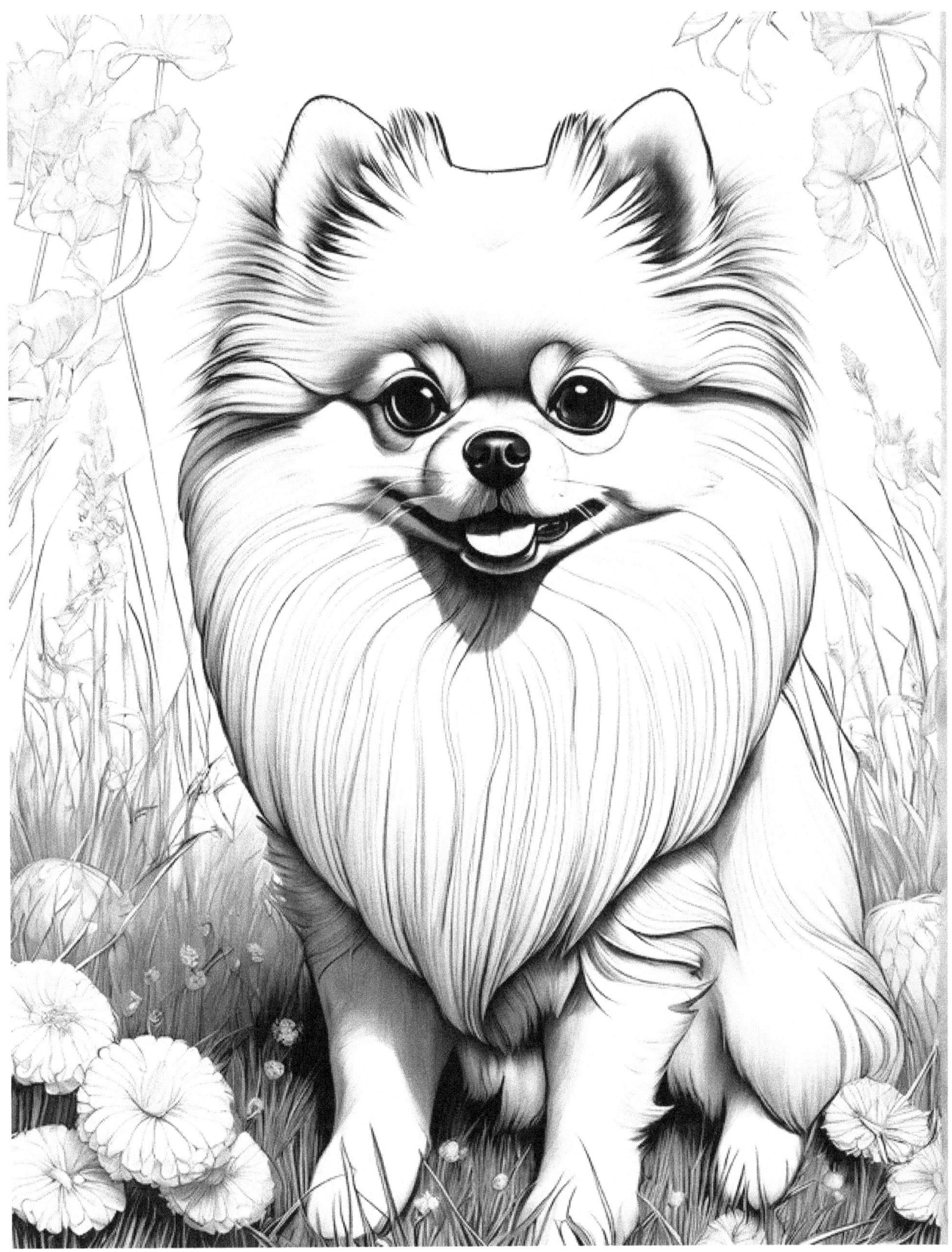

ROBERTO BARONDI

POODLE

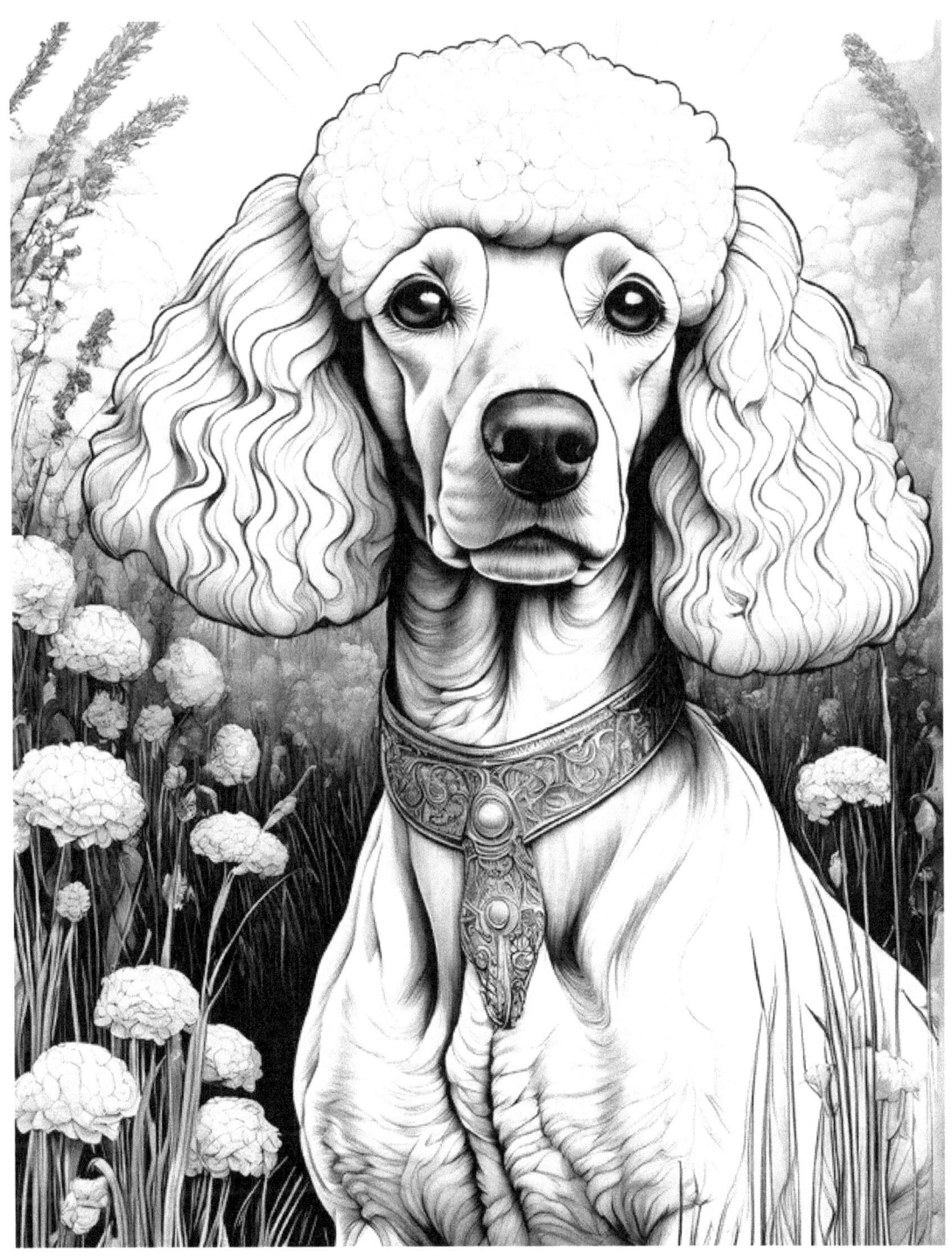

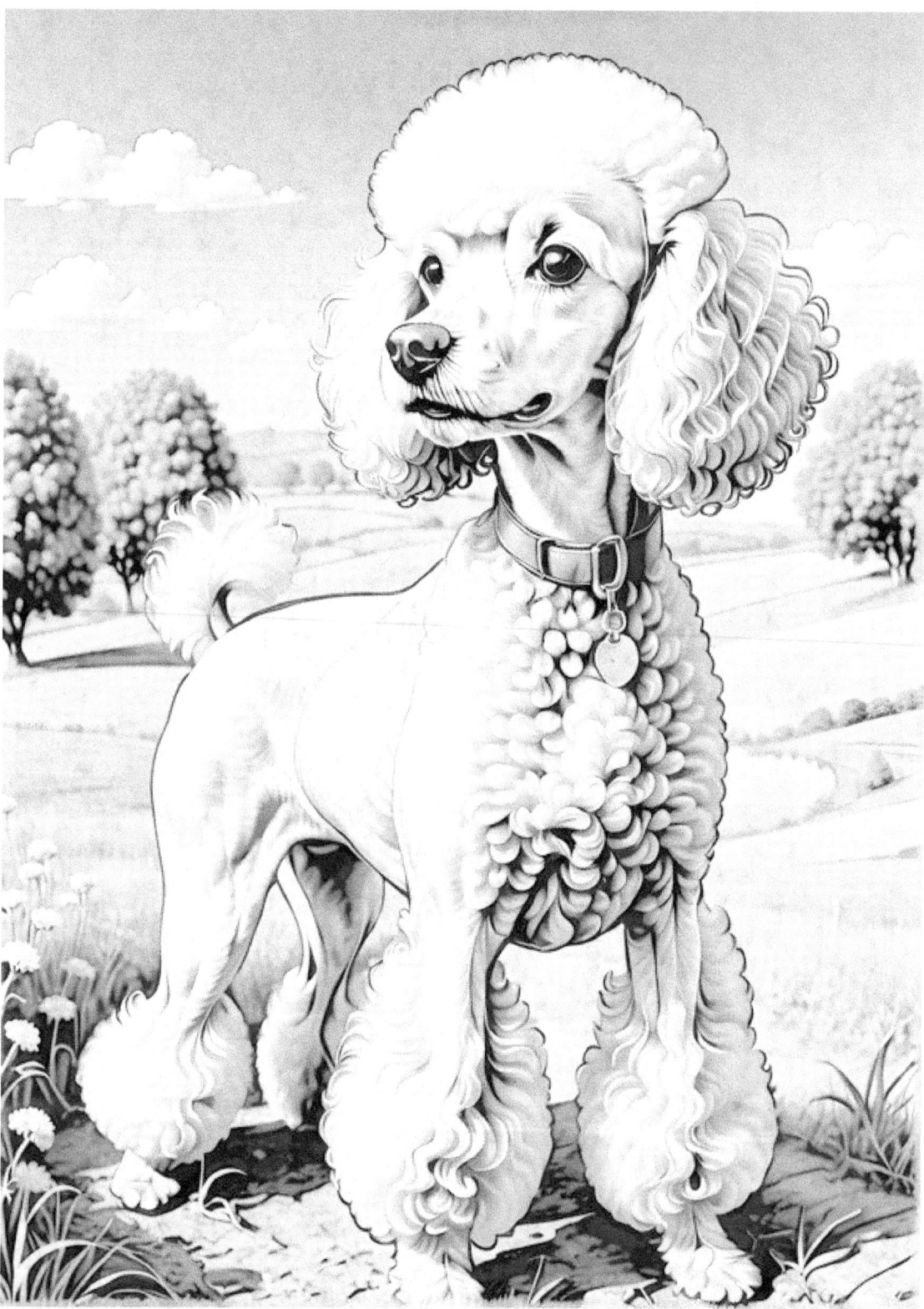

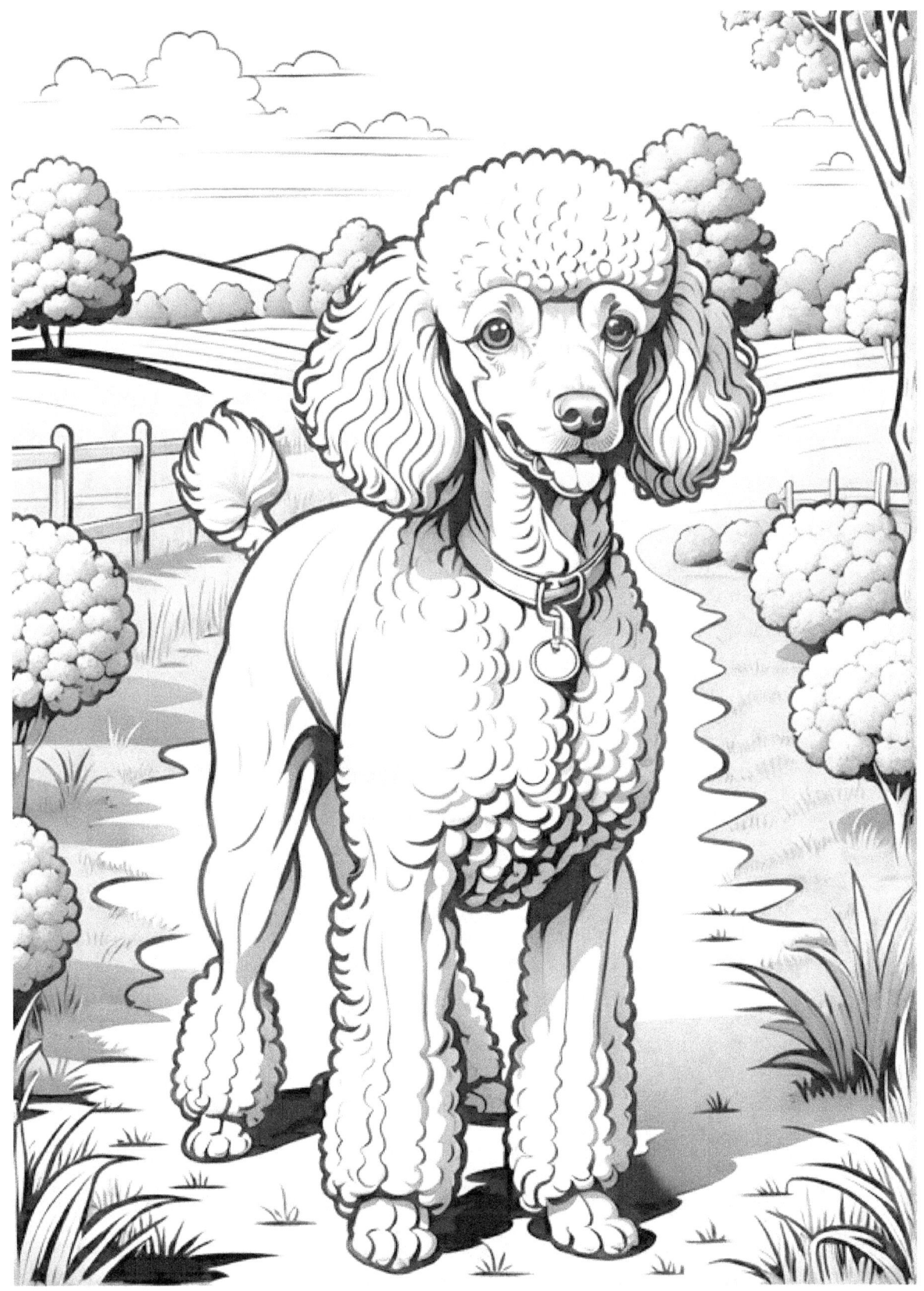

ROTTWEILER

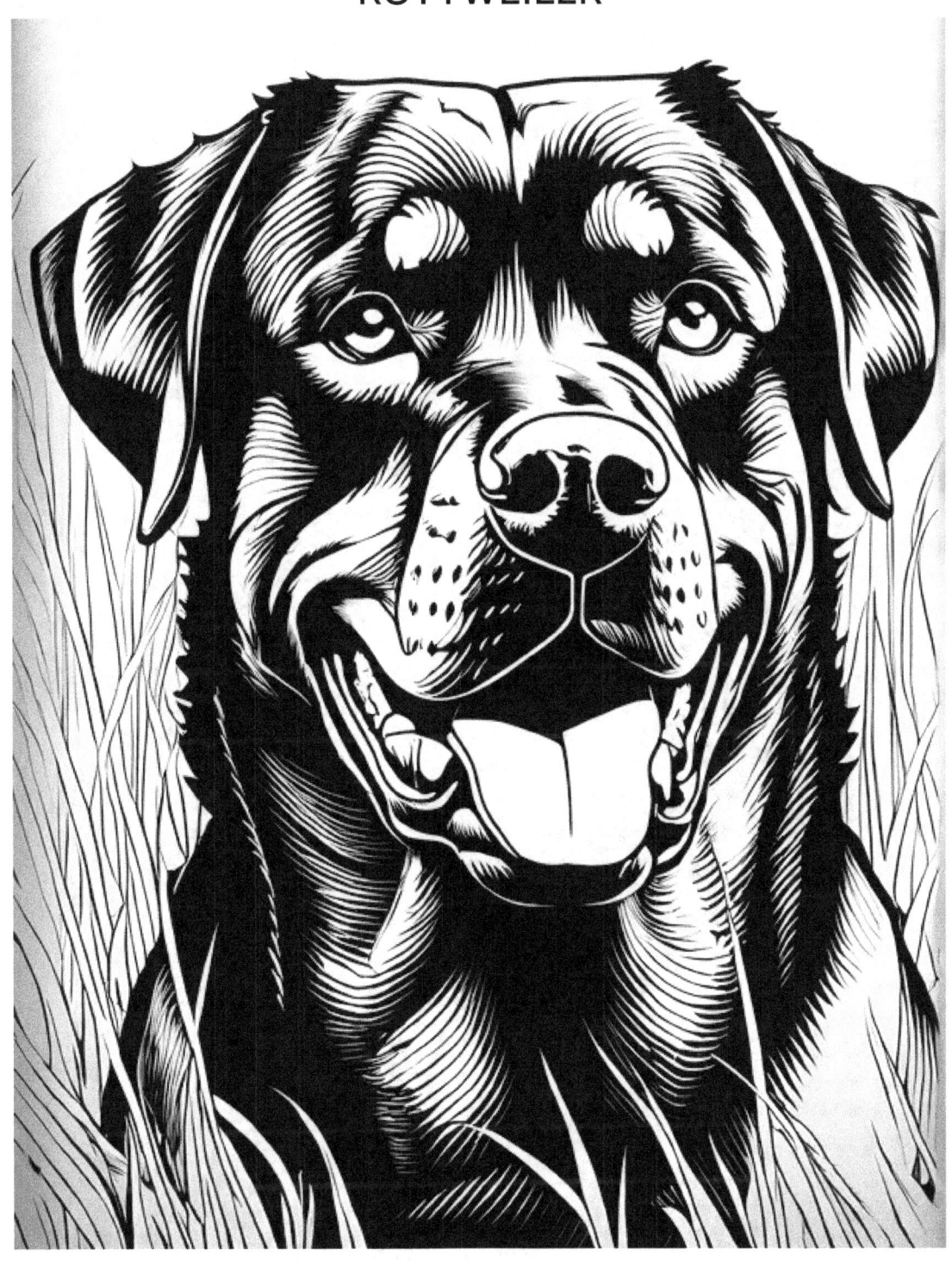

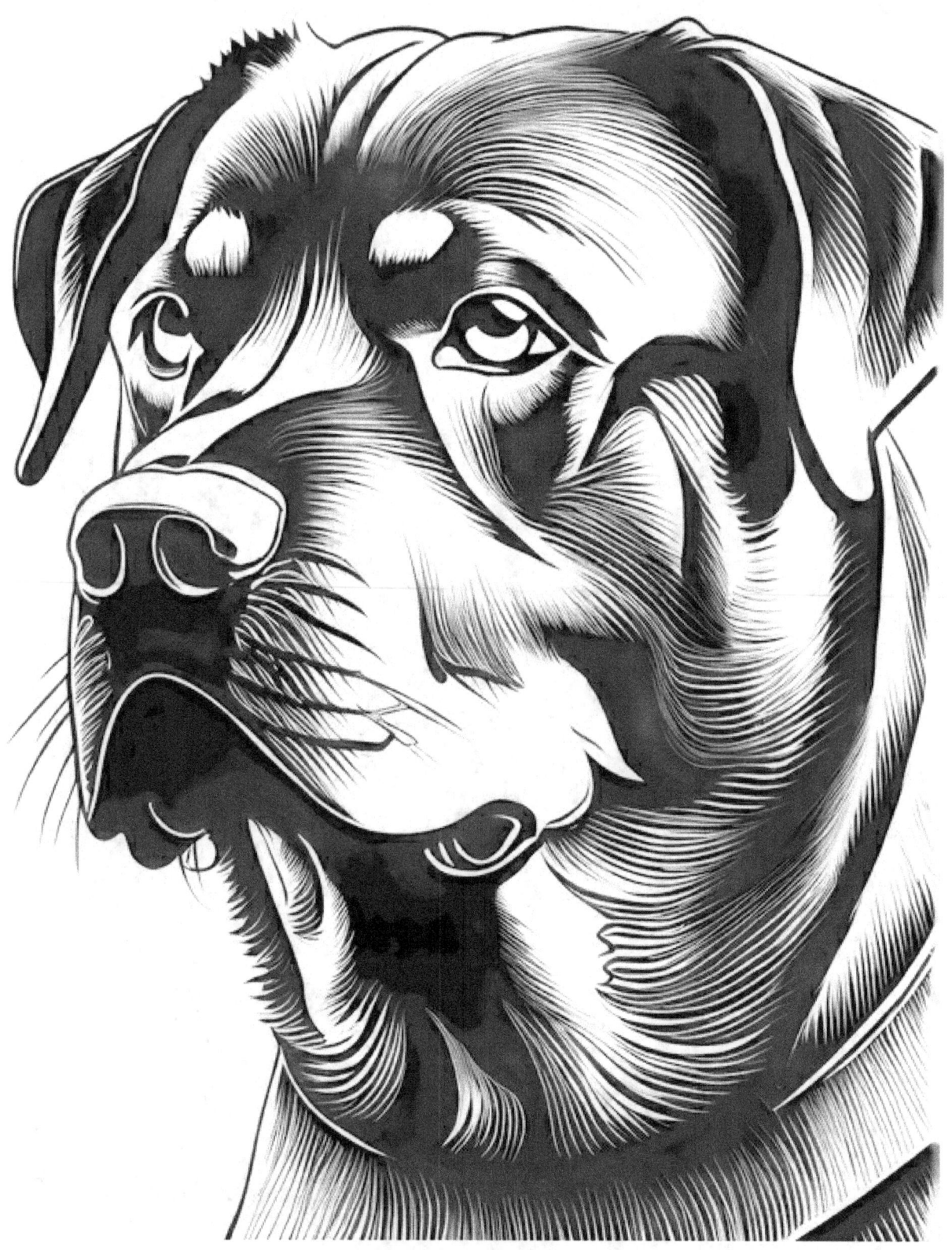

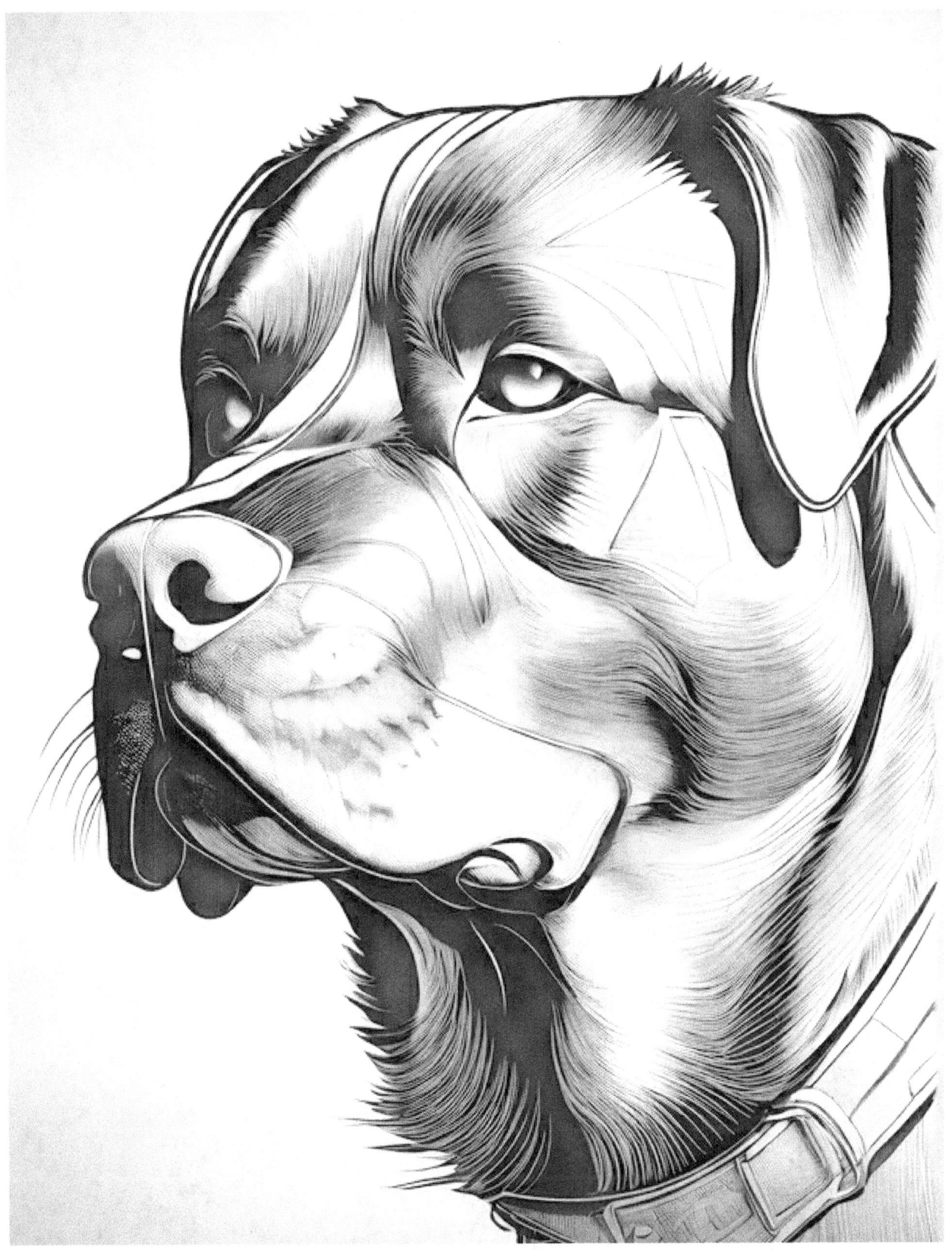

SETTER

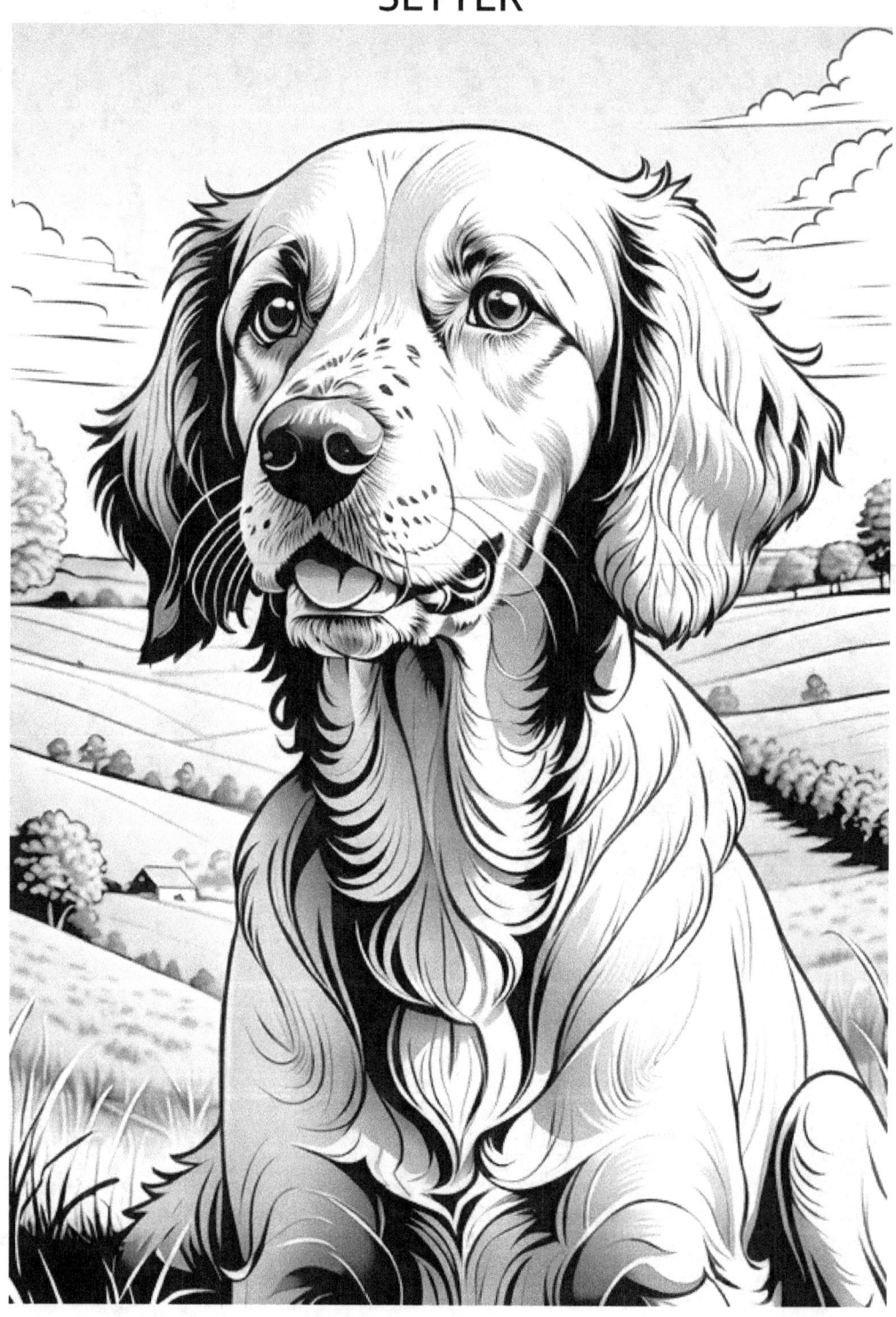

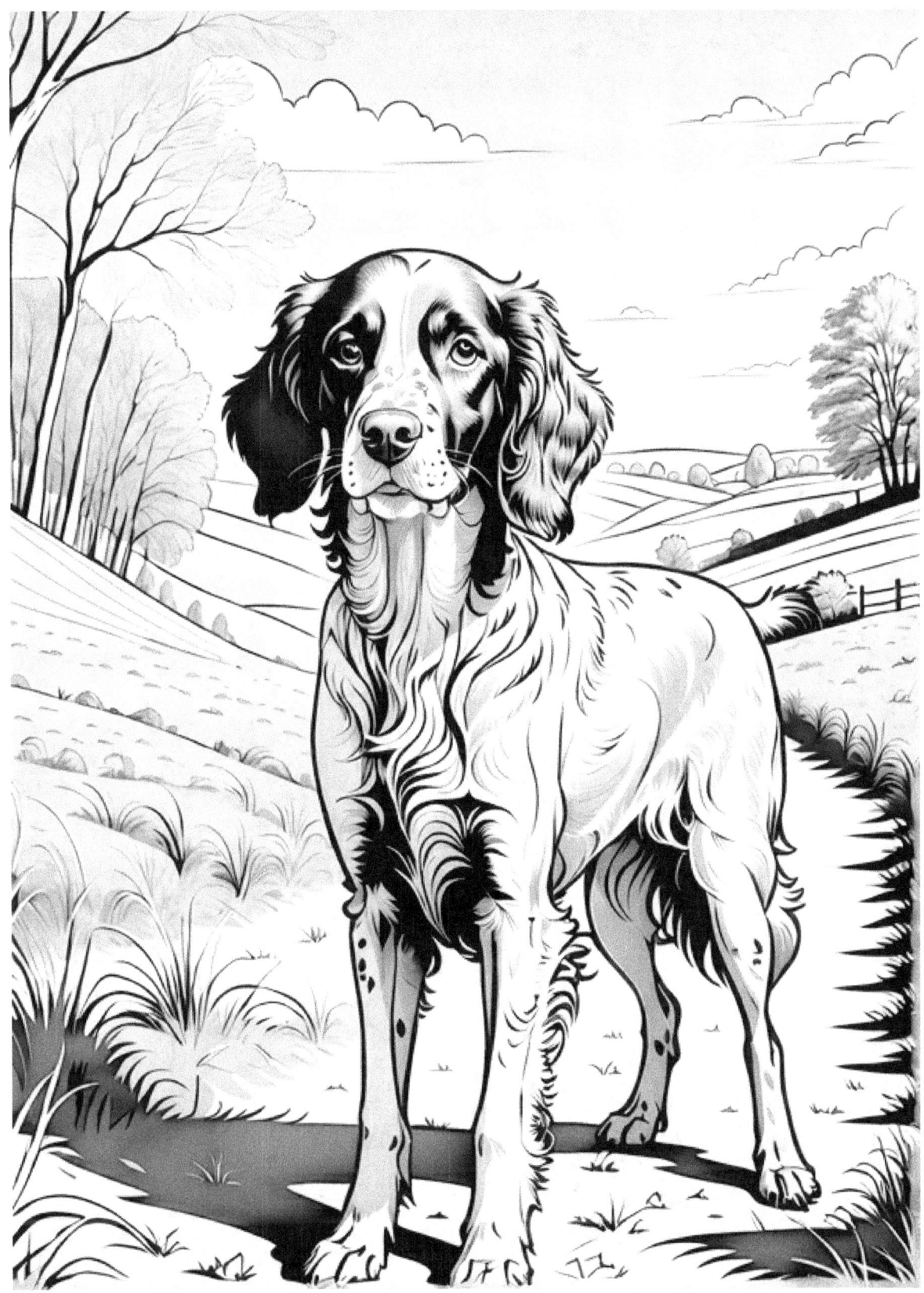

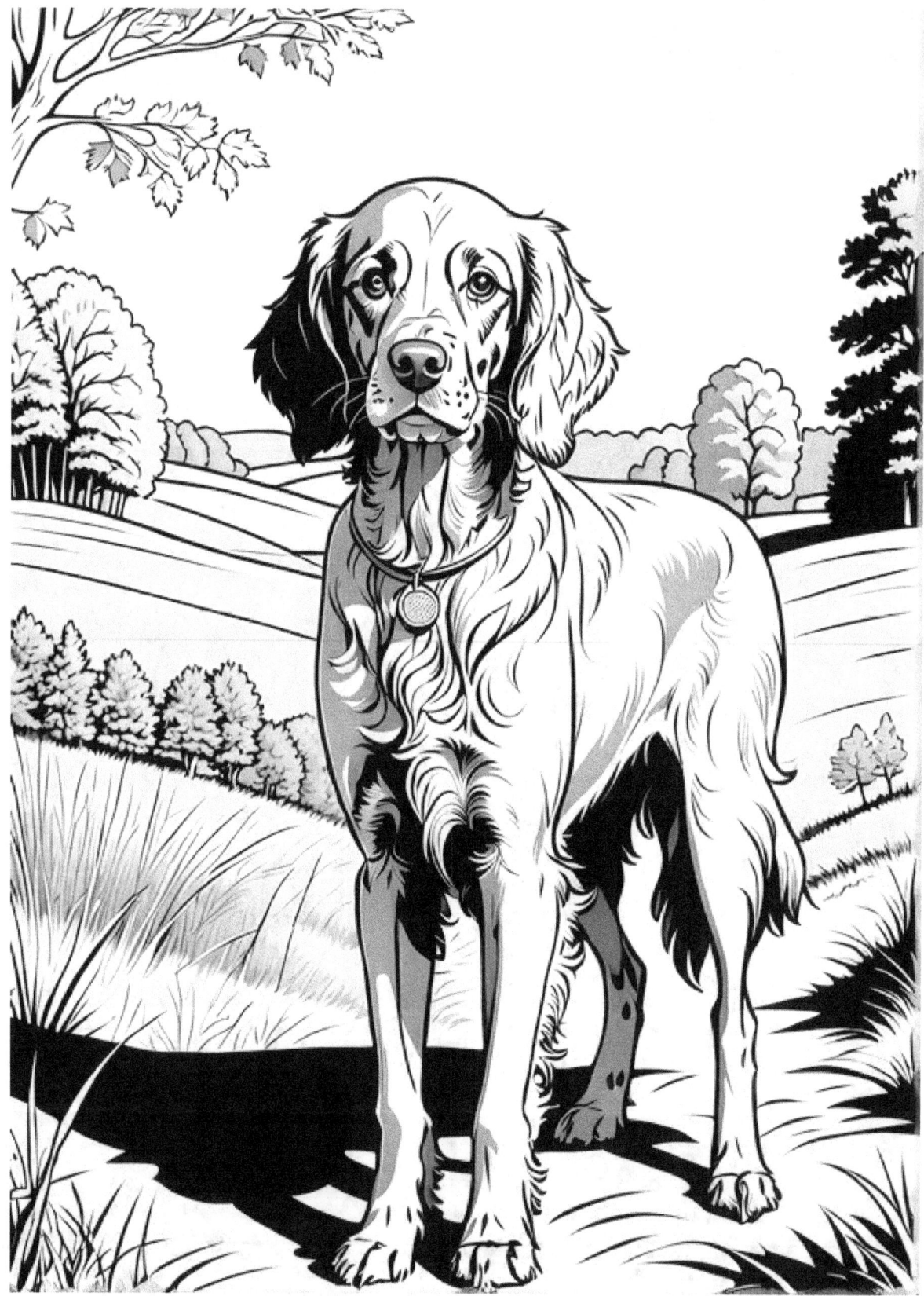

SHIH-TZU

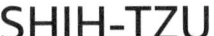

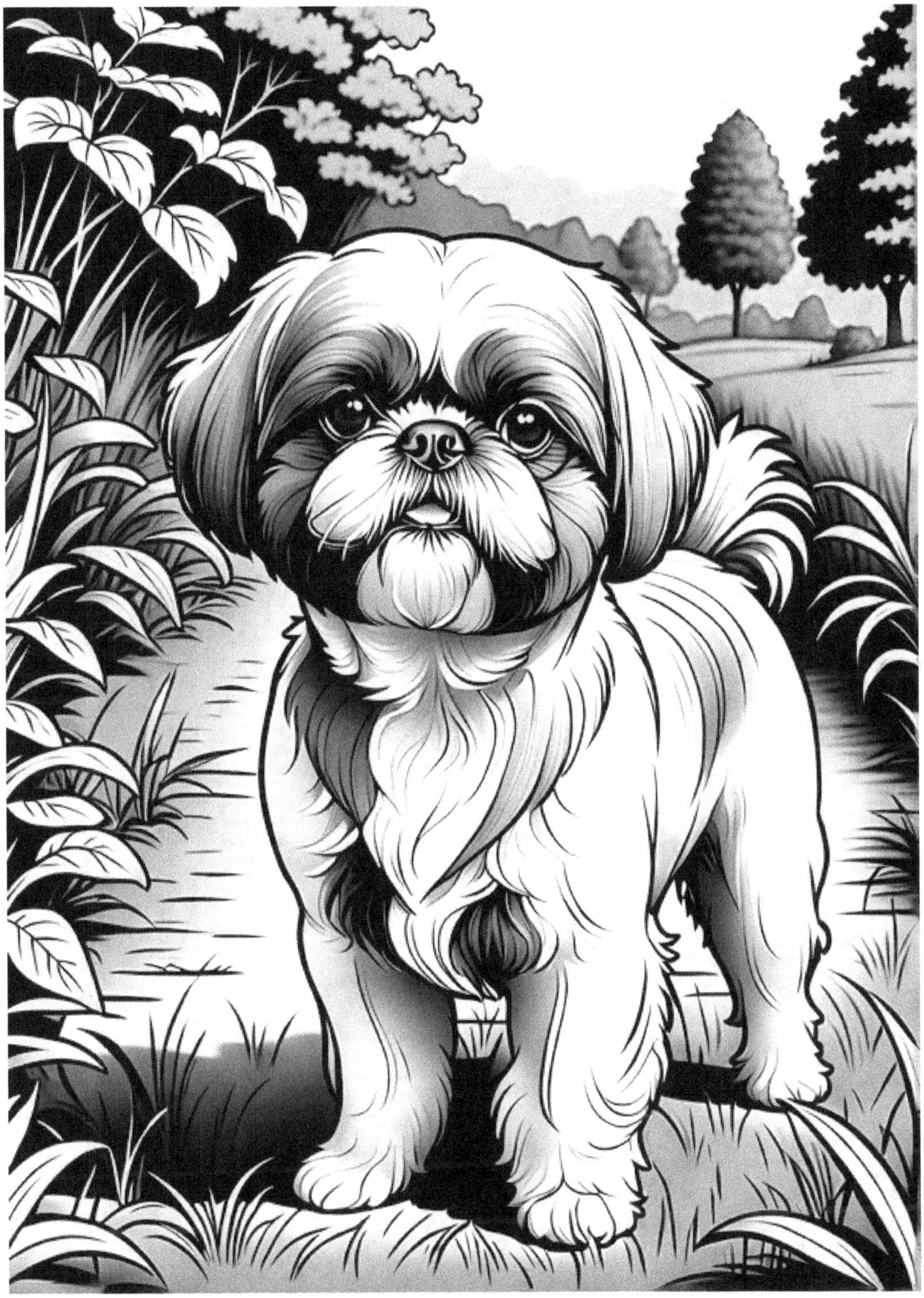

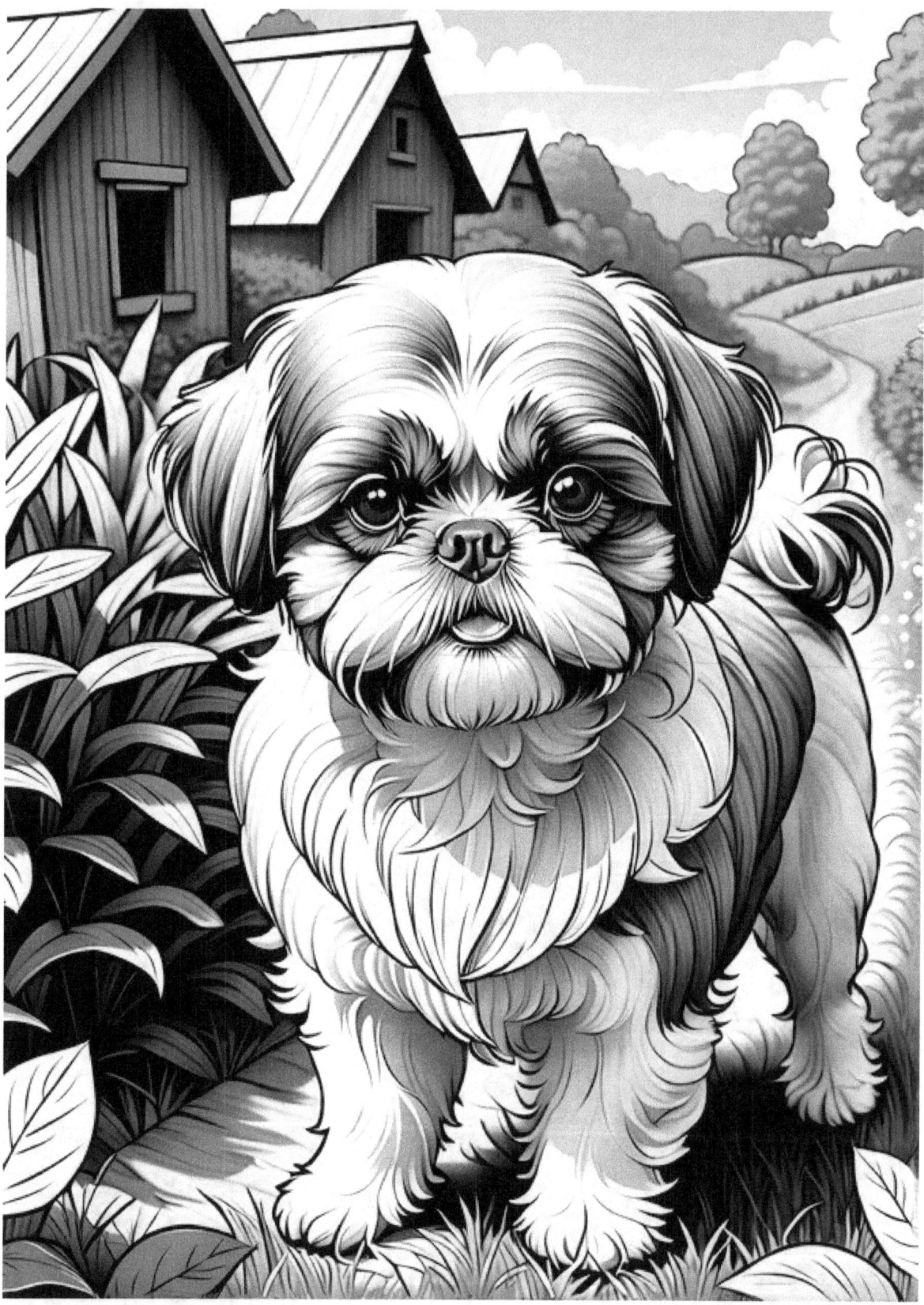

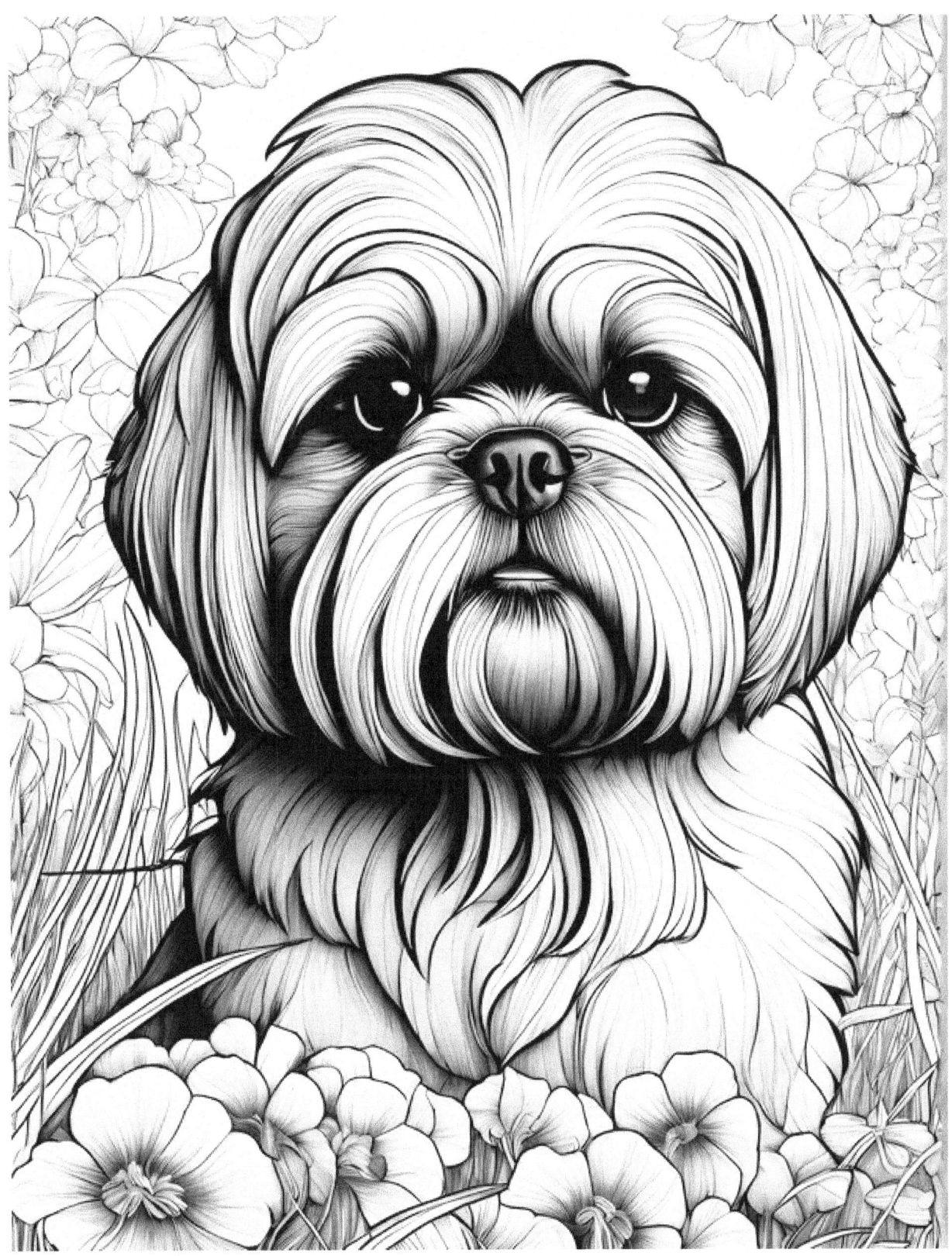

ROBERTO BARONDI

SIBERIAN HUSKY

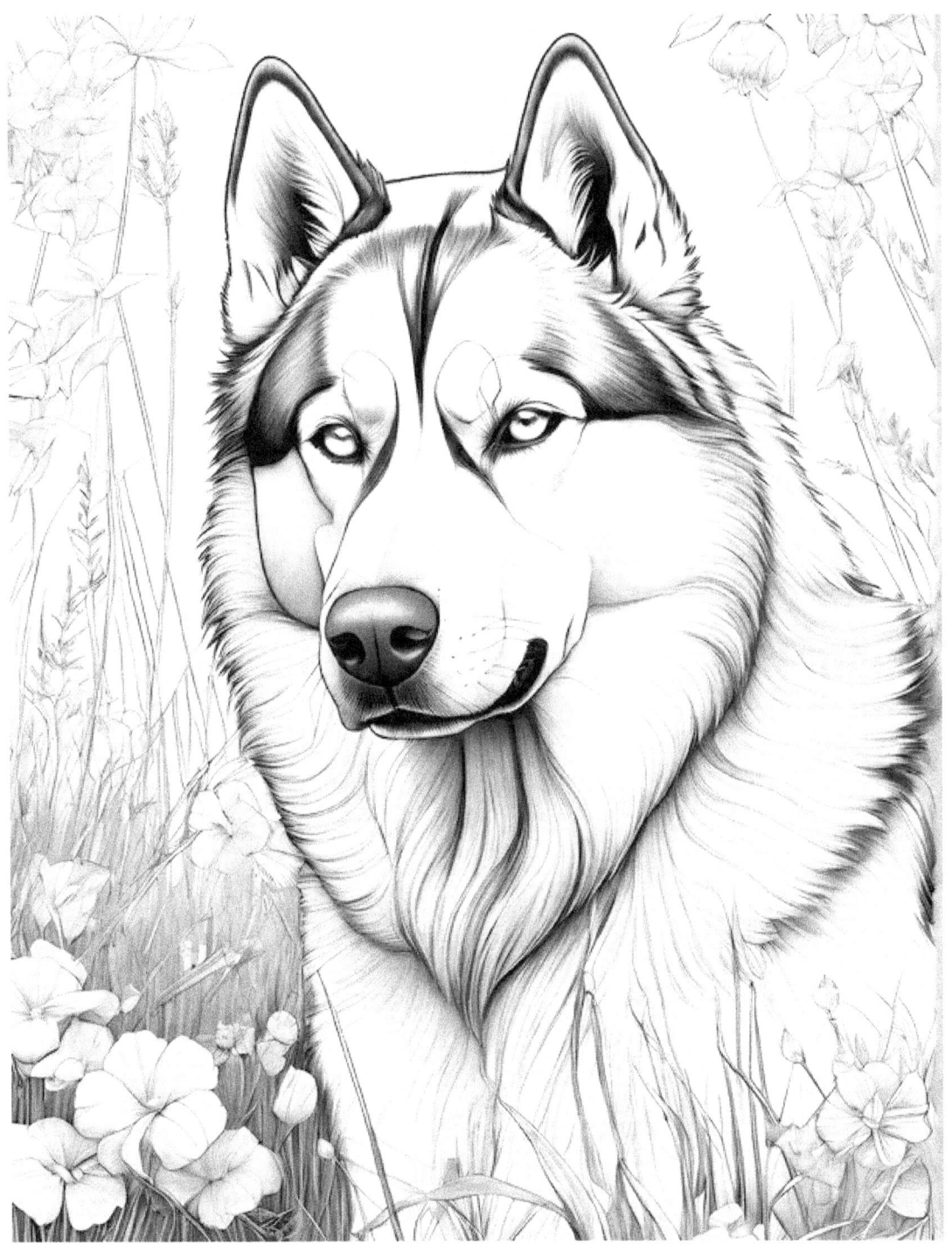

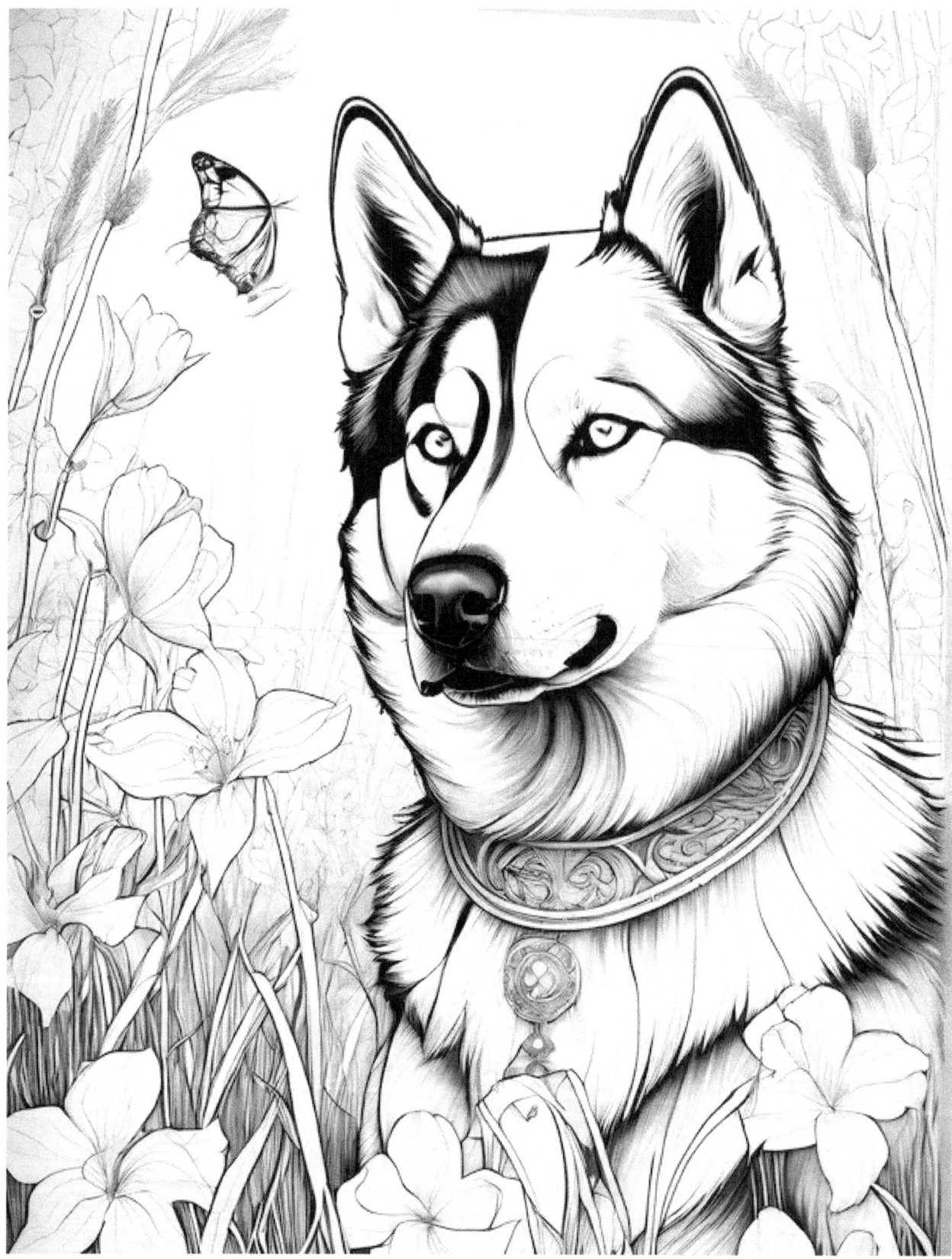

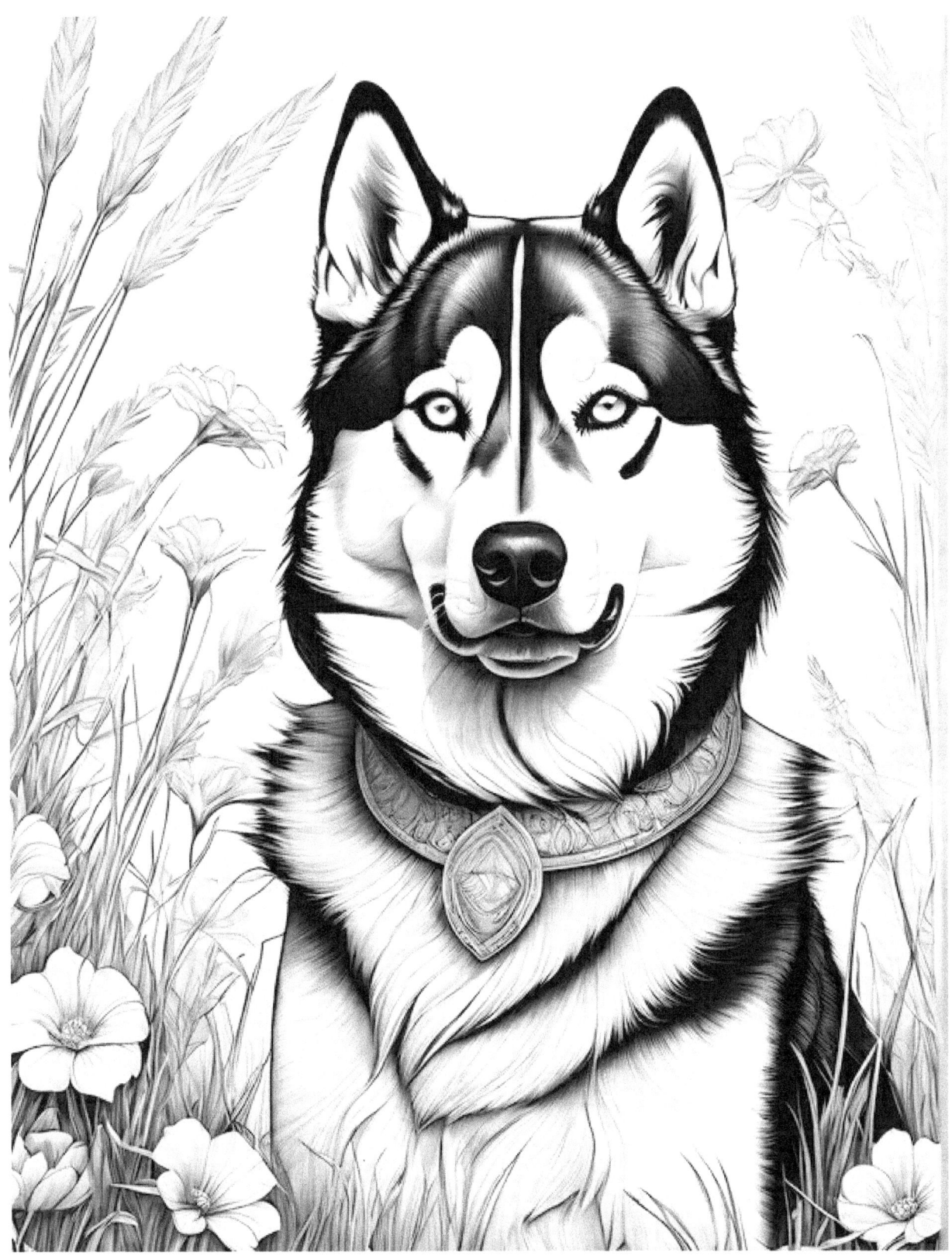

ROBERTO BARONDI

THAI RIDGEBACK

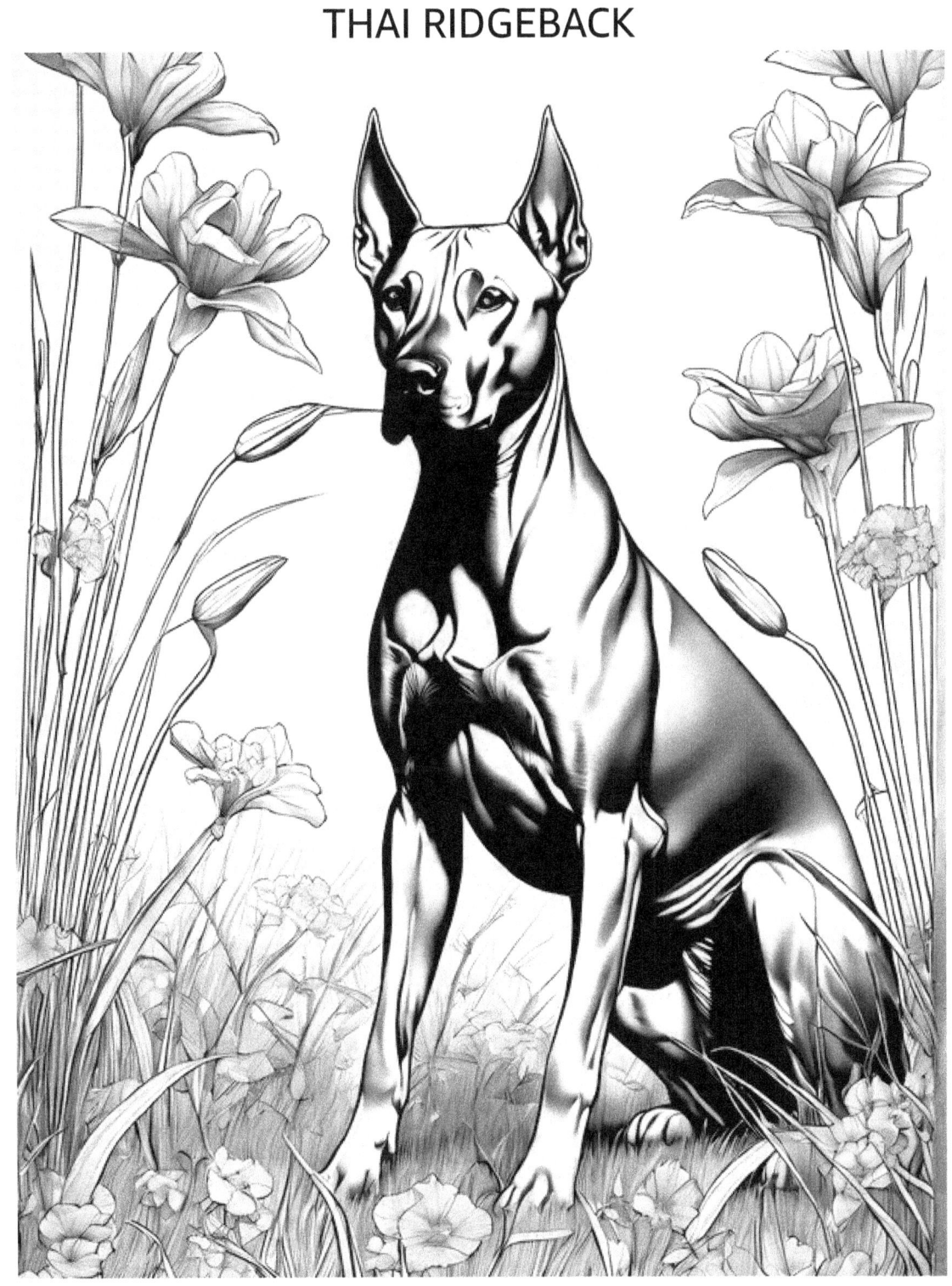

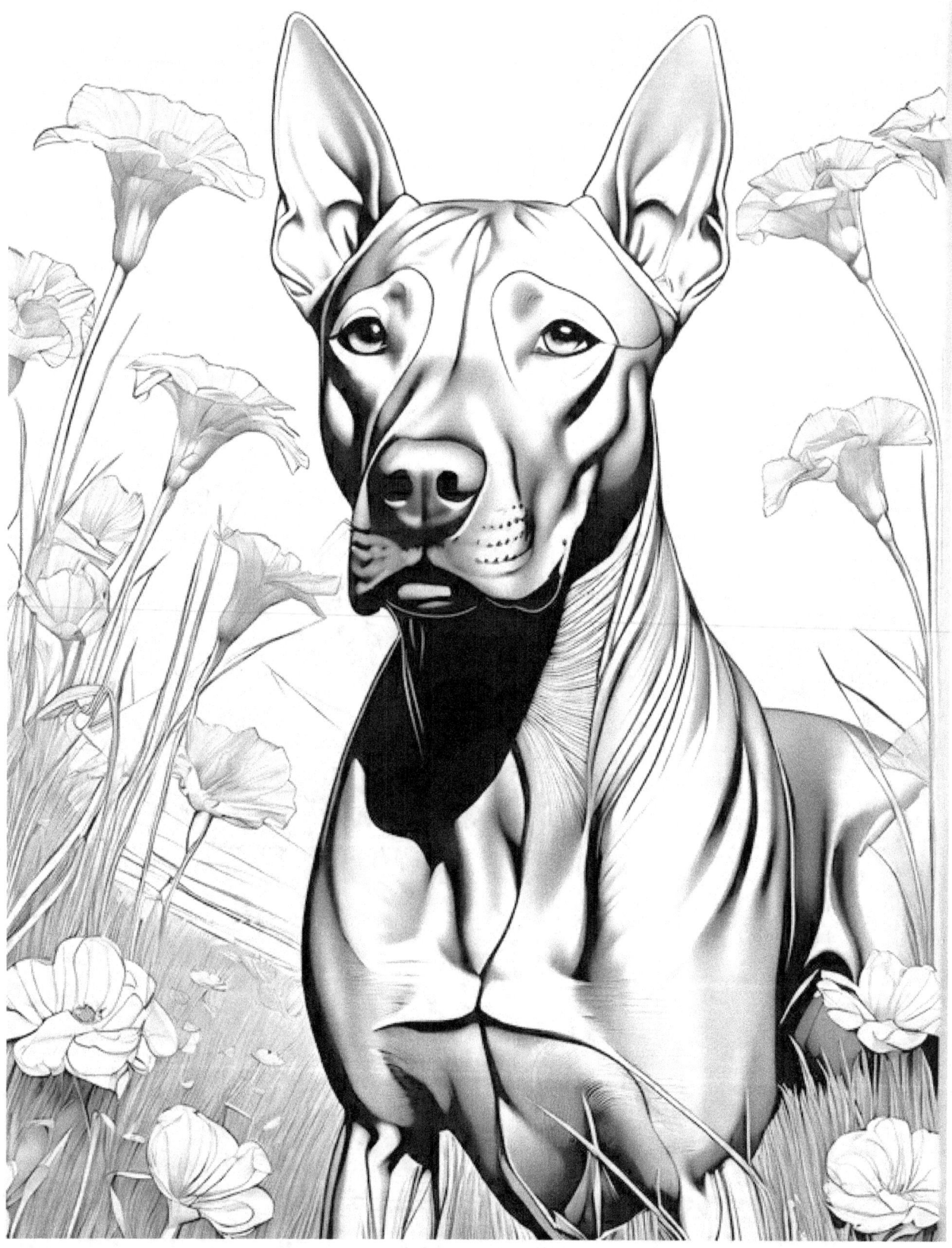

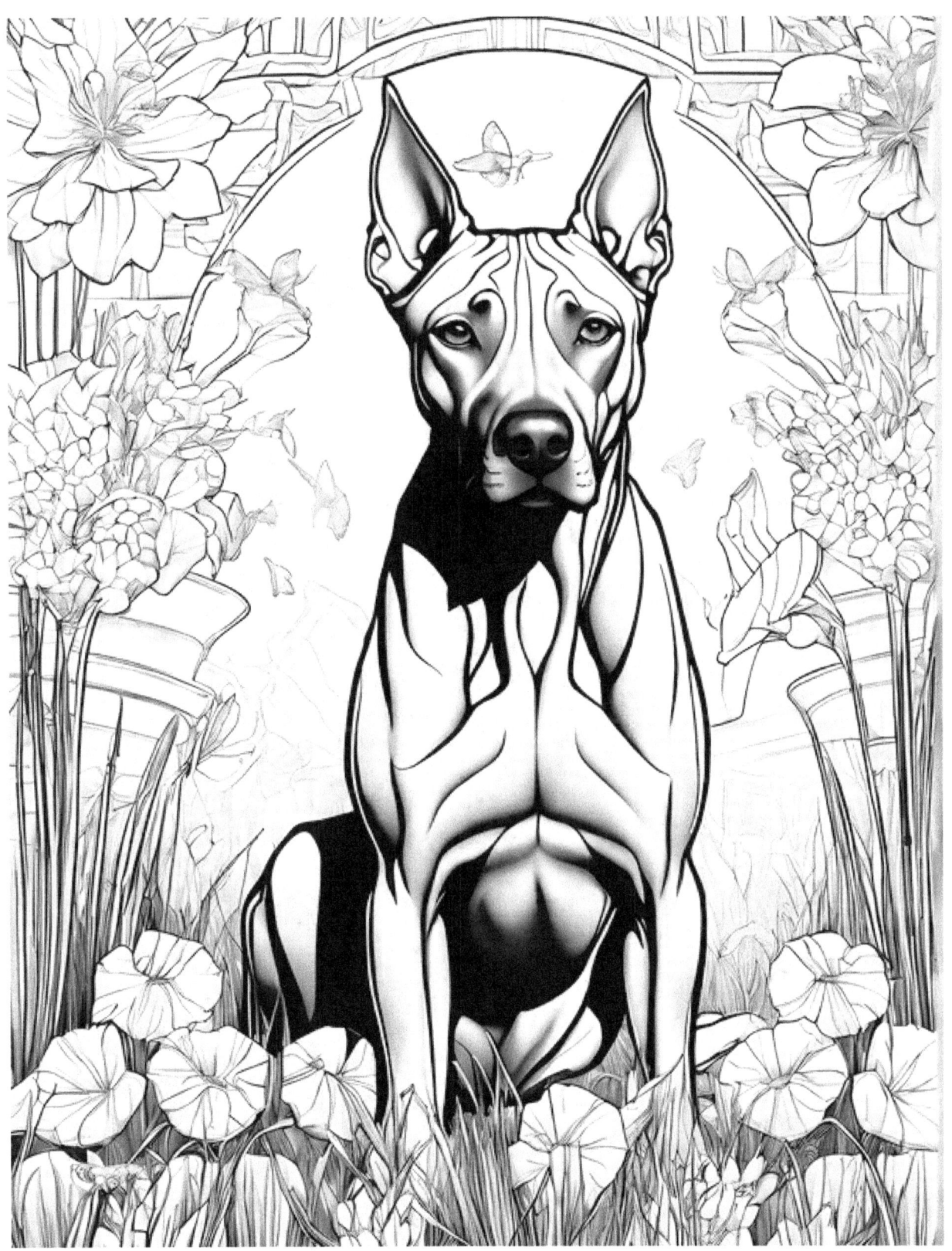

TTIBETAN MASTIFF

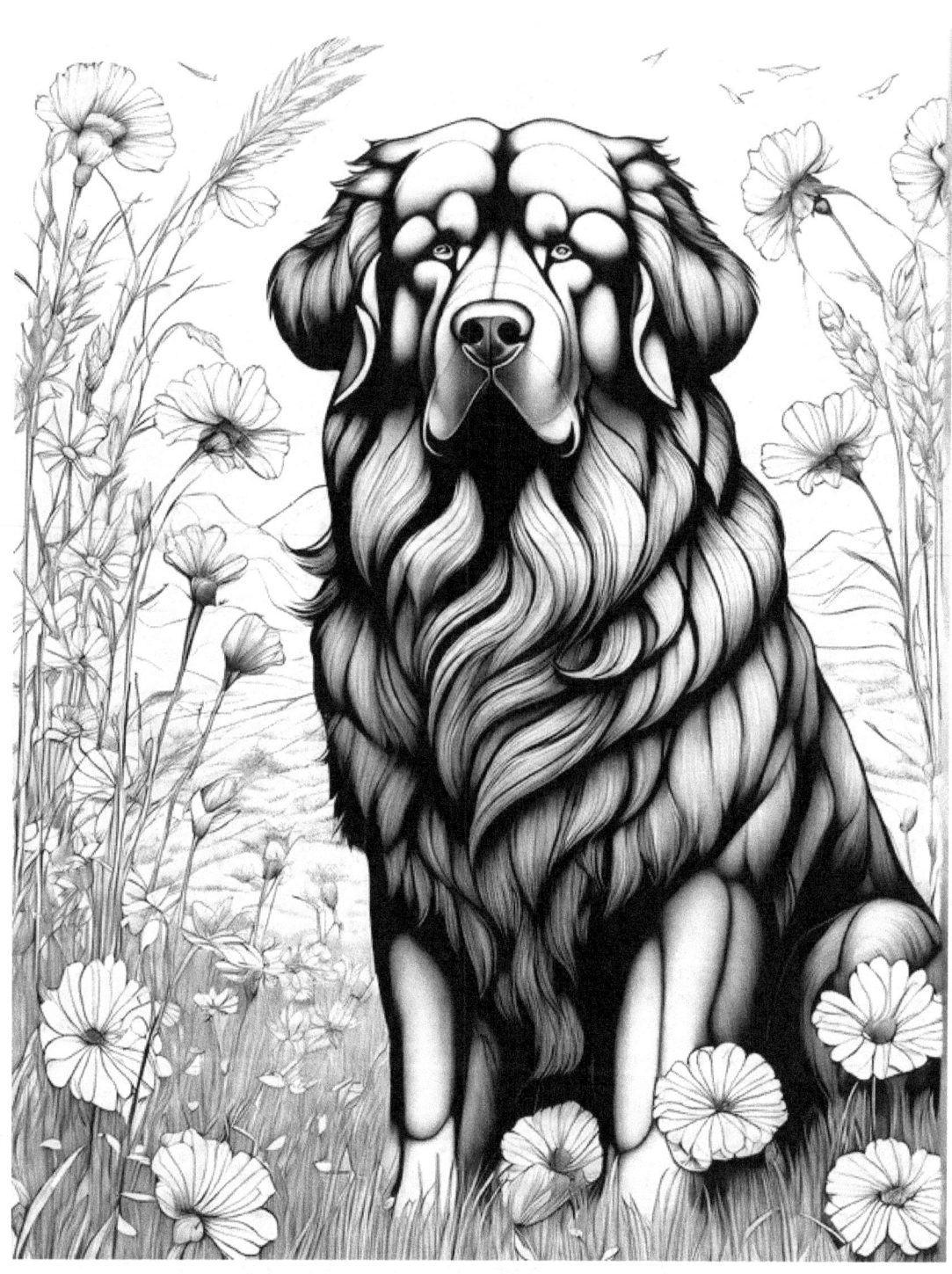

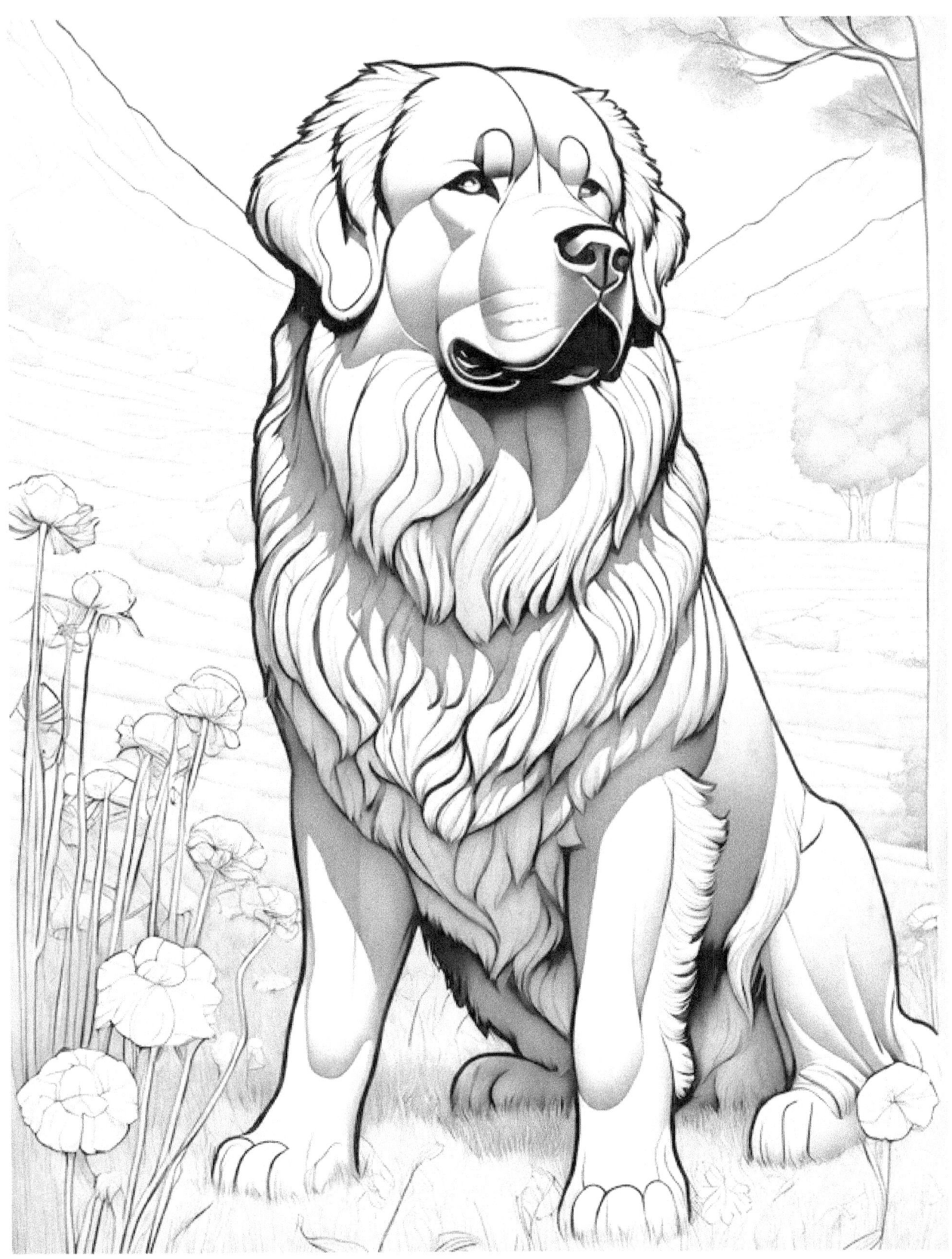

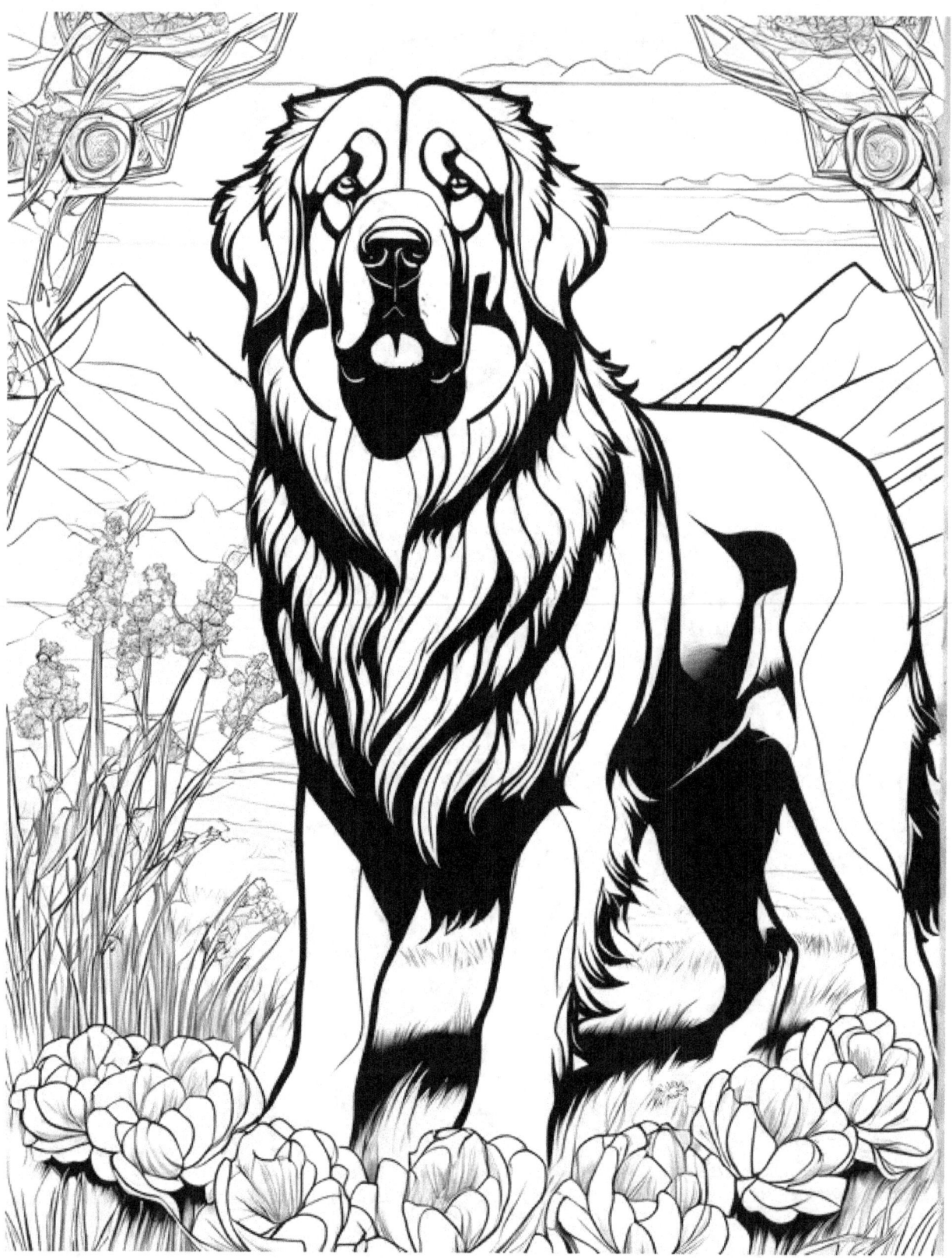

XOLOITZCUINTLI

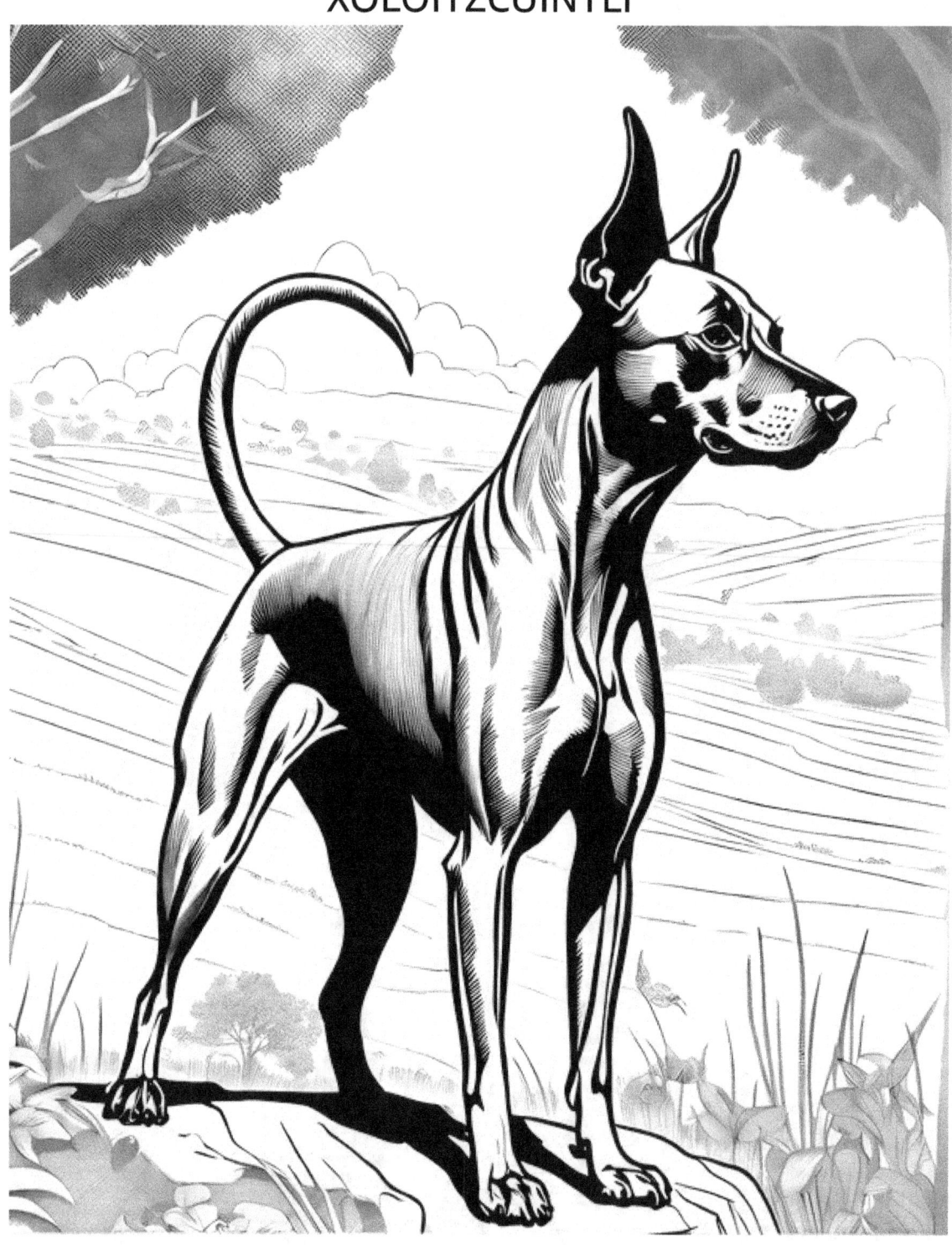

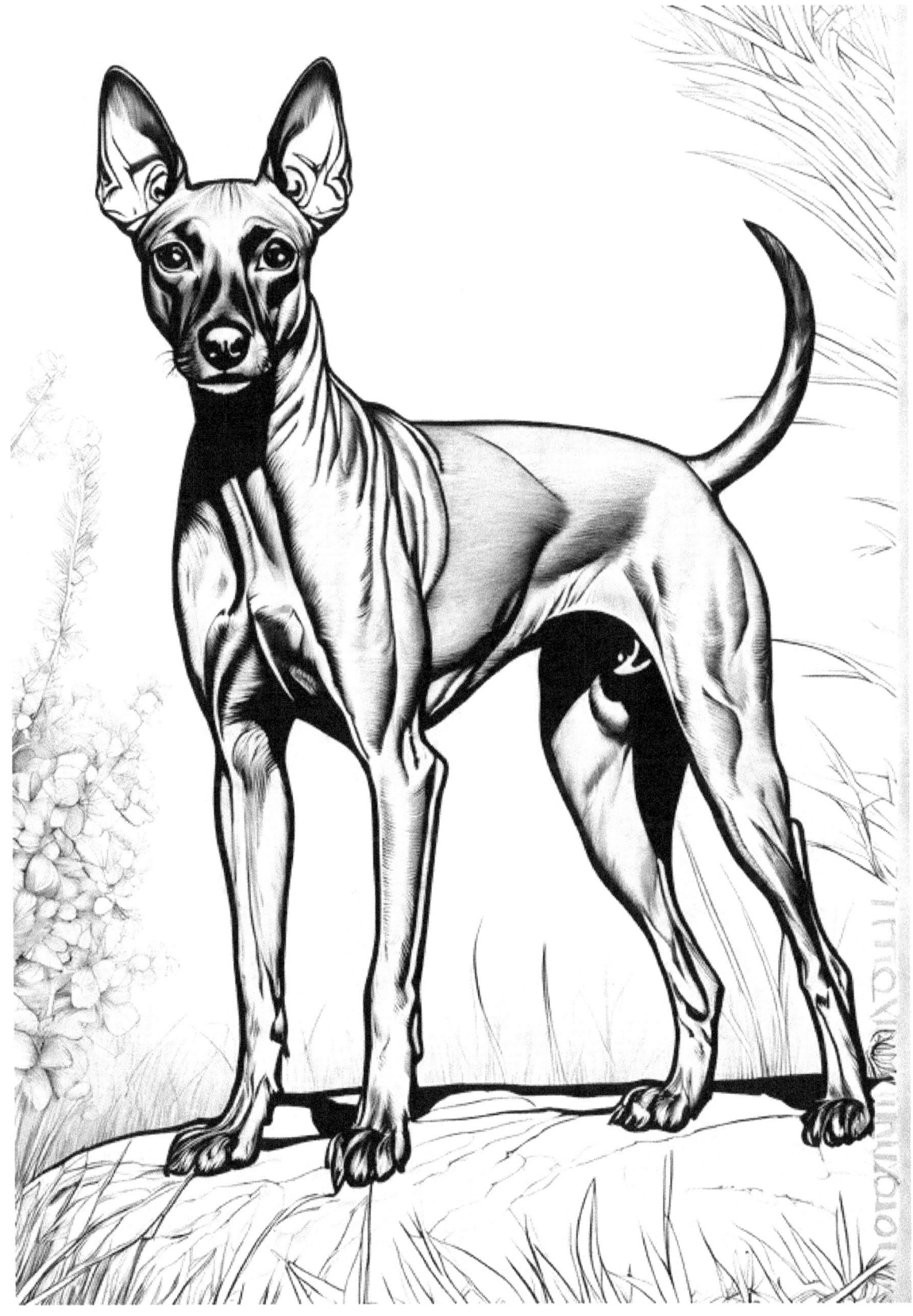

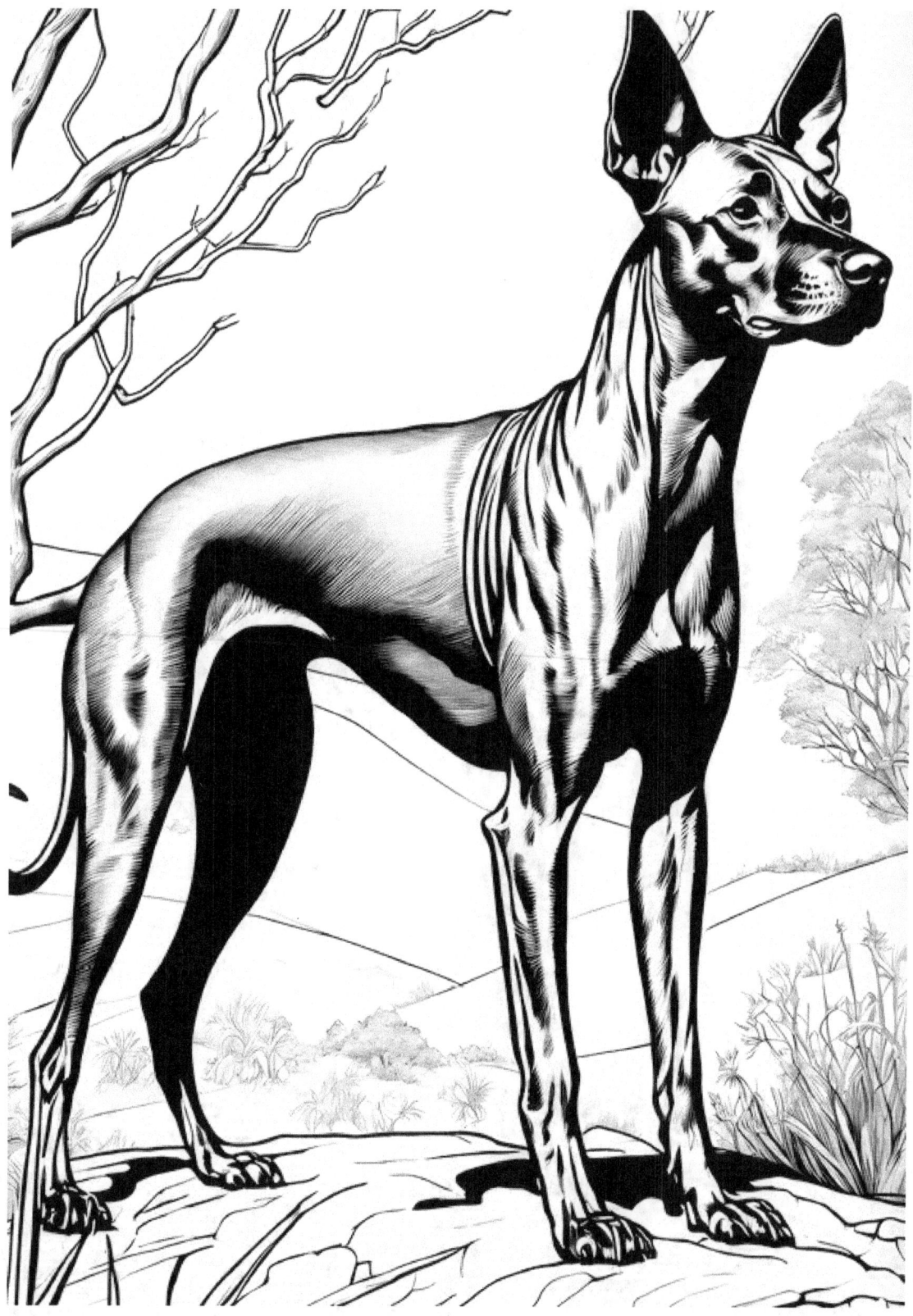

YORKSHIRE TERRIER

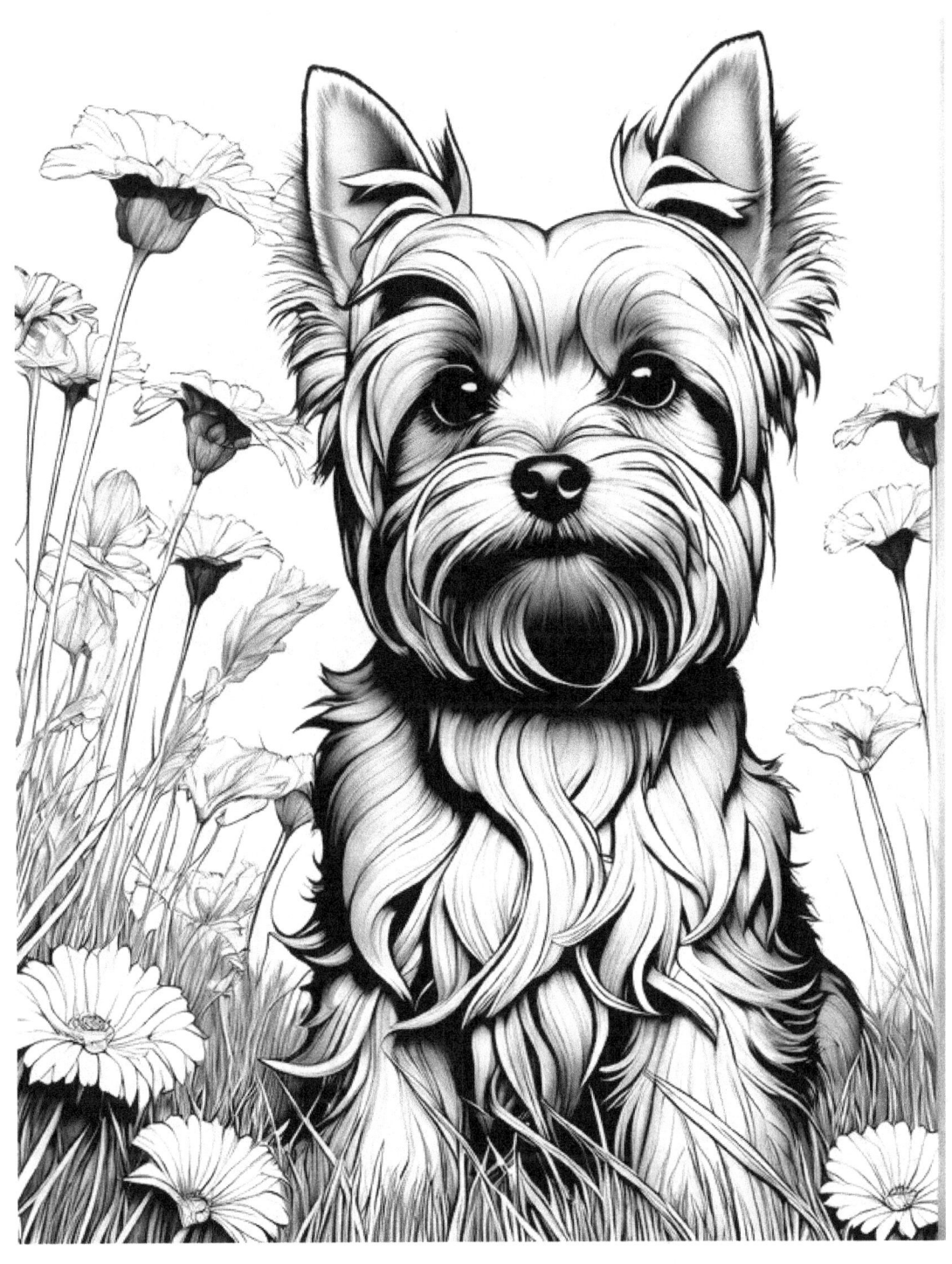

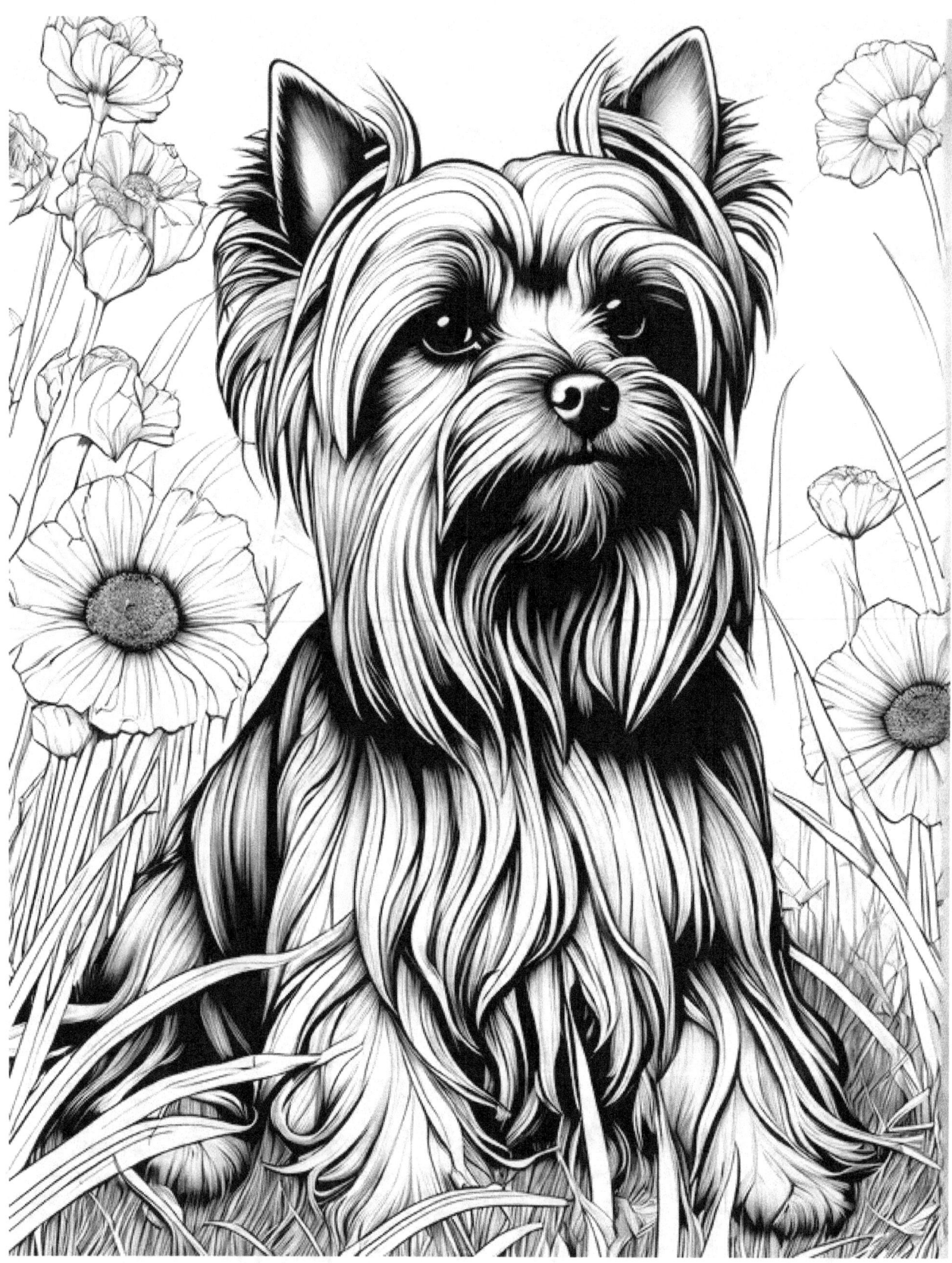

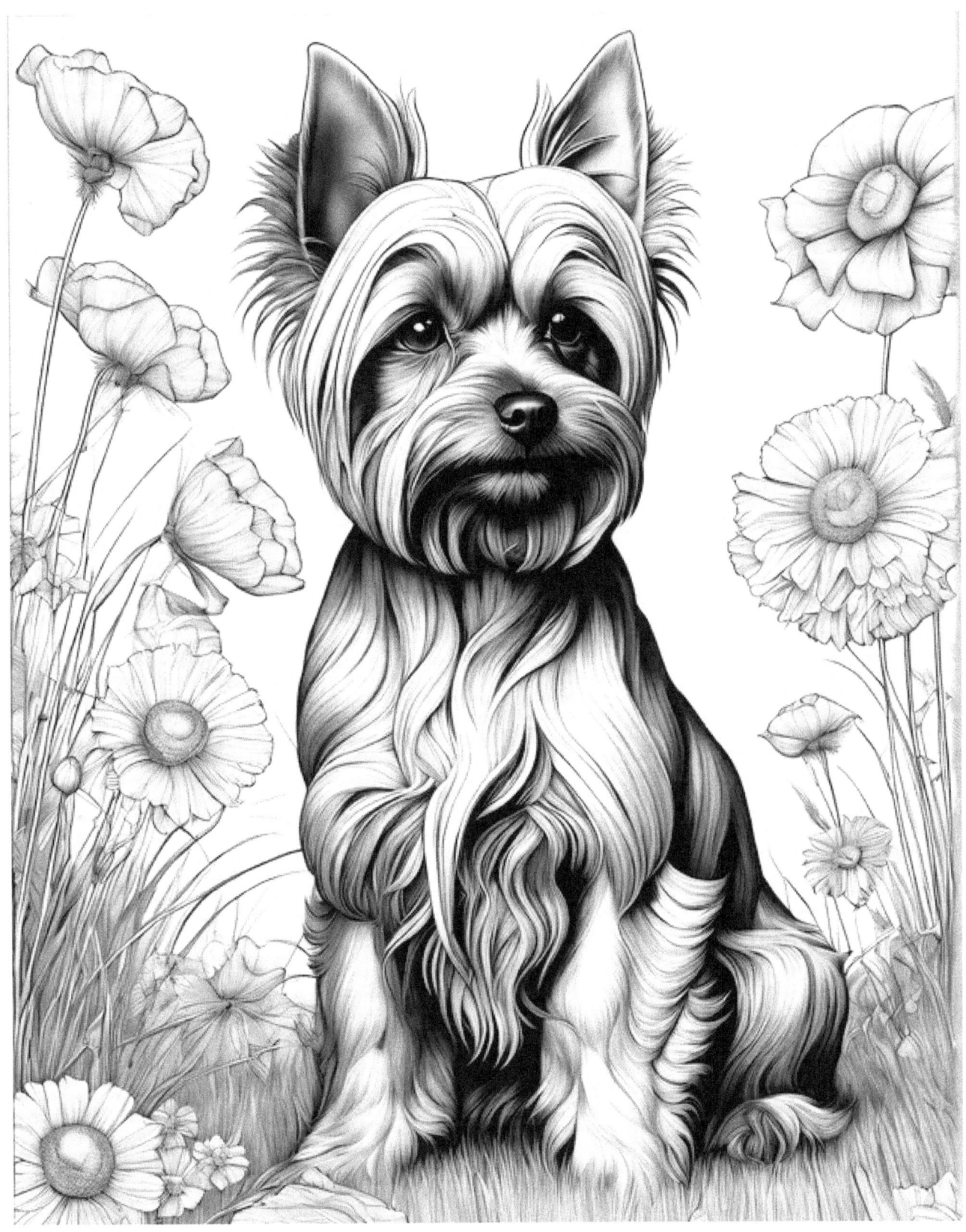